THE MEDIEVAL MYSTICAL TRADITION IN ENGLAND

The essays collected in this volume explore the mystical tradition in both written texts and material culture. There is a particular focus on Julian of Norwich (her use of biblical language; her influence on the *Book of Margery Kempe*; her concept of the soul and learning; and as representative of her time), and on Syon Abbey and the Bridgettine tradition. Other topics explored include the *Cloud*-texts; the idea of the body in anchoritic writing, and the influence of Continental writers on the English tradition.

Dr E. A. JONES teaches in the Department of English at the University of Exeter.

The Medieval Mystical Tradition in England

Exeter Symposium VII

Papers read at
Charney Manor, July 2004

Edited by E. A. Jones

D. S. BREWER

First published 2004
D. S. Brewer, Cambridge

ISBN 1 84384 007 3

ISSN 0950–7299

D. S. Brewer is an imprint of Boydell & Brewer Ltd
PO Box 9, Woodbridge, Suffolk IP12 3DF, UK
and of Boydell & Brewer Inc.
668 Mt. Hope Avenue, Rochester NY 14620, USA
website: www.boydellandbrewer.com

A catalogue record for this title is available
from the British Library

Library of Congress Cataloging in Publication Data
Exeter Symposium (7th : 2004 : Charney Manor)
The Medieval mystical tradition in England : Exeter Symposium VII : papers read at Charney Manor, July 2004 / edited by E.A. Jones.
p. cm.
Includes index.
ISBN 1–84384–007–3 (alk. paper)
1. Mysticism – England – History – Middle Ages, 600–1500 – Congresses. 2. Julian, of Norwich, b. 1343 – Congresses. I. Jones, E. A. (Edward Alexander), 1968– II. Title.
BV5077.E54E94 2004
248.2'2'09420902 – dc22 2003023036

This book is printed on acid-free paper

Printed in Great Britain by
Antony Rowe Ltd, Chippenham, Wiltshire

CONTENTS

for Marion
flores of a longer-lasting kind

FOREWORD

When Marion Glasscoe organised the first Exeter Symposium in 1980, study of the medieval mystical tradition was (at best) a marginal pursuit, whether one's vantage point was the field of literary studies, history or theology. What Marion realised was that the liminal nature of the 'Mystics' both demanded a broad-based interdisciplinary approach (of the sort that she was, at the same time, building into her undergraduate teaching at the University of Exeter) and enabled them to act as a conduit for the different disciplines to talk to each other.

That first Symposium brought together scholars from Britain, Europe and the United States; literary, historical, theological and psychological approaches to the texts; established and new names. It paid full attention to the five 'Middle English Mystics' (Hilton, Rolle, Julian (two papers), Kempe, and – though there was no paper devoted solely to his works – the *Cloud*-author), but also tested the boundaries of the received canon, and particularly those between mystical and other sorts of writing (Langland, homiletic literature, religious drama).[1] For those of us who were not in Exeter in 1980, the papers read at the Symposium were published in the series Exeter Medieval Texts and Studies immediately afterwards, so that their work of stimulating further research could both begin at once, and continue to influence future generations of scholars.

Over the next twenty years, five further Symposia followed (in 1982, 1984, 1987, 1992 and 1999). Though there have been changes in venue and publisher over that time, and in 1999 a change to the published volume's title to reflect a broadening of focus to include Irish and Welsh mystical traditions, the series has kept to Marion's original conception of providing, in the Symposia themselves, a forum for 'healthy, relaxed and open inter-disciplinary exchanges' and, in the resultant volumes, a series of 'windows on to current research on the medieval mystical tradition', with the overall aim of 'seeking to promote greater understanding for our own time of the medieval English mystics, and the cultural context to which they belong'.[2]

Marion's openness to new approaches to, and new configurations of, the 'Medieval Mystical Tradition', her discerning eye for the best papers and the brightest emerging scholars, and her hard editorial work combined to make the volumes of Exeter Symposia not only the most prestigious, authoritative and lastingly valuable of publications on the 'Middle English Mystics', but one of the best-respected series in English medieval studies. It is, if not entirely, then in very

1 See *MMT* I.

2 These quotations are taken seriatim from the Forewords to *MMT* III, *MMT* VI and *MMT* IV.

large measure, due to her efforts that, a quarter of a century after the first Exeter Symposium, a medieval studies that can safely ignore the 'Mystics' seems unthinkable.

For this seventh collection, I have tried not to depart significantly from what has been such a successful formula. There is once more a variety of disciplinary approaches – literary, historical, theological, art historical – and a mix of well-known scholars (including colleagues, collaborators and former students of Marion's) and the as yet less-published. As with previous volumes in the series, I have not set out to produce a themed collection (the absence of essays on Celtic mysticism, and the reversion to the title *Medieval Mystical Tradition in England*, is a function only of those papers and contributors who came forward, and is not irreversible). The sequence in which the essays are arranged has been designed primarily to provide a varied and pleasurable reading experience, rather than to point up (or to impose) particular patterns and structures on the collection. One of the strengths of the Symposia has been the way their relaxed, intimate, country-house-weekend atmosphere has allowed conversations to develop among speakers, papers and approaches, and I hope that readers of this volume will similarly make productive connections of their own among its various essays.

Nevertheless, certain groupings suggest themselves to me. Most obviously, there are clusters of essays on Julian of Norwich (Sutherland, Baker, Kukita Yoshikawa, Barratt), Syon Abbey and the Bridgettines (Hutchison, Gillespie), and the continental *mulieres sanctae* as they appear in England (Grisé, Griffith). Thematic links include the spirituality of the religious orders (Edden, Gillespie); gender, class and mystical discourse (McAvoy, Chewning, Barratt); the theological precision of mystical language (Sutherland, Baker, Cré, Steinmetz), and the translation (in the sense both of literary translation, and the more generous medieval sense of *translatio* from one culture, genre, or medium to another) of the continental mystics into English cultural forms – often accompanied by a 'toning down' of their more daring and characteristic aspects (Baker, Cré, Grisé, Griffith).

I should like to offer my thanks to the contributors for letting me have their papers early enough for us to keep to Marion's practice of enabling the rapid dissemination of the Symposium's proceedings more or less as soon as it has taken place; to Roger Ellis and Vincent Gillespie for their advice and encouragement; to Caroline Palmer of Boydell & Brewer for her expertise and enthusiasm at all stages of the project, and, above all, to Marion Glasscoe for entrusting the series to me. This book is dedicated to her, from all the contributors – who will be joined in this by the whole community of students of medieval mysticism – with appreciation, gratitude and affection.

LIST OF ABBREVIATIONS

CCSL	Corpus Christianorum Series Latina
Dict. spir.	*Dictionnaire de spiritualité, ascétique et mystique, doctrine et histoire*, ed. M. Viller et al. (Paris, 1932–)
EETS	Early English Text Society
ES	Extra Series
OS	Original Series
SS	Supplementary Series
MED	*Middle English Dictionary*, ed. Hans Kurath, Sherman M. Kuhn and John Reidy (Ann Arbor, 1952–2001)
MMT I	*The Medieval Mystical Tradition in England*, ed. Marion Glasscoe, Exeter Symposium I (Exeter, 1980)
MMT II	*The Medieval Mystical Tradition in England*, ed. Marion Glasscoe, Exeter Symposium II (Exeter, 1982)
MMT III	*The Medieval Mystical Tradition in England*, ed. Marion Glasscoe, Exeter Symposium III (Cambridge, 1984)
MMT IV	*The Medieval Mystical Tradition in England*, ed. Marion Glasscoe, Exeter Symposium IV (Cambridge, 1987)
MMT V	*The Medieval Mystical Tradition in England*, ed. Marion Glasscoe, Exeter Symposium V (Cambridge, 1992)
MMT VI	*The Medieval Mystical Tradition: England, Ireland and Wales*, ed. Marion Glasscoe, Exeter Symposium VI (Cambridge, 1999)
PL	*Patrologia Latina*, ed. J.-P. Migne, 221 vols (1844–65)
STC	*A Short-Title Catalogue of Books Printed in England, Scotland, & Ireland, and of English Books Printed Abroad, 1475–1640*, first compiled A. W. Pollard and G. R. Redgrave, 2nd rev. edn begun by W. A. Jackson and F. S. Ferguson, completed by Katherine Pantzar, vol. I (London, 1986), vol. II (London, 1976)

NOTES ON CONTRIBUTORS

Denise Baker, Professor of English at the University of North Carolina at Greensboro, is author of *Julian of Norwich's Showings: From Vision to Book* and editor of *Inscribing the Hundred Years' War in French and English Cultures*. She has published articles on the Middle English mystics, Gower, Langland, and Chaucer.

Alexandra Barratt is Professor in the Department of English, University of Waikato, New Zealand. She has published on Middle English women writers (Julian of Norwich, Dame Eleanor Hull) and is currently working on texts written or translated for female audiences and patrons.

Susannah Mary Chewning teaches British Literature, Women's Studies, and writing at Union County College. She has published on various topics including Chaucer, Shakespeare, anchoritic literature, and medieval devotional poetry and has recently edited a collection of critical essays on the intersections of sexuality and spirituality in medieval culture.

Marleen Cré is a research and teaching assistant at the University of Antwerp. Her main research interest is Middle English mystical texts in their manuscript contexts. She has published on two fifteenth-century manuscripts containing Julian of Norwich material: Westminster Cathedral Treasury MS 4 and British Library, MS Additional 37790.

Valerie Edden is honorary Senior Lecturer in the Theology Department Centre for the Editing of Texts in Religion, Birmingham (and formerly of the Department of English). Publications include an edition of Richard Maidstone's Penitential Psalms, *Index of Middle English Prose: Handlist XV* and a number of articles on the English Carmelites.

Vincent Gillespie is a Fellow of St Anne's College and Reader in English at the University of Oxford. His edition of the library registrum of the English Birgittine house Syon Abbey was published in 2001. His research interests include mystical writing, pastoral manuals, and the History of the Book. He is currently exploring the textual and spiritual culture of the Syon Brethren.

David Griffith is Lecturer in English at the University of Birmingham. He is particularly interested in text-image relations, iconoclasm, networks of artistic patronage and connections between textual and material culture. He is currently writing a book about medieval roodscreens.

C. Annette Grisé is Assistant Professor of English at McMaster University. She has published on Syon Abbey and late-medieval devotional literature, and is currently conducting research on texts by and about continental female mystics in late-medieval England.

Ann M. Hutchison is a Visiting Professor at the Pontifical Institute of Mediaeval Studies where she assists with the licence theses of the post-doctoral fellows. She is also a member of the Department of English at York University in Toronto. Most recently, she has published an edition of British Library, Additional MS 18650, 'The Life and Good End of Sister Marie', concerning an English nun of the Bridgettine Order, in *Birgittiana*.

Eddie Jones is Lecturer in English Medieval Literature and Culture in the University of Exeter School of English. He works on late-medieval devotional texts, and the literature and history of hermits and anchorites.

Liz Herbert McAvoy is currently Lecturer in Medieval Language and Literature at the University of Leicester. She has published widely on Margery Kempe and Julian of Norwich, including an abridged translation of *The Book of Margery Kempe*, and has recently completed a book on both writers.

Karl-Heinz Steinmetz is Lecturer in Medieval Theology and Spirituality at the Ludwigs-Maximilians-University and in Medieval Philosophy at the Jesuit University for Philosophy in Munich. His book on contemplation in the *Cloud*-Texts is in print, and he is currently working on medieval concepts of corporeality.

Annie Sutherland is Lecturer in Old and Middle English at Somerville College, Oxford. She has published on vernacular devotional literature and is currently working on medieval English Psalters.

Naoë Kukita Yoshikawa is Professor of English Medieval Literature and Culture at Shizuoka University, Japan. She has published articles on Margery Kempe, and has recently completed a book on Margery Kempe and her meditations, written in Japanese.

‘OURE FEYTH IS GROUNDYD IN GODDES WORDE’ – JULIAN OF NORWICH AND THE BIBLE[1]

ANNIE SUTHERLAND

Thanne hadde I wonder in my wit what womman it weere
That swiche wise wordes of Holy Writ shewed.[2]

I

OF THOSE ENGLISH AUTHORS deemed to be participants in ‘the medieval mystical tradition’, Julian of Norwich is arguably the most opaque.[3] Richard Rolle and Walter Hilton are recognised historical figures, the *Cloud*-author leaves us with undeniable clues as to his identity, and Margery Kempe is explicit in her autobiographical references. Further, while we can locate Rolle within the *girovagus* tradition in which he places himself, while we can read Hilton as heir to a form of Augustinian spirituality, while we can speculate legitimately on the Pseudo-Dionysian affinities of the *Cloud*-author and while Margery’s *Book* foregrounds the influence of continental hagiography and insular devotion, we are provided with only the most minimal frame of reference in approaching Julian.[4] She allows us little personal information (the few self-referential remarks that the Short Text contains are deleted in the Long Text) and such frames as have been constructed by scholars and readers are inevitably speculative. Indeed, we are not even in possession of her proper name.

[1] This paper examines both the Short and Long Texts of the *Revelations*, quoting from E. Colledge and J. Walsh, eds, *A Book of Showings to the Anchoress Julian of Norwich*, Pontifical Institute of Medieval Studies, Studies and Texts XXXV (Toronto, 1978). I abbreviate the Short Text and Long Text respectively as *ST* and *LT*.

[2] A. V. C. Schmidt, ed., *The Vision of Piers Plowman* (London, 1978), Passus I, 71–2. Also quoted in A. Blamires, ‘The Limits of Bible Study for Medieval Women’, *Women, the Book and the Godly*, ed. L. Smith and J. H. M. Taylor (Cambridge, 1995), pp. 1–12 at p. 1.

[3] Some scholars have argued that Julian was not directly responsible for the writing of her *Revelations*, but used an amanuensis. However, it is the assumption of this paper that the composition of both texts is entirely Julian’s own.

[4] There is minimal external evidence of Julian’s existence. Such as there is can be found in extant wills (for references, see Colledge and Walsh, *Showings*, pp. 33–35) and in S. B. Meech and H. E. A. Allen, eds, *The Book of Margery Kempe*, EETS OS CCXII (1940 for 1939), p. 42/7–p. 43/20.

In such a climate, it is extremely difficult to contextualise Julian's *Revelations* without feeling that one is doing violence to a deliberately self-deprecating author, who desired that attention was focused on her message and not on its literary sources, let alone on herself. However, while not denying that Julian's text is what it says it is (a revelation from a divinity outside time, space and language), it is surely legitimate for the scholar to speculate on the context within which this revelation was received.

It is on the biblical background of Julian's *Revelations* that this paper focuses, and in the light of which it attempts to contextualise them. This is a difficult task, for although Julian's prose in both *ST* and *LT* is informed by persistent scriptural echoes, it is only on very rare occasions that she foregrounds their biblical origins. Further, she never distinguishes biblical language from her own by quoting from the scriptures in Latin; all of her biblical allusions are in English. Yet the extent to which biblical language is embedded in Julian's own vernacular is so remarkable when compared with that found in the writings of her mystical near-contemporaries that an exploration of its background and significance is imperative.[5]

Any examination of the scriptural resonances which inform so much of Julian's prose leads us inevitably towards the issue of her learning; was she, as characterised in London, British Library MS Sloane 2499, 'a simple creature that cowde no letter'?[6] Or might she have been the scholar whom Colledge and Walsh portray:

> Before she began to compose the short text, Julian already knew all the Vulgate; especially, she can be seen to be deeply familiar with all four gospels, the Pauline and Johannine epistles and Hebrews, the Psalms, the sapiential books and Deutero-Isaias. . . . [Furthermore] when young, Julian had received an exceptionally good grounding in Latin, in Scripture and in the liberal arts, and . . . thereafter she was able and permitted to read widely in Latin and vernacular spiritual classics.[7]

The obvious route for Colledge and Walsh to take in justifying their presentation of a latinate and biblically learned Julian is to claim that in her youth she was 'already serving God in the religious state', possibly in the Benedictine house at

5 This is not to say that other mystical texts do not contain scriptural reference; but unlike Julian, Richard Rolle alternates between referring to the Bible in the vernacular and in Latin in his English treatises. The same can be said of Walter Hilton, though the exegesis of the biblical material in his vernacular writings is more conventionally academic than that of Rolle. In *The Cloud of Unknowing*, the anonymous author only alludes to the scriptures in the vernacular, yet *Privy Counselling* is marked by its exegetical use of the Latin Bible. (See my unpublished doctoral thesis 'Biblical Citation and its Affective Contextualisation in some English Mystical Texts of the Fourteenth Century' (Oxford, 2000).)

6 See M. Glasscoe, ed., *Julian of Norwich – a Revelation of Love*, Exeter Medieval English Texts and Studies (Exeter, 1976. Revd edn 1986 and 1993), p. 2. See also 'a symple creature vnlettyrde' in Paris, Bibliothèque nationale MS Fonds Anglais 40 (Colledge and Walsh, *Showings*, *LT* 2/2).

7 *Showings*, pp. 43 and 44.

Carrow.[8] However, the supposition that Julian was a religious is by no means shared by all critics; Norman Tanner, for example, points out that in references to her in wills, Julian is never styled *domina* or *dame*, which she probably would have been had she been a nun.[9] And why, Benedicta Ward asks, if Julian was a member of a religious community, did her order apparently do nothing to preserve or propagate the written record of her visionary experience?[10] Furthermore, it is misguided to assume that a monastic environment would inevitably have provided Julian with either a latinate education or unmediated access to the Vulgate and patristic material; as Blamires points out, on the strength of library data and wills, evidence for 'the availability of Vulgates in nunneries' is 'rather slight'.[11]

Yet if this is the case, then how can we explain Julian's intricate biblical knowledge and understanding? Again, various critics have broached this question in different ways. Benedicta Ward, for example, posits the theory that Julian *never* belonged to a religious order, and suggests that she did not become an anchoress until *after* the composition of *LT* (which she, in agreement with Colledge and Walsh, dates to around 1393). She circumvents the problems that this theory poses to Julian's learning by suggesting that 'as a married woman in her own home [Julian] would . . . need to read and write for the management of her household'.[12]

As will become clear, it is obvious that, even when composing *ST*, Julian's scriptural familiarity was profound. Yet if she wrote this text as a laywoman with no religious background, immediately after her illness and the 1373 receipt of her showings, then we must ask ourselves from where she may have gleaned this biblical learning.[13] For the ability to 'read and write for the management of her household' is at some remove from the capacity to apprehend and interpret scriptural complexities (presumably in Latin). Nicholas Watson's 1993 article 'The Composition of Julian of Norwich's *Revelation of Love*' provides a speculative answer to this dilemma. As he states, Colledge and Walsh's analysis of the dating of the two texts of the *Revelations* is rather complex, leading them to suggest that *LT* was actually composed in two versions, one after the revelation of 1388 (the

8 *Showings*, p. 72.

9 N. Tanner, *The Church in Late Medieval Norwich, 1370–1532*, Pontifical Institute of Medieval Studies, Studies and Texts LXVI (Toronto, 1984), p. 60.

10 K. Leech and B. Ward, *Julian Reconsidered* (Oxford, 1988), p. 21.

11 Blamires, 'The Limits of Bible Study', p. 4.

12 Leech and Ward, *Julian Reconsidered*, p. 26. G. Jantzen, *Julian of Norwich: Mystic and Theologian* (London, 1987. Revd edn 2000) also entertains this possibility, though she seems to lean toward the likelihood that Julian was living the anchoritic life before the composition of *ST* (chapter 2).

13 That Julian is most likely to have composed *ST* soon after 1373 has become something of a critical commonplace. See, for example, F. Beer, ed. and trans., *Revelations of Divine Love: translated from British Library Additional MS 37790; the Motherhood of God: an excerpt translated from British Library MS Sloane 2477*, Library of Medieval Women (Cambridge, 1998), p. 1.

peroration of *LT*) and one after 1393. Their dating of *ST* is even more confused. On occasion, they assume that the production of the 'well-composed and highly-finished' *ST* 'must have taken some time', yet elsewhere they state that 'we may suppose, though we cannot prove, that the short text was written soon after the event'.[14]

Watson's solution is radically different; *ST*, he argues, may have been composed some 'ten to fifteen years later than is supposed' (i.e. the mid to late 1380s rather than the commonly assumed 1370s), shifting the composition of *LT* forward by a comparable time period (i.e. to the late 1390s or early 1400s).[15] If Watson's re-dating of *ST* is correct, then it could be the case that Julian did indeed receive her revelations when living in the secular world – probably a woman of the status and education which Ward envisages. At the time of the receipt of her visions (1373), Julian may thus have been a devout laywoman, familiar with the scriptures and the tenets of the religious life, through both preaching and her own devotions. As Norman Tanner has pointed out, medieval Norwich is known to have been home to several devout laywomen.[16] And that such laywomen enjoyed active spiritual lives and participated in the exchange of biblical and devotional books is well attested by late medieval evidence.[17]

Upon recovery from her illness, Julian may well not have retreated directly to the anchorhold. Instead, she may have taken time to ponder the significance of her visions, exploring and confirming their biblical and ecclestiastical orthodoxy.[18] It might only have been when she had achieved this to her satisfaction that she decided to commit her revelations to the page and thus prepare herself for enclosure. Indeed, it has been speculated that *ST* may originally have been intended to function as a written guarantee of Julian's orthodoxy, submitted to an ecclesiastical 'examination committee' prior to the granting of the right to enclosure.[19] Yet although this interpretation of *ST* goes some way towards explaining its defensive and repeated insistence on its own orthodoxy, and its two references to the contemplative life (excised in *LT*), it could legitimately be argued that *ST* is too self-consciously *literary* a text to have been intended for such an apparently prosaic purpose.[20]

[14] N. Watson, 'The Composition of Julian of Norwich's *Revelation of Love*', *Speculum* lxviii (1993), pp. 637–83 at p. 639.

[15] Watson, 'Composition', pp. 640–1.

[16] Tanner, *The Church in Late Medieval Norwich*, p. 112.

[17] M. C. Erler, *Women, Reading and Piety in Late Medieval England*, Cambridge Studies in Medieval Literature XLVI (Cambridge, 2002).

[18] For compelling evidence that Julian's *ST* is not an immediate response to her revelations, see Watson, 'Composition', pp. 657–72.

[19] Personal communication with Vincent Gillespie. For evidence of the requirement of a diocesan licence for 'official recognition as a recluse' see F. D. S. Darwin, *The English Mediaeval Recluse* (London, 1944), p. 53. Yet note also that there does not seem to have been any single widely recognised rite of enclosure in use in medieval England.

[20] For *ST* references to the contemplative life, see chapter 4/lines 41–4 and 13/25–8.

However, for all *ST*'s 'self-consciousness', *LT* is undoubtedly composed with more 'meditative assurance' than its predecessor.[21] Bearing this in mind, it is possible that the period of 'twenty yere . . . saue thre monthys' to which Julian alludes in *LT*, during which she 'had techyng inwardly' (51/86–7), is a reference to a time of enclosed contemplation, subsequent to the completion of *ST*.[22] Only after this solitary period of almost twenty years did Julian feel sufficiently confident to compose *LT*. Indeed, as will become clear, the biblical echoes contained in *LT* bear witness to an extended period of meditation and rumination consistent with a lengthy time of solitude.

Yet all of this speculation leaves one important question unanswered – if Julian was (as I assume) sufficiently literate to be able to compose her own vernacular *Revelations*, could she also have been latinate? In other words, would she have been personally capable of reading the Vulgate? And, indeed, under what circumstances can we assume that she might have had personal access to the same? And if she did not, from whence can we assume that her biblical familiarity arose?

II

As mentioned above, it is Colledge and Walsh's firm belief that Julian was personally familiar with the Vulgate. This is a belief that is based at least in part on the negative outcome of their investigations into the possibility that she might have used a Wycliffite version of the scriptures.[23] In their 1976 article, they do entertain the feasibility of her having had access to a vernacular version of the scriptures no longer extant, and do suggest that a scholar may have orally translated the Bible for her.[24] Yet such possibilities are no longer entertained in the introduction to their 1978 edition. Here, their simple claim is that, on several occasions, Julian makes 'her own translation[s] direct from the Vulgate', in support of which they adduce the following example:

> when in the short text she writes: *Swilke paynes I sawe that alle es to litelle þat y can telle or saye, for itt may nouȝt be tolde, botte ylke saule aftere the sayinge of saynte Pawle schulde feele in hym þat in Criste Jhesu* (234.23) she is providing an exact reproduction of the Latin syntax of Philippians 2.5: Hoc enim sentite in vobis quod et in Cristo Iesu.[25]

21 B. A. Windeatt, 'Julian of Norwich and her Audience', *Review of English Studies* xxviii (1977), pp. 1–17 at p. 3.

22 '51' refers to the chapter number and '86–7' to the line numbers. This system of numeration is used throughout the paper.

23 E. Colledge and J. Walsh, 'Editing Julian of Norwich's *Revelations*. A progress report', *Medieval Studies* xxxviii (1976), pp. 404–27.

24 Colledge and Walsh, 'Editing Julian', p. 410. They also suggest that she may have known French and used an Anglo-Norman Bible, yet this seems an unnecessarily circuitous explanation for her scriptural familiarity.

25 *Showings*, p. 45.

However, Julian's words do not *exactly reproduce* those of the Vulgate. Not only does she turn the scriptural imperative into reported speech ('after the sayinge of saynte Pawle . . .'), but she produces no equivalent of the Vulgate's 'quod *et*'. Indeed, this inaccurate reading of Julian's biblical voice effectively highlights the dangerous generalisations which characterise Colledge and Walsh's understanding of Julian's scriptural debt.

What is also extraordinary about this inaccurate reading of Julian is the fact that Colledge and Walsh do not address the possibility that the 'translation' of Philippians 2:5 could very easily have been made orally by a party other than Julian, who then committed it to memory. For as they have already stated (probably accurately), 'when Julian uses Scripture, she relies largely on her memory'.[26] In a predominantly oral environment, there is no reason to assume that Julian would not have heard read such devotional authors as those to whom Margery Kempe refers (i.e. Richard Rolle and Walter Hilton, amongst others).[27] In addition to hearing scriptural texts translated, it is perfectly possible that she would have gleaned a degree of biblical knowledge from such treatises; they are, after all, prolific in their use of scriptural quotation. What can also be said with certainty is that much of Julian's biblical knowledge is likely to have arisen from her close familiarity with the scriptural resonances of the liturgy which would have played a central role in her devotional life.

Of course, given the breadth and depth of her scriptural familiarity, it is tempting to surmise (as Colledge and Walsh initially did) that Julian might have had access to a vernacular version of the scriptures. However, there is no evidence that this is so, and admitting the unlikelihood of her accessing a Wycliffite Bible, there is no extant complete scriptural vernacularisation to which she could be indebted. Arguably, the only biblical text which she might have encountered in translation is the Psalter; the popularity of Rolle's *English Psalter* bears obvious witness to the fact that such texts were in circulation in the late Middle Ages.[28]

Finally, it is possible that Julian might have been familiar with the Vulgate at first hand; some late medieval women do indeed seem to have owned Latin texts.[29] But I remain agnostic on this issue, for while Julian is clearly both learned in and sensitive to the complexities of biblical theology, it is not necessarily imperative to attribute this to a first-hand acquaintance with the Vulgate.

26 *Showings*, p. 37.

27 B. Windeatt, ed., *The Book of Margery Kempe* (Harlow, 2000), 17/1251–61. Watson's re-dating of *ST* and *LT* makes Hiltonian influence possible; *Scale I* is thought to have been composed in the mid 1380s and *Scale II* in the 1390s (before Hilton's death in 1396). See J. P. H. Clark and R. Dorward, eds and trans, *Walter Hilton – The Scale of Perfection*, Classics of Western Spirituality (New Jersey, 1991).

28 H. R. Bramley, ed., *The Psalter translated by Richard Rolle of Hampole* (Oxford, 1884).

29 C. M. Meale, ' ". . . alle the bokes that I haue of latyn, englisch, and frensch": Laywomen and their Books in Late Medieval England', *Women and Literature in Britain 1150–1500*, ed. C. M. Meale (Cambridge, 1993), pp. 128–58.

Furthermore, at a time when, due to the cost and labour of production, Vulgate Bibles were few and far between, it would be utterly misguided to imagine that scriptural knowledge was inevitably gained through first-hand familiarity with the Bible as a material entity.

In addition, it must be recognised that, as both devout laywoman and enclosed contemplative, Julian would have fed night and day on the words of the scriptures, presented in various guises and by various means. This being the case, it is inevitable that her language should become infused with that of the Bible to such an extent that we need not assume that whenever she echoes scriptural terminology, she is always doing so consciously and deliberately. For in claiming divine inspiration for herself, it is arguably inevitable that Julian should echo canonical authors who made similar claims. For example, in chapter 79 of *LT*, she states:

> ther was I lernyd to be dradfull for vnsykernesse of my selfe, for I wot nott how I shalle falle, ne I know not the mesure ne þe gretnesse of my synne. For that wolde I awyst dredfull, and therto I had no answere. (11–14)

In this phrase, Colledge and Walsh locate an allusion to I Corinthians 2:3 ('And I was with you in weakness and in fear and in much trembling'). Yet it is surely ill-judged to infer that whenever Julian refers to her own sin and inadequacy, she is consciously casting herself in the Pauline mould. After all, to accentuate one's failings so as to emphasise God's mercy is a typical Christian device. Further, when Julian states that 'No tonge may telle ne herte fully thynke the paynes that our savyoure sufferde for vs' (*ST* 11/11–12), it is tempting to posit a deliberate echo of I Corinthians 2:9 ('But, as it is written: that eye hath not seen, nor ear heard, neither hath it entered into the heart of man, what things God hath prepared for them that love him'). Yet it is salutary to bear in mind that the similarity may be due simply to the fact that Julian (and other mystical writers) grappled with the ineffability of their experience in much the same way as did Paul.

However, it would be naïve to read either text of the *Revelations* as having been composed without deliberate literary artifice. In this light, it is imperative to examine Julian's biblical self-characterisation in both books of the *Revelations*, to ascertain the degree of imaginative licence which may have informed her re-presentation of her experience. For any experience (whether real or imaginary) becomes, as soon as it is uttered or committed to the page, to some extent a fiction, in that its authenticity can never be objectively gauged. This fictionality of language is compounded by the fact that one can always choose to articulate oneself and one's experiences in words borrowed from others' articulation of themselves and their experiences. Julian's frequent characterisation of herself as a figure of scriptural resonance should be read as part and parcel of this capacity of language to re-invent and even fictionalise the individual.

III

Evidence of Julian's propensity to articulate her experience in terminology of Christ-like resonance can be seen in the first chapter of *ST*, offering an early example of the extent to which her consciousness is steeped in biblical language. Echoing the words of Matthew 26:39 ('he fell upon his face, praying and saying: My Father, if it be possible, let this chalice pass from me. Nevertheless, *not as I will but as thou wilt*' (italics mine)), she writes:

> Lord, thowe woote whate I wolde. ȝyf it be thy wille that I have itt, grawnte itt me, and ȝyf it ne nouȝt thy wille, goode lord, be nought dysplesede, for *I wille nought botte as thowe wille*. (42–5; italics mine)[30]

And her tendency to frame Christ-like phrases as her own can be heard again, slightly later in *ST*, when she states:

> þan thouȝt me *I knewe fulle lytylle whate payne it was that I askyd*
> (10/34–5; italics mine)[31]

echoing in the first person the words of Christ to the mother of the sons of Zebedee, as recorded in Matthew 20:22 ('And Jesus, answering, said: *You know not what you ask*. Can you drink the chalice that I shall drink? They say to him: We can' (italics mine)).

Not only does Julian describe her own experiences and emotions with the assistance of biblical phraseology, but she also represents herself as the recipient of words of comfort and encouragement which appear to have their basis in scripture. Perhaps most notably, in chapter 36 of *LT*, Julian writes:

> tendyrly oure lorde towchyth us and blysydfully callyth vs, seyeng in oure soule: Lett me aloone, my derwurdy chylde, intende to me. I am inogh to þe (45–7)

And in this statement, a clear echo of II Corinthians 12:9a ('My grace is sufficient for thee') can be heard. Further, for a fascinating possibility that, in *ST*, Julian likens her experience to that of doubting Thomas, it is instructive to compare her report of Christ's words to her:

> My childe, ȝif thow kan nought loke in my godhede, see heere how I lette opyn my *syde* and my harte be clovene in twa and lette oute blude and watere, alle þat was thare yn; and this lykes me and so wille I that it do the (13/2–6; italics mine)

with John 20:27 ('Then he saith to Thomas: Put in thy finger hither and see my hands; and bring hither thy hand and put it into my *side*; and be not faithless but believing').

It would be tempting to draw a comparison between Richard Rolle's biblical self-fashioning and this tendency of Julian's to frame her visionary experience in language of biblical resonance. Yet the hermit's scriptural posturing is fundamen-

30 See also Mark 14:36 and Luke 22:42. Cf. *LT* 2/36–8.
31 Cf. *LT* 17/53–4 and 19/21–2.

tally more dramatic than that of Julian, and his use of biblical *figurae* (in reference to both himself and his addressee) is calculated to have an almost seductive effect on his reader, luring her towards the admiration of him and the imitation of Christ. Julian's scriptural mannerisms are, by contrast, less deliberately rhetorical in intent and effect. In fact, although there is (as stated above), a degree of imaginative licence in Julian's biblical self-framing, it could be that her adoption of Christ-like language is in some sense an inevitable by-product of her intense identification with the suffering Christ. Just as she adopts Christ's pain as her own ('I wolde that his paynes ware my paynes' *ST* 3/4), so she, perhaps necessarily, adopts his terminology of suffering.

It is, however, the *Revelations*' minute echoes of biblical terminology that provide us with the most compelling evidence of Julian's intricate scriptural knowledge. When, for example, she writes:

> and suerly I saw that in to this *hye depnesse* our good lorde hym self ledyth vs (*LT* 56/28–9; italics mine)

she is, without a doubt, recollecting the terminology of Ecclesiastes 7:24–5:

> I have tried all things in wisdom. I have said: I will be wise: and it departed further from me. Much more than it was: it is a great depth [*alta profunditas*]. Who shall find it out?

Although it would be tempting to speculate that the very literal phrase 'hye depnesse' suggests that the translation may be Julian's own work, the evidence is minimal.[32] In addition, when she says: 'and thus maye we saye, enioyande: Oure parte is oure lorde' (*ST* 14/26)[33] she is clearly recalling the words of Psalm 15:5a ('The Lord is the portion of my inheritance and my cup').[34] Further, the closing words of Julian's comment in *LT*:

> for that ech kynde that hevyn shall be fulfylled with behovyd nedes of goddys rygh(t)fulnes so to be knytt and onyd in hym that there in were kepte a substannce whych myght nevyr nor shulde be partyd from hym, and that thorow his awne good *wyll* in his endlesse forse(ing) *purpose*. (53/18–22; italics mine)

are undoubtedly indebted to the phrasing of Ephesians 1:11 ('In whom we also are called by lot, being predestinated according to the purpose of him who worketh all things according to the counsel of his will').

Nonetheless, the *Revelations*' biblical echoes are not always so verbally precise. In fact, they are frequently of a more generalised nature. On occasion, for example, Julian can be heard to frame her experience in a form strikingly akin to

32 The Early Version (*EV*) of the Wycliffite Bible also translates 'alta profunditas' literally as 'heeȝ depnesse'. The Late Version (*LV*), however, renders it as 'the depthe is hiȝ'. J. Forshall and F. Madden, eds, *Wycliffite Versions of the Bible,* 4 vols (Oxford, 1850), III, p. 64.

33 Cf. *LT* 30/10–11.

34 Rolle translates this verse, 'Lord is part of myn heritage . . .' (Bramley, *The Psalter*, p. 53) as do both *EV* and *LV* of the Wycliffite Bible (Forshall and Madden, *Wycliffite Versions*, II, p. 750).

that of the New Testament parables. There is a notable instance of this in chapter 79 of *LT*, where the language in which the following account is cast:

> And than wylle he [i.e. God] that we se oure wrechydnesse and mekely be it aknowen; but he wylle nott that we abyde therwith, ne he wylle nott þat we besy vs gretly aboute oure accusyng, ne he wylle nott that we be to wrechydfulle on oure selfe. But he wylle þat we hastely entende to hym, for he stondyth alle aloone, and abydeth vs contynually, monyng and mornyng tylle whan we come. And he hath haste to haue vs to hym, for we are his joy and his delyght, and he is oure salue of oure lyfe (32–9)

recalls unmistakably Luke's parable of the Prodigal Son ('And when he was yet a great way off, his father saw him and was moved with compassion and running to him fell upon his neck and kissed him' Luke 15:20). Similarly, her visual image of God:

> as a lorde in his owne howse, whych lorde hayth callyd alle hys derewurthy frendes to a solempne fest (*LT* 14/5–7)

recalls, among several other scriptural precedents, Matthew's parable of the king who held a marriage feast for his son.[35] Typically, however, Julian is not bound by the possible constraints of the parable form ('Than I saw the lorde takyng no place in his awne howse'), but uses it as a starting point for theological speculation:

> but I saw hym ryally reigne in hys howse, and all fulfyllyth it with joy and myrth, hym selfe endlesly to glad and solace hys derewurthy frendes fulle homely and fulle curtesly, with mervelous melody in endelesse loue in hys awne feyer blessydfulle chere, which glorious chere of the godhede fulfyllyth alle hevyn of ioy and blysse (7–12)

Such assured negotiation of biblical frameworks is also striking in terms of the doctrinal competence that it reveals. Indeed, throughout both *ST* and *LT*, Julian evinces a familiarity with a wide spectrum of biblical doctrine. This is particularly true of her acquaintance with the scriptural background of the Last Judgement. For example, when, in chapter 33 of *LT*, she writes:

> I vnderstond þat alle the creatures þat be of the devylles condiscion in thys lyfe and ther in endyng, ther is no mencyon made of them before god and alle his holyen then of the devylle, notwythstondyng that they be of mankynde (11–14)

she is obviously recalling the biblical principle expressed in texts such as Psalm 68:29 ('Let them be blotted out of the book of the living: and with the just let them not be written') and Revelation 20:15 ('And whosoever was not found written in the book of life was cast into the pool of fire'). In addition, when she states:

[35] Matthew 22:1–14. See also echoes of Matthew 20:1–16's parable (the workers in the vineyard and the inscrutability of God's favour) in *LT* 14/32–5.

> as it es punysched here with sorowe and with penannce, it schalle be rewarded in heuen be the curtayse loue of oure lorde god (*ST* 18/40–1)[36]

she is clearly recollecting gospel sentiments such as those expressed in Luke 6:22–3a ('Blessed shall you be when men shall hate you . . . Be glad in that day and rejoice; for, behold, your reward is great in heaven').

It should, of course, be admitted that such eschatalogical familiarity does not, in itself, present a strong case for Julian's *personal* familiarity with the Bible. After all, as Carol Meale has pointed out, apocalyptic literature was very popular among late medieval women.[37] Yet Julian's doctrinal echoes of the Bible stretch much further than an obvious familiarity with the Last Things, revealing at times what can only be termed an intricate understanding of scriptural theology. In this context, perhaps most striking is her firm grasp of doctrine contained in the New Testament Epistle to the Hebrews, a text rarely cited in contemporary mystical literature.

At the end of the fifth chapter and the beginning of the sixth, Hebrews, equating itself with a certain degree of doctrinal complexity, reads:

> But strong meat is for the perfect; for them who by custom have their senses exercised to the discerning of good and evil. Wherefore, leaving the word of the beginning of Christ, let us go on to things more perfect.

Indeed, devotional authors such as Hilton and the author of *The Chastising of God's Children* warn their female readers away from complexities such as those contained in Hebews, encouraging them to learn to drink 'milk' before embarking on the consumption of 'strong meat'. Yet Julian appears, even in *ST*, to have begun to digest such 'strong meat'. This may be seen, for example, in her allusions to the singularity of Christ's passion ('I wate weele he suffrede nouȝt botte aneȝ' (*ST* 10/27); 'the swete manhode of Crist myght suffer but oonse' (*LT* 22/34)), a point of doctrine emphasised in Hebrews 9:12 and 10:10:

> Neither by the blood of goats or of calves, but by his own blood, [he] entered *once* into the Holies, having obtained eternal redemption . . . we are sanctified by the oblation of the body of Jesus Christ *once*' (italics mine).

An even more striking example of Julian's theological familiarity with Hebrews can be seen in her statement, unique to *LT*, that:

> The precious plenty of his [Christ's] dereworthy blode ascendyth vp into hevyn in the blessed body of our lorde Jesu Crist, and ther is in hym, bledyng, preyeng for vs to the father, and is and shal be as long as vs nedyth. (12/26–9)[38]

This notion of Christ as man's intercessor before the father in heaven clearly has

36 Cf. *LT* 39/32–4.

37 Meale, *Women and Literature*, p. 151 n. 40.

38 *The Prickynge of Love* contains similar statements regarding the intercessory nature of Christ's blood. See H. Kane, ed., *The Prickynge of Love*, Salzburg Studies in English Literature, Elizabethan and Renaissance Studies XCII:10, 2 vols (Salzburg, 1983), p. 35/18–22.

its roots in Hebrews ('Whereby he is able also to save for ever them that come to God by him, always living to make intercession for us'), as does the notion of Christ's blood playing a specific intercessory role in securing the redemption of mankind ('For if the blood of goats and of oxen and the ashes of an heifer, being sprinkled, sanctify such as are defiled, to the cleansing of the flesh; How much more shall the blood of Christ, who by the Holy Ghost offered himself unspotted unto God, cleanse our conscience from dead works, to serve the living God?).[39] In fact, in Hebrews 12:24, we see Christ's blood represented as *speaking*, in a manner similar to the *interceding* blood of Julian's *LT.*

Leaving Hebrews aside, Julian's *LT* doctrine of the motherhood of both God and Christ provides us with another example of her familiarity with biblical theology (this time that of Isaiah). But, in addition, her use of this particular doctrine can be seen as evidence of her willingness to creatively exploit scriptural tenets in order to produce her own distinctive theology. In chapter 60 of *LT,* she writes:

> We wytt that alle oure moders bere vs to payne and to dyeng. A, what is that? But oure very moder Ihesu, he alone beryth vs to joye and to endlesse levyng, blessyd mot he be (18–20)

and she goes on to exploit to the full this comparison between human and divine motherhood. Whereas an earthly mother 'may geue her chylde sucke hyr mylke', Julian claims that Christ feeds us 'with hym selfe' (60/29–32). And whereas an earthly mother 'may *ley* hyr chylde tenderly *to* hyr brest', Julian's Christ 'may homely *lede* vs *in to* his *blessyd* brest' (60/38–9; italics mine). She appears to conclude the comparison thus:

> And in oure gostly forth bryngyng he vsyth more tendernesse in kepyng *without ony comparyson*, by as moch as oure soule is of more pryce in his syght
> (61/2–4; italics mine)

yet cannot resist the pull of the analogy, proceeding to claim that although an earthly mother 'may suffer hyr chylde to peryssch, oure hevenly moder Jhesu may nevyr suffer vs þat be his chyldren to peryssch' (61/28–9).

It should be noted that the comparison which Julian and other medieval authors make between divine and earthly motherhood has its biblical roots in Isaiah 49:15 ('Can a woman forget her infant, so as not to have pity on the son of her womb? And if she should forget, yet will I not forget thee').[40] So, additionally, does Julian's unwillingness, for all her emphasis on Christ's maternal uniqueness, to abandon the terminology of contrast. For even though the writer of Isaiah claims above that the messiah's faithfulness surpasses that of a human mother, neither can he resist reverting to comparison in Isaiah 66:13a:

> As one whom the mother caresseth, so will I comfort you.

[39] For the first biblical reference, see Hebrews 7:25; for the second, see Hebrews 9:13–14.

[40] For historical background, see C. Walker Bynum, *Jesus as Mother: Studies in the Spirituality of the High Middle Ages* (Berkeley, 1984).

IV

It is, however, impossible to explain fully the doctrine of the *Revelations* by means of reference to biblical precedent. For Julian's theology is nothing if not creative; although it can often be clarified by comparison with a scriptural archetype, it cannot always be paralleled by the same. She seems to enjoy moments of inspiration which cannot be explained fully by recourse to biblical precedent. For example, Colledge and Walsh argue that in stating:

> And god shewed me that synne shalle be no shame, but wurshype to man
> (*LT* 38/2–3)[41]

Julian is recalling the sentiment of Romans 4:7–8 ('Blessed are they whose iniquities are forgiven; and whose sins are covered. Blessed is the man to whom the Lord hath not imputed sin'). However, although Julian's phrase echoes that of Paul insofar as they both emphasise the paradoxical profitability of sin, any resemblance ceases beyond this point. For while the scriptural text implicitly distinguishes between those whose sins are forgiven, and those whose are not, suggesting that blessing is only extended to the former, Julian somewhat daringly makes no distinction of this kind.

A similar attempt to 'tame' Julian's adventurousness may also be seen in Colledge and Walsh's reading of Julian's words in chapter 22 of *LT*:

> For yf he seyde he wolde for my loue make new hevyns and new erthys, it ware but lytylle in regarde, for this myght he do ech day, yf that he wolde, without any traveyle. But for to dye for my loue so often that the nomber passyth creatures reason, thys is the hyghest profer that our lorde god myght make to mannes soule, as to my syght (36–41)

and the comparison that they draw with Isaiah 65:17a ('For, behold, I create new heavens and a new earth'). Of course, it is undeniable that Julian does, at this point, echo this particular verse. Yet what Colledge and Walsh's wholesale biblicalisation does not register is Julian's implicit claim that the Christ of her Revelations surpasses the messianic figure of Isaiah. For while the latter is capable (as promised in Isaiah) of making 'new heavens and a new earth', this is, according to Julian, 'but lytylle' in comparison with his willingness, revealed to her own 'syght', 'to dye for my loue so often that the nomber passyth creatures reason'.

Additionally, in Christ's professed willingness to die repeatedly, we can also hear a fascinating expansion on the previously noted doctrine of the singularity of Christ's passion (Hebrews 9:12 and 10:10). For while in both *ST* and *LT* Julian demonstrates an awareness of this doctrinal point, in both texts she also presents the Christ of her visions as surpassing (without contradicting) it:

[41] Cf. *ST* 17/17.

> And in these wordes: If I myght suffer more I wolde suffer more, I saw truly þat as often as he myght dye, as often he wolde, and loue shulde nevyr lett hym haue rest till he hath done it. And I behelde with grete dyligence for to wet how often he wolde dye yf he myght. And truly the number passyd my vnderstandyng and my wittes so ferre that my reson myght nott nor cold nott comprehende it ne take it.
> (*LT* 22/25–31)[42]

In drawing on, but outdoing, the precedent of Hebrews, Julian presents her own doctrine as biblically learned *and* theologically daring.

V

Having established Julian's profound scriptural familiarity, there remains to be explored the nature of the shift in biblical hermeneutic between *ST* and *LT*. In this context, it is noteworthy that while the earlier and briefer of the two treatises contains no explicit reference to the Bible as the Word of God, the latter refers twice (in chapter 32) to 'God's Word'. The first allusion is found when Julian states:

> oure feyth is groundyd in goddes worde (38–9)[43]

and the second occurs when she writes:

> and it longyth to oure feyth that we beleue that goddys worde shalle be sauyd in alle thyng . . . I shalle saue my worde in alle thyng . . . he shalle saue his worde in alle thyng. (39–40, 50–1, 56)[44]

Of interest in both of the above statements are the simple facts that they reflect openly on the value of 'goddes worde' and that they are unique to *LT*. For in this tiny discrepancy between the two treatises, it may be that we have found the key to the alteration in scriptural hermeneutic between *ST* and *LT*.

As discussed, it is highly likely that *LT* was composed after a lengthy period of solitude, during which Julian would have occupied herself at least partially in rumination on the 'ground' of her 'feyth', the Word of God. Indeed, also unique to *LT* are her words:

> In theyse vj wordes that folowyth where he seyth: Take it [i.e. the 'feyth' that she has gained through her visionary experience], his menyng is to fasten it feytfully in oure hert (71/2–3)

which are significant insofar as they reflect openly on the value of inward thought and rumination. In fact, on several occasions, the scriptural usage of Julian's *LT* as compared with that of *ST* appears to bear witness to such an

42 Cf. *ST* 12/33–6.

43 Note the possible echo of Romans 10:17 '*Faith*, then, comes by hearing; and hearing by the *word* of Christ' (italics mine).

44 Note the possible echo of Matthew 24:35 'Heaven and earth shall pass; but my words shall not pass.'

extended period of biblical rumination.[45] To offer just a few examples, it is fascinating to examine Julian's *LT* deployment of language reminiscent of I Corinthians (which, incidentally, of all books of the New Testament, is the one whose phraseology she uses most repetivitely and ruminatively). For example, echoing the terminology of verses such as I Corinthians 3:11 ('For other foundation no man can lay, but that which is laid, which is Christ Jesus'), she writes, in *ST*:

> For Criste hym selfe is grownde of alle the lawe of crysten menn (17/15)

and this statement is reproduced in *LT* (40/45). However, *LT* contains further and repeated allusions to this biblically inspired notion ('he is ground of alle oure hoole lyfe in loue' (39/44); 'I am grounde . . .' (42/5); 'we know not truly that oure lorde is grounde in whom that oure prayer spryngyth' (42/18–9)), all of which may suggest an extended period of rumination on the same.

Of course, in opposition to this theory of rumination could be raised the simple objection that *LT* is six times the length of *ST*, and that it is thus bound to contain more scriptural allusions. However, what is interesting about the biblicalism of *LT* is not so much the increased *variety* of allusion as the increasingly detailed and creative exploration of scriptural terminology which had already been introduced in *ST*. For example, in *ST*, Julian writes:

> There was none ese ne na comforthe to my felynge botte hope, faythe and charyte (9/25–6)

and again:

> for in this oure lorde lered me the same, to hafe of goddes gyfte faith, hope and charyte (19/7–8)

both of which contain straightforward echoes of the Pauline triad of I Corinthians 13:13, such as are commonplace in religious literature of the period. However, although Julian continues to allude to this verse in *LT*, it becomes increasingly woven into the texture of her own prose, suggesting a greater ease and familiarity with biblical terminology. For example, in chapter 7 of *LT*, she writes:

> But feyth and beleue with charyte deserue the mede (58–9)

and she goes on to incorporate the phrase within an affective context:

> The sekyng with feyth, hope and charitie plesyth oure lord (10/72–3)

before allowing herself to alter the syntactic relationship between the words, as in chapter 36:

> and that for strenghyng of our feyth, and encrese oure hope in charyte (69–70)

and in chapter 65:

> Which presence in all thing is most desyrid, for it worketh that mervelous sekernesse in true faith and seker hope by greatnes of charitie in drede that is sweet and delectable. (13–15)

45 This is particularly true of Julian's use of the New Testament epistles.

Julian's fluent adaptation of biblical language to her own vernacular is not the only point of difference between the scriptural echoes contained in her two texts, but should be viewed together with the *LT exemplum* of the lord and servant, an expansion of *ST*'s fourteenth revelation. It is the evidence provided by this *exemplum*, together with that provided by the increased biblical assimilation apparent in much of *LT*, which provides the most compelling argument in favour of a period of biblical exploration and rumination between the composition of the two texts.

Julian herself foregrounds the distinctive nature of this particular showing by referring to it as a wonderful 'example', a term not used in reference to any other of her visions, and by claiming that it took 'twenty yere . . . saue thre monthys' (51/36–7) to comprehend its significance. It forms *LT*'s most comprehensive expansion of *ST*, and chapter 51 as a whole bears witness to the fact that it is not only this showing, but also (and perhaps more significantly) Julian's response to it, which is distinctive. Around the simple image of a servant sent on an errand by his master, and injured by falling into a 'slade', she constructs a theological exploration of considerable complexity.

What is most striking about the *exemplum*'s distinctive biblicalism is the fact that, in chapter 51, Julian stands *outside* the scriptural text in a way which is not paralleled elsewhere in the *Revelations*. There is little, if any, of the biblical self-characterisation that has been noted in other parts of her text. In fact, Julian herself plays a very small part in this *exemplum*, other than to remind her audience that she did not reach a full understanding of it for nearly two decades. Her retelling of the *exemplum* contains little of her earlier expressed affective desire to suffer with Christ. On the contrary, she watches him (represented by the servant) with relative dispassion, and draws logical conclusions from his actions. Near the outset of chapter 51, she claims that:

> an inwarde goostely shewyng of the lordes menyng descendyd in to my soule
> (54–5)

and, as Colledge and Walsh note, this is the only place in the *Revelations* when Julian writes of a showing coming down from on high. That she chooses this occasion to speak of the 'descent' of revelation is significant since it supports the theory that she is, in the retelling of this *exemplum*, standing at a distance from the material of her showing, and adopting something of an objective perspective on the same. It implies a definite distinction between herself and her subject-matter.

Indeed, this gesture towards objectivity releases Julian to 'inhabit' several perspectives other than simply her own in the retelling of the vision; at specific times, she inhabits the mind of the lord, at others, that of the servant, and, at still others, that of the 'commentator' upon the actions and attitudes of both. This is, of course, an explicitly exegetical device, the deployment of which suggests strongly that by the time she came to write *LT*, Julian had gained some familiarity with the conventions of allegorical interpretation.

That Julian's awareness of the conventions of allegorical reading was fairly mature is indicated by her choice of terminology in the retelling of her fourteenth revelation. Not only does she call the vision an *exemplum*, a technical term in itself, but she also refers to 'þe propertes and the condescions' revealed in this 'example' (88).[46] Further, that she speaks, more than once, of the 'doubyll vnderstandyng' with which she views the matter of her revelation indicates that she is fully aware of the duality of signification comprehended by conventionally allegorical reading. The way in which she 'reads' individual objects and instances in the revelation also bears witness to a competent familiarity with the conventions of exegetical allegory – nothing simply 'means' on a literal level. She interprets allegorically, for example, not only 'the manner of syttyng of the lorde and the place he satt on':

> his syttyng on the erth, bareyn and desert, is thus to mene: he made mannes soule to be his owne cytte and his dwellyng place (143–6)

but also 'the coloure of his clothyng and the manner of shape':

> The blewhed of the clothyng betokenyth his stedfastnesse, the brownhed of his feyer face with the semely blackhede of the eyen was most accordyng to shew his holy sobyrnesse, the largenesse of his clothyng, whych was feyer flammyng about, betokenyth that he hath beclosyd in hym all hevyns and all endlesse joy and blysse. (153–7)

Similarly, she reads the 'manner of stondynge of the seruannt' and 'his manner of clothyng' (96–7) as possessing some significance beyond themselves.

This 'doubyll vnderstandyng' also reveals itself in her more explicitly doctrinal reading of her vision. Her interpretation of 'the servant', for example, is competent in its articulation of the dual nature of Christ:

> In the servant is comprehendyd Adam, that is to sey alle men. And therfore whan I sey the sonne, it menyth the godhed whych is evyn with the fader, and whan I sey the servannt, it menyth Crystes manhode whych is ryghtfull Adam. (211–15)

Indeed, in this awareness of Christ as at once servant and son, human and divine, Julian's *Revelations* (and, in particular, the fourteenth of these) can be said to have much in common with the biblical presentation of Christ in Hebrews. In addition, the eschatological crescendo with which her retelling of the revelation concludes is painstaking in its theological accuracy:

> The body ley in the graue tyll E(as)ter morow; and fro that tyme he ley nevyr more. For ther was ryghtfully endyd the walowyng and the wrythyng, the gronyng and the monyng; and oure foule dedely flessch . . . then by oure savyoure was made feyer, new, whyt and bryght . . . Now syttyth nott þe lorde on erth in wyldernesse, but he

46 The MED definition most appropriate to Julian's use of 'exaumple' is (3) 'A story which teaches a lesson; a nature fable or parable; an instructive instance from Scripture, history or the classics' (the MED actually dates the first deployment of 'exaumple' in this context to 1420). The definition most appropriate to Julian's use of 'propertes' is (5c) 'details of a story or report, particulars' (the MED dates the first deployment of 'properte' in this context to 1387). 'Condescion' is understood to mean 'condition'.

> syttyth on hys ryche and nob(lest) seet, whych he made in hevyn most to his lykyng . . . Now stondyth not the sonne before the fader on the lyfte syde as a laborer, but he sytteth on the faders ryght hande in endlesse rest an pees. (302–23)

What is also remarkable in biblical terms is the very shape in which the vision is cast. For while the revelation itself is a profoundly original narrative, its mode recalls that of several New Testament parables. Not only is it redolent of the parable of the prodigal son, but, in its characterisation of Christ as gardener, it recalls the several parables centred around vineyards and the relative merits of those who tend them.[47] In fact, its allegorical presentation itself may be said to draw on New Testament precedent. For just as Christ's parables offer themselves up for exegetical reading, so Julian's *exemplum* demands an analysis which ventures beyond the literal. The sheer simplicity of its ostensible events, coupled with the profunditiy of its theological significance, is in itself an *imitatio* of a Christ-like mode of address.

Yet for all its borrowings from the terminology and style of academic exegesis and for all its echoes of parabolic utterance, Julian's retelling of this *exemplum* is remarkably idiosyncratic. It is, furthermore, characteristic of the ease with which she eludes conventional categorisation. For the fact remains that while echoing the New Testament parables, the showing of the lord and the servant is apparently wholly original. And while recalling the trends of academic exegesis, what Julian is allegorising is not a *text* but an intangible product of her own visionary experience. What sets her apart from the traditions on which she draws as well as from her contemporaries is, therefore, the consummate skill with which she manages to occupy the positions of both *interpreter* and *interpreted*, of both *exegete* and *text*. Without straying from the bounds of orthodoxy, she turns her back on conventional textual exegesis and chooses, instead, to extract significance from her own 'vnderstandyng'. Of course, if she did not have access to academic and exegetical texts, if her allegorical awareness was simply a result of aural instruction or a product of her own memory, then all that was ruminatively available to her was her own visionary experience.

The blurring of boundaries between authorial prose as *commentary* and the Bible as *that which is commented upon* in the writings of the Middle English mystics is at its most effective in Julian's *Revelations*. For it is only in this text that a scriptural mode of utterance is subsumed almost entirely to the authorial narrative, and that the conventional tools of biblical interpretation are applied to the 'living' text of personal visionary experience.

[47] See, for example, Matthew 9:37–8; 13:31–2; 13:44; 20:1–16; 21:28–41; Luke 13:6–9; 20:9–17 etc.

VI

It has been the task of these pages to examine the 'embedded' nature of Julian's vernacular biblicalism, the extent to which a scriptural mode of expression becomes an unconscious adjunct of her own voice. However, not *all* of Julian's biblical allusions are incorporated deliberately into the texture of her own prose; there are, in *ST*, three identifiable occasions on which Julian alludes directly to scriptural narrative and sets these allusions apart from her own voice. The first occurs in chapter 9, when she claims:

> And in the tyme of ioye I myght hafe sayde with Paule: Nathynge schalle departe me fro the charyte of Cryste (33–4)

a statement which plainly echoes the terminology of Romans 8:38–9 ('For I am sure that . . . [nothing] . . . shall be able to separate us from the love of God which is in Christ Jesus our Lord'). The second highlighted allusion to the scriptures occurs immediately afterwards, when Julian remarks that:

> in payne y myght hafe sayde with saynte Petyr: Lorde, save me, I perysche. (35–6)

As Colledge and Walsh suggest, it is probable that this statement is a conflation of Matthew 8:25 ('And they came to him and awaked him, saying: Lord, save us, we perish') and Matthew 14:30 ('But, seeing the wind strong, he [Peter] was afraid; and when he began to sink, he cried out, saying: Lord, save me'). The third of *ST*'s highlighted biblical references is to Philippians 2:5 ('For let this mind be in you, which was also in Christ Jesus') and is found in chapter 10:

> Swilke paynes I sawe that alle es to litelle þat y can telle or saye, for itt maye nouȝt be tolde, botte ylke saule aftere the sayinge of saynte Pawle schulde feele in hym þat in Criste Jhesu. (23–6)

When composing *LT*, Julian retains the first two of *ST*'s scriptural allusions, but deletes the third. Colledge and Walsh's speculations on the reasons behind this deletion are interesting:

> Perhaps [Julian] or a later scribe removed this rare direct Scriptural quotation, with its source adduced, because of the contemporary controversies which culminated in the 1408 Oxford condemnation and prohibition of such translation without episcopal licence.[48]

Indeed, it does seem highly unlikely that Julian could have remained unconscious of and unaffected by the contemporary translation controversies. For if one accepts that *ST* was written in the mid to late 1380s and *LT* in the late 1390s or early 1400s, then it becomes more imperative than ever to recognise that even when composing *ST*, Julian could not have been unaware of the potentially

48 *Showings*, p. 93. If this is the case, then presumably it would have been more acceptable for Julian (or a scribe) to have retained the two other direct allusions, referring, as they do, to well-known biblical phrases and characters, rather than to demonstrate familiarity with the more subtle thought of Philippians 2:5.

dubious nature of scriptural translation. Further, it is conceivable that *LT* could have been written around the time of the 1409 promulgation of Arundel's Constitutions, a possibility which would go some way towards explaining *LT*'s omission of the Philippians reference. Indeed, it could be possible to argue that behind Julian's tendency to weave scriptural language seamlessly into her own prose there is not only the vaguely romantic notion of the solitary with a consciousness steeped in the Bible, but the far more prosaic fact that political considerations dictated the camouflage of all but the most basic of scriptural familiarity.

'WE ARE UNITED WITH GOD (AND GOD WITH US?)': ADAPTING RUUSBROEC IN *THE TREATISE OF PERFECTION OF THE SONS OF GOD* AND *THE CHASTISING OF GOD'S CHILDREN*

MARLEEN CRÉ

JAN VAN RUUSBROEC (1293–1381) was introduced to the Middle English readership of *The Treatise of Perfection of the Sons of God* as 'dan john rusbroke, the first prior of the chartyrhowse in valle viridi iuxta bruxellam'.[1] The anonymous translator of *De calculo candido*, the Latin translation of Ruusbroec's *Vanden blinckenden steen* (*The Sparkling Stone*) was right about both Ruusbroec's function and location, but mistakenly presented him as a Carthusian.

Ruusbroec was the prior of the monastery of Augustinian canons regular at Groenendaal, not far from Brussels. He was one of a community of five men, three priests and two laybrothers, who in 1434 were given permission by Duke Jan III of Brabant to start a religious community in an abandoned hermitage in the forest of Soignes. While still at Brussels, the three priests – Vranke van den Coudenberg, Jan Hinckaert, the chaplain who had been responsible for his kinsman Ruusbroec's upbringing, and Ruusbroec – had already given up the worldly life of the clergy associated with the wealthy cathedral chapter in favour of an apostolic life of poverty and contemplation. The move to Groenendaal added the physical solitude of the forest to the spiritual solitude the men had chosen and lived amid the hustle and bustle of the Cathedral town.[2] The community soon adopted the rule of St Augustine and became a monastery of Augustinian canons. It grew and prospered, with the astute organizer Vranke van den Coudenberg as dean, and Ruusbroec as prior.

When the community settled at Groenendaal, Ruusbroec had already written five of his eleven works: *Dat rijcke der ghelieven* (*The Kingdom of Lovers*), *Die geestelike brulocht* (*The Spiritual Espousals*), *Vanden blinckenden steen* (*The Sparkling Stone*), *Vanden vier becoringhen* (*The Four Temptations*) and *Vanden*

1 See *The Chastising of God's Children and The Treatise of Perfection of the Sons of God*, ed. Joyce Bazire and Eric Colledge (Oxford, 1957), p. 229, lines 4–5. Subsequent references to this edition are by page and line numbers, given in the text.

2 Geert Warnar, *Ruusbroec: Literatuur en mystiek in de veertiende eeuw* (Amsterdam, 2003), pp. 171–4. See also Paul Verdeyen, *Ruusbroec and his Mysticism* (Collegeville, 1994), pp. 31–40.

kerstenen ghelove (*The Christian Faith*).[3] In Groenendaal, he would finish *Vanden geesteliken tabernakel* (*The Spiritual Tabernacle*) and compose *Vanden seven sloten* (*The Seven Enclosures*), *Een spieghel der eeuwigher salicheit* (*A Mirror of Eternal Blessedness*), *Van seven trappen* (*The Seven Rungs in the Ladder of Spiritual Love*), *Boecsken der verclaringhe* (*The Little Book of Clarification*) and *Vanden XII beghinen* (*The Twelve Beguines*). It was Ruusbroec's reputation as a saintly man and inspired author that attracted many visitors to Groenendaal, Geert Grote (d. 1384), the founder of the *Devotio moderna*, and the German Dominican and mystic Johannes Tauler (1300–1361) among them.

Soon Ruusbroec's works began to be disseminated beyond the author's immediate circle. The Benedictines of Ter Doest in Western Flanders asked for a Latin translation of the *Brulocht*, arguing that they had difficulties understanding the Brabant vernacular. The Latin translation was undertaken by Willem Jordaens (d. 1372), Ruusbroec's fellow-Augustinian, who also translated *Vanden blinckenden steen*, *Vanden geesteliken tabernakel* and *Van seven trappen* into Latin. Geert Grote translated *Die geestelike brulocht*, *Van seven trappen* and *Een spieghel der eeuwigher salicheit.* A Premonstratensian of Park, near Leuven, translated *Vanden vier becoringhen* and *Boecsken der verclaringhe. Die geestelike brulocht*, *Vanden blinckenden steen*, *Vanden vier becoringhen* and *Boecsken der verclaringhe* were translated into High German by the Godfriends in Strasbourg.[4] The Middle Dutch works were probably taken there by Johannes Tauler.[5]

Two of Ruusbroec's texts survive in Middle English to this day: the anonymous translation into Middle English of Ruusbroec's *Vanden blinkenden steen*, a single copy of which occurs in British Library, MS Additional 37790, and fragments of the *Die geestelike brulocht* which were translated to form part of *The Chastising of God's Children*.[6] Both attestations of Ruusbroec material in Middle English appear to have been translated from Latin versions of the Middle Dutch originals that travelled across the Channel at the end of the fourteenth or the beginning of the fifteenth century. The *Treatise* was translated from *De calculo candido*, the Latin version of the *Steen* usually, though probably mistakenly,

3 See Paul Mommaers and Jan Van Bragt, *Mysticism Buddhist and Christian: Encounters with Jan van Ruusbroec* (New York, 1995), p. 2.

4 See Guido De Baere, 'Ruusbroec's "Spieghel" in de Latijnse vertaling van Geert Grote', in *Boeken voor de Eeuwigheid: Middelnederlands geestelijk proza*, ed. Thom Mertens (Amsterdam, 1993), pp. 157–8. Also see Thom Mertens, 'Ruusbroec onder de Godsvrienden', in *Die Spätmittelalterliche Rezeption Niederländischer Literatur im Deutschen Sprachgebiet*, Amsterdamer Beiträge zur Älteren Germanistik XLVII (1997), pp. 109–30 and Warnar, *Ruusbroec*, pp. 128–30 and 134–41.

5 Warnar, *Ruusbroec*, p. 127.

6 References to Ruusbroec's Middle Dutch originals can be found in *Jan van Ruusbroec: Die Geestelike Brulocht*, ed. J. Alaerts (Turnhout, 1988) and in *Jan van Ruusbroec: Vanden blinkenden steen, Vanden vier becoringhen, Vanden kerstenen ghelove, Brieven*, ed. G. de Baere, Th. Mertens and H. Noë (Turnhout, 1991). References are to line numbers. Passages from these texts quoted in English translation have also been taken from these editions.

attributed to Willem Jordaens,[7] and the fragments of the *Brulocht* from Grote's translation *Ornatus spiritualis desponsationis*.[8]

In this paper, I will discuss the translators' reactions to one particular theme in Ruusbroec's *Steen* and *Brulocht*, i.e. the equal partnership of God and the soul in contemplation, an experience Ruusbroec characteristically describes as a dynamic process with two moments, union and unity.

The *Treatise*-translator's identification of Ruusbroec as a Carthusian is one clue among many pointing towards the role of the Carthusian Order in the transmission of Ruusbroec's works to and in England. MS Additional 37790 (Amherst), the manuscript in which the unique copy of the *Treatise* occurs, can be associated with the Carthusian Order in so many ways that it seems extremely likely it was produced by Carthusians for Carthusians. Containing the Carmelite Richard Misyn's translations of Rolle's *Emendatio Vitae* and *Incendium Amoris*, the short text of Julian of Norwich's *Revelations*, the translation of Ruusbroec's *Steen* and M. N.'s Middle English translation of Marguerite Porète's *Mirror of Simple Souls*, Amherst focuses on the solitary contemplative life. This singleness of purpose, expressed in a quite radical sense in these texts, is repeated and strengthened in the many shorter compilations and fragments of texts that have been inserted between the authorial texts.[9] The life described, then, eminently agrees with the radical vocation of the Carthusian monk. Though it could be argued that this anthology was originally intended to serve a female audience – all but one of the texts in the anthology are in English, the copyist leaves in Misyn's dedication of the *Fire of Love* to 'Sister Margarete' and put in the *Revelations*, a text by a female author[10] – the rewriting of parts of Rolle's *Ego Dormio*

7 The attribution is questioned in Hilde Schreel-Noë, 'Jan van Ruusbroec *Vanden blinkenden steen* – Willem Jordaens *De calculo candido*: Een vertaaltechnisch onderzoek' (Wijchen, 1980) (Unpublished paper, University of Nijmegen), pp. 126–7. See also Guido De Baere, 'Een Latijnse Deelvertaling van Ruusbroec's "Tabernakel" in handschrift Wenen, Österreichische Nationalbibliothek, series nova 12.899', in *Ons Geestelijk Erf* lxx (1996), pp. 143–56. The edition of the *Calculus* used here is *Jan van Ruysbroeck: Vanden Blinckenden Steen, met W. Jordaens' Latijnsche vertaling*, ed. D. Ph. Muller (Leuven, 1921). References to this edition are to page and line numbers.

8 In their 1957 edition of *The Chastising*, Bazire and Colledge incorrectly assume that the compiler used Jordaens' translation of the *Brulocht*. This erroneous assumption was rectified in G. B. De Soer, 'The Relationship of the Latin Versions of Ruysbroek's "Die Geestelike Brulocht" to "The Chastising of God's Children" ', *Mediaeval Studies* xxi (1959), pp. 129–46. The edition of the *Ornatus* used here is *Ioannis Rusbrochii Ornatus Spiritualis Desponsationis Gerardo Magno Interprete*, ed. Rijcklof Hofman, Corpus Christianorum Continuatio Mediaevalis CLXXII (Turnhout, 2000). References to this edition are to book and line numbers.

9 See Marleen Cré, 'Vernacular Mysticism in the Charterhouse: An Analysis of BL MS Additional 37790 in its Religious and Literary Context' (University of Fribourg Doctoral Dissertation, 2001).

10 Marguerite Porète's *Mirror of Simple Souls* circulated as an anonymous text until the identification of its author by Romana Guarneri in 1946. M. N., who translated the *Mirror* into Middle English, thought its author was a man, and the text did not circulate

for a male, rather than its original female audience, suggests a male readership. That the Carthusian textual critic James Grenehalgh left annotations in both the *Fire of Love* and the *Mirror* further corroborates this hypothesis. In addition, the *Mirror of Simple Souls* survives in two manuscripts besides Amherst, Bodleian Library, Oxford, MS Bodley 505 and St John's College, Cambridge, MS 71, both of which originated in the London Charterhouse. Next to the Middle English *Mirror*, MS Bodley 505 also contains a copy of *The Chastising of God's Children*, which also places the Middle English fragments of Ruusbroec's *Brulocht* within the Carthusian sphere.

The identification of Ruusbroec as a Carthusian by the *Treatise*-translator was probably borrowed from the *Confirmacio ordinis cartusiensis*, a text found in Trinity College, Cambridge, MS 1401. Ruusbroec is mentioned in a section entitled 'Si sanctis ac miraculis personarum ordinis carthusiensis queratur, qui habet aures audiendi, audiat.'[11]

> So many shone in La Grande Chartreuse and in other Houses of the Order by signs and wonders, of whom the deeds were and are considered miraculous. Some are remarkable for the fervour of their contemplation, as if they were set ablaze by fire. Others are lifted up from the earth. *Thus master Johannes Rusbroke, Prior of the House Vallis Viridis close to Brussels, of the Carthusian Order* [*Item dominus Johannes Rusbroke Prior domus uallis viridis iuxta Bruxellam ordinis Carthusiensis*], was a man of miraculous holiness and contemplation.[12]

The *Treatise*-translator's identification of Ruusbroec seems clearly inspired by this notice of him. The English Carthusians would seem to have confused the Augustinian priory Groenendaal near Brussels with the Charterhouse of Vauvert near Paris.[13]

The *Confirmacio* lists some of Ruusbroec's works.

as a *woman's book*. See Nicholas Watson, 'Melting into God the English Way: Deification in the Middle English Version of Marguerite Porète's *Mirouer des simples âmes anienties*', in *Prophets Abroad: The Reception of Continental Holy Women in Late Medieval England*, ed. Rosalynn Voaden (Cambridge, 1996), p. 26.

11 See Eric Colledge, '*The Treatise of Perfection of the Sons of God*: A Fifteenth-Century English Ruysbroeck Translation', *English Studies* xxxiii (1952), p. 52. The passages from this text quoted here were taken from this article. In Trinity MS 1401 they can be found on fols 86r–v.

12 For the Latin of this and the following quotation see Colledge, '*The Treatise*', p. 52.

13 Dr Cees Schepers, who edited Jordaens' translation of Ruusbroec's *Brulocht* has shown that the Carthusians of Vauvert copied Jordaens' Ruusbroec translations *De ornatu* and *De calculo sive De Perfectione filiorum Dei*. He has shown that Paris, Bibliothèque Mazarine MS 921, containing Jordaens' Ruusbroec translations and several works by Gerson, was copied from a Vauvert model, arguing convincingly that in the Mazarine colophon 'valluicide' is a scribal misreading of 'vallis viridis'. The Vauvert manuscript is no longer extant. Though it is tempting to start speculating about the involvement of Vauvert Charterhouse in the dissemination of Ruusbroec's texts, there is not enough evidence at the moment to establish whether *De calculo* reached England through contacts between the English Charterhouses and Vauvert.

> [Johannes Rusbroke] was believed to be simple as an unlettered person, yet the style and subject matter of the books he composed, such as *The Seven Enclosures* and *The Taking of the Eucharist*, and – very much so – *Of the Perfection of the Sons of God* or *Of the Genealogy of Virtues*, prove him to have been a man of the greatest wisdom, be it infused or acquired. He also wrote a greatly edifying treatise for men dedicated to the contemplative life and for others, which divides into three books: the first is entitled *Of the Active and Moral Life*, the second *Of the Spiritual and Affective Life*, the third *Of the Supernatural and Contemplative Life*. Search him more fully in his books and writings, and you will find a man filled with the Holy Ghost, as it will be most clearly obvious from his doctrine. There have been, and still are many saints that neither performed, nor perform miracles, and that have not been canonized.

The works mentioned here are *The Seven Enclosures*, *The Sparkling Stone* (under its alternative title *The Perfection of the Sons of God*, with as another alternative title *The Genealogy of Virtues*) and *The Spiritual Espousals*, untitled, but correctly described as 'a treatise for men who dedicated themselves to the contemplative life', and as consisting of three books. Warnar, Ruusbroec's most recent biographer, presupposes a continental Carthusian source for the *Confirmacio*'s information on Ruusbroec's works,[14] which were eagerly read and copied in the Order. It is likely, however, that the works mentioned were the ones circulating among the English Carthusians.

It would seem that the first origins of the transmission of Ruusbroec's works across the Channel lie in personal contacts between the Groenendaal priory and members of (or people associated with) the Carthusian Order. The Carthusians of Herne, living within walking distance of Groenendaal, produced several manuscript anthologies of a selection of Ruusbroec's works in the last quarter of the fourteenth century. In describing a visit Ruusbroec made to the Charterhouse, Brother Geeraert of Saintes' prologue to one of these anthologies provides an important early biographical account of the mystic.[15] Geert Grote, whose Latin translation of the *Brulocht* was used as the source text for the fragments of Book II selected and translated by the compiler of the *Chastising*, stayed at the Charterhouse of Monnikhuizen (Arnhem) from 1375 to 1379, and it seems likely that he translated the *Brulocht* there. Significantly, seven of the thirteen manuscripts in which Grote's *Ornatus* survives are of Carthusian provenance.[16] In addition, on the foundation of Sheen Charterhouse in 1415, some of the Monnikhuizen monks moved to the new house because there were not enough English monks to fill it.[17] Though it seems most likely that these monks brought Grote's translation of Ruusbroec's *Brulocht* to England, the dating of the *Chastising* as a text probably written before 1400 does suggest earlier intensive

14 Warnar, *Ruusbroec*, p. 263.

15 The Middle Dutch prologue has been edited in W. De Vreese, 'Bijdragen tot de kennis van het leven en de werken van Jan van Ruusbroec', *Het Belfort* x/2 (1895), pp. 7–20.

16 Most of these come from continental Charterhouses. The only copy of Grote's *Ornatus* currently in a British Library is British Library MS Royal 6 B. IX, a fifteenth-century manuscript. The provenance of this manuscript is unknown.

17 Colledge, '*The Treatise*', p. 55.

contacts between Monnikhuizen and the Charterhouses of the English Province.[18] The Latin translation of the *Steen* would equally have been carried across the Channel by Carthusians.[19]

The Treatise of Perfection of the Sons of God and *The Chastising of God's Children* differ as to purpose and audience. *The Treatise* is a complete translation of its source text. On the whole, it keeps the original's structure intact and keeps Ruusbroec's concise but complete account of the different moments of spiritual ascent. The *Chastising*, on the other hand, is a compilation that discusses one aspect of the religious life, i.e. temptation. It is deftly put together by a translator-compiler who does not seek in the first place to render his source texts for their own sake, but to fit the fragments he selected and edited into the structure and contexts of his own design. As such, the Middle English Ruusbroec texts exemplify two types of fifteenth-century English literary activity: translation of authorial texts and translation-compilation.[20] If, as I suspect and tentatively suggest, the *Treatise*-translator and the *Chastising*-compiler were Carthusians, the shape in which they passed on the *Brulocht* and the *Steen* also teaches us about two kinds of pastoral care practised by the Carthusian Order in fifteenth-century England: a specialised pastoral care within the order, that focused on making challenging mystical texts available to readers within the Charterhouse; and a more popularising pastoral care steering clear of any texts that could be called speculative to dispense to readers outside the Charterhouse. In spite of the differences between *The Treatise* and the *Chastising*, and the differences between the translator and the translator-compiler,[21] they both react in a very similar way to Ruusbroec's description of the being one of the soul and God in contemplation.

18 See Bazire and Colledge, *Chastising of God's Children*, pp. 34–7. See also Nicholas Watson, 'Middle English Mystics', in *The Cambridge History of Medieval English Literature*, ed. David Wallace (Cambridge, 1999), pp. 539–65 at p. 561. Here Watson refers to the *Chastising* as one of 'the classics of the years before 1410'. I intend to deal with these matters more fully elsewhere.

19 One clue here is the presence of the *Treatise* in Amherst. The only manuscript that contains *De calculo* that is currently in a British library, and was probably in England in the medieval period as well, is MS Heneage 3083 (MS DD/WHb/3083), which was deposited in the Somerset County Record Office at Taunton until 1991, when it was returned to its owners, the Heneage Family of Coker Court, Somerset. See Michael G. Sargent, 'The Heneage Manuscript of *Calculus De Perfectione Filiorum Dei* and the Middle English *Treatise of Perfection of the Sons of God*', *Ons Geestelijk Erf* lix/4 (1985), pp. 533–59. This manuscript contains a Rolle compilation that is similar to the compilation *De Excellentia Contemplationis*, 'which seems to have been a product of the Charterhouse of Sheen, near London, or the neighbouring Brigittine convent of Syon' (ibid., p. 533).

20 Watson, 'Middle English Mystics', p. 560.

21 I discuss the differences between the Latin and Middle English texts as the result of the translators' decisions. If any variant readings in the manuscripts suggest that the omission or change possibly occurred at another stage in the transmission of the texts, I signal the variant reading.

Central to Ruusbroec's work is his understanding of the relationship between the contemplative and God as a highly personal, dynamic experience in which the soul and God are equal partners. Ruusbroec describes the soul being one with the divine as a dynamic process of 'union' and 'unity' alternating. In the contemplative experience the soul finds a dynamic balance between work and rest. The soul's desire for God makes it work its way to him in inner activity. This inner activity is a response to God's outflowing touch of the mystic's soul. God's outflowing touch, and the mystic's reaction to it is what Ruusbroec calls 'union'. The Middle Dutch term Ruusbroec uses here is *eeninghe*, the present participle, a verb form signifying a process: the meeting of the soul and God. Next to union there is another aspect of the being one of the soul and God. The soul can rise to a state above union, defined by Ruusbroec as 'unity', Middle Dutch *eenicheit*. Unity comes about because the soul is touched by God's indrawing touch, as opposed to the outflowing touch the soul feels in its experience of union with the divine. When the soul feels unity with the divine, it is in a state of blessedness and idleness and does not experience any difference with God.[22] Thus the experience of being one is a constant alternation of union and unity, the soul's drawing to God in union, and God's drawing in of the soul in a brief and fleeting moment of stable rest that cannot last, and needs to revert to union again. The soul's being one with God is a process characterized by movement and the simultaneity of opposites.

> Wherfore vs behoues to grownde oure lyfe vpon a profounde depenesse; and so we may in euerlastynge loue drowne, and alle of oure selfe into inserchable depnesse be drownde, in þe whiche loue we schalle be alterate into ane incomprehensible height. And also with that loue whiche is wantynge maner we schalle grope, and it schalle lede vs and brynge vs agayne into the gate of the incomprehensible depnesse of charite, in the whiche we schalle flowe frome oureselfe, and flowe agayne in vnknawyn swetnesses thorowe the spirit of the goodness of god, in the whiche we schalle be made liqued and stable euerlastyngly be the ioye of god.
>
> (*Treatise* 233/21–31)

The *Treatise*-translator seems uneasy with Ruusbroec's descriptions of equal partnership of God and the soul in their loving unity, as he more than occasionally omits passages that describe their intimacy.[23] When Ruusbroec describes the process of spiritual ascent in which the soul, first a mercenary, can grow to become a true servant, a secret (or dear) friend, and a hidden son of God,

22 The phrase 'without difference' is problematic as a formal, theological statement. Ruusbroec himself qualifies the phrase by stressing that this 'deification' is a momentary aspect of the (paradoxical) play of contemplative love. In the *Treatise*, he speaks out against quietism (*Treatise* 249/19–26), affirms that the soul will forever remain other than God (*Treatise* 250/9–16) and that the soul will not feel the bliss of heaven in this life (*Treatise* 252/1–5).

23 In the following discussion, I quote from the editions of the texts mentioned above. Occasionally, I refer to readings of *De calculo* found in MS Heneage 3083. See Sargent, 'The Heneage Manuscript'. Some of the readings in the *Treatise* can be clarified by a reading found in the Heneage manuscript as listed by Sargent.

Ruusbroec writes that God 'roept ons weder inne alse sine heimelijcke vriende' (*Steen* 525–6; 'God calls us inwards as his secret friends'). The Latin text reads 'Huiusmodi quippe amicos vocat et invitat deus deorsum' (*De calculo* 42/4–5). The Middle English text renders this sentence in truncated form: 'Thees manere of men oure lorde calles his frendys' (*Treatise* 239/31–2). The translator omits the following passage in which the contemplative's loving embrace with the Trinity is described.[24]

> For you must know that the Father with the Son and the Son with the Father have taken eternal pleasure in that the son should assume our humanity and die and bring all the chosen back to their beginning. And therefore, when we are elevated into our origin by the Son, we hear the voice of the Father that draws us in and enlightens us with truth eternal [beyond doubt]. And the truth shows us the wide open pleasure of God, in which all pleasure begins and ends. There all our powers fail and we fall down headlong into our open vision, and we all become one, and one all in the loving embrace of the unity of the three.[25]

The interpretation of these omissions as reflecting the translator's unease with the intimacy between the contemplative and God is further supported by omissions that affect Ruusbroec's descriptions of the reciprocity of the relationship between the contemplative and God. These omissions could be indicative of the translator's reluctance to talk about God as an active partner in the contemplative's spiritual life, engaging in a reciprocal relationship with the contemplative.

In Ruusbroec's description of the soul's growth from a mercenary into a hidden son of God, we learn that the best happens to the secret friends of God, 'quoniam ipsi placent deo et e regione deus placet eis' (*De calculo* 54/3–4). The Middle English text translates only the first half of the sentence, omitting the reference to God's role in the relationship: 'for thay plese god' (*Treatise* 243/4). The omission in the following passage also seems to illustrate the translator's unwillingness to allow for reciprocity in the contemplative relationship, as he leaves out a reference to God's immense greatness as the source of the contemplative's spiritual food and a sentence in which the interdependence of God and the soul in contemplation is expressed.

> Hac estuatione commoti, cogimur incomprehensibili [amore] inhyare: nam *de eius immensitate* pascimus quam nimirum absorbere nequimus, eiusque infinitati inhyamus quam apprehendere non valemus. *Sic nec in deo possumus, nec deus in nobis*: quoniam estuante amoris impatientia nobismetispsis abrenunciare nequimus.
> (*De calculo* 86/19 – 88/2)[26]

> In this heete we are knowen to abyde be incomprehensible loue, þorowe þe whiche we be fedde; and no mervayle ȝif we may not swalowe it, for we be abowte his

[24] The passage should have followed onto the sentence 'This, he says, is my welbeloued sonne, in whome I am wele plesed' (*Treatise* 256/8–9).

[25] Translated by Helen Rolfson, *Sparkling Stone* (English translation printed on the facing page of the edition of the *Steen* referred to above, n. 6), pp. 739–47. For the Latin see *De calculo* 106/12–108/4. Sargent points out that this passage can be found in the Heneage manuscript. Sargent, 'The Heneage Manuscript', p. 557.

[26] 'Amore' is a Heneage reading. See Sargent, 'The Heneage Manuscript', p. 553.

> infynytenesse, bot we maye not reche it, and for burnynge impacyence of loue we may not forsake oureselfe. (*Treatise* 250/32–251/2)[27]

In the following passage, the translation does not have the sentences in which God's touching of the soul is described. Although, in this case, the omission could be the result of eye-skip (as the omission occurs between the first and second 'amplius'), the result of it is, again, that a description of the closeness between the soul and God has been left out.

> quam quo amplius gustamus eo magis degustare desideramus. [Et quo amplius *degustare desideramus*], *eo profundius ipsius tactui inhyamus. Et quo amplius divino tactui inhyamus, eo magis sue dulcedinis flumina nos transfluunt et perfundunt. Quo vero amplius* transfundimur et perfundimur, eo clarius agnoscimus divinam dulcedinem incomprehensibilem esse et infinitam.
>
> (*De calculo* 90/11–18)[28]

> the whiche the more we tayste, the more we desyre to taste, and the more that we be made depe and þyrlde be loue, the more clerely we knowe the incomprehensible swetnesse of god to be infynyte. (*Treatise* 251/29–32)

These omissions do seem to reflect a recurrent unease with Ruusbroec's insistence on the partnership between God and the soul in contemplation. However, the translator did not consistently edit out all descriptions of the dynamic play of contemplative love.

> And this is the fourt difference, in the whiche we fele oureselfe and god; for we fele vs stondynge in the presence of god, that is to saye, the trewe conscyence whiche of the chere of god we take berys vs witnesse þat we wille oure lorde to be alletogydre oures and lykewyse hym to wille vs to be alletogydre his. For in the same instant in the whiche we fele vs wille god to be alle oures, sprynges in vs a glad abydynge desyre frome god, welle smellynge, depe and wyde; so that ȝif god gaffe vs alle thynge owtsepte hymselfe, ȝit thay may not suffice to sacyat the desyre.
>
> (*Treatise* 250/14–23)

Thus, passages that are close translations of *De calculo* alternate with passages that are much more cautious than both the Middle Dutch original and the intermediate Latin translation.

If we read the *Treatise* as the translator's reception of Ruusbroec's ideas, we can conclude that he toned down Ruusbroec's optimistic affirmation of the equality of God and the soul in contemplation in several instances. That the translator repeatedly seems to shy away from some of the high subject matter in 'the treatise he is translating for his own learning' (cf. *Treatise* 229/2–3), might also be symptomatic of his own inability to understand the text completely.

27 The translator here also translates 'cogimur' as 'we are knowen', as if his original read 'cognoscimur'. A correct translation of 'cogimur' would have been 'we are made'.

28 The omitted passage translates: 'and the more we desire to taste, the more deeply we crave to be touched by him; and the more deeply we crave to be touched by God, the more the flowing of his sweetness flows through us and over us' (Rolfson, *Sparkling Stone*, pp. 619–21). Heneage lacks the phrase between brackets. Sargent, 'The Heneage Manuscript', p. 554.

Though he is obviously amassing all his powers to render Ruusbroec's concise and dense, yet comprehensive account of what it is to live the contemplative life, he has apparently been struggling with Ruusbroec's mystical terminology. Significantly, his rendering of the concepts 'union' and 'unity' is not precise. Because they do not stand for the same thing in Ruusbroec's description of the contemplative experience, this is problematic.

Throughout the Middle English text the translator uses the word 'oned' to translate both the Latin 'unio' and 'unitas'. The word 'oned' seems the more correct translation of the word 'unitas' and the Middle Dutch word *eenicheit*, as it lacks the suggestion of a dynamic process of renewal implied in Middle Dutch *eeninghe* and Latin 'unio'. In Middle English one could express this dynamism with the words 'knyttynge' or 'oning'. It seems that the translator, because he had already used the word that would have been the best choice of Middle English word to translate 'unitas', gets into trouble whenever he comes across the word 'unitas' in the Latin text. In each of the cases where the word occurs in the Latin text, the translator either translates it as 'oned' or 'vnycioun', or he avoids translating the term. 'Vnycioun', incidentally, is also used to translate Latin 'unitio', which is used to refer to 'unio' that is renewed by the soul's activity. The translator's failure to distinguish between union and unity results in a blurring of Ruusbroec's and Jordaens' articulate expression of the core of Ruusbroec's mystical doctrine as it is presented in the *Treatise*.[29] In the following passage the translator solves the problem he has with the distinctions among 'unio', 'unitio' and 'unitas' simply by obliterating them. (The translator's additions are in italics.)

> This knyttynge or vnycioun, *that is to saye oned*, that a spiritualle man felys with god, somme tyme he felys in spyrit with hymselfe as a felyng vnable to be borne, so he thynkys it withoute mesure, and in that felynge or openynge of the spyrrit, be the meene of loue, persayues hymselfe frome hymselfe, errynge in wisdome atte alle tymes, felynge hym one lyfe with god, so stedfastly he abydes in that vnknawen knawlege. (*Treatise* 232/6–13)

Let us compare this with the Latin:

> Ipsa quippe unio, quam spiritualis homo sentit cum deo, quandocumque se pandit spiritui quasi abyssum impercontabilem: hoc est sine modo altam, longam, latam et profundam; in ea ipsa apparitione percipit se spiritus in ipsa profunditate a se profundatum, in altitudine inaltatum, in longitudine prolungatum et in ipsa amplitudine pervagatum. Sentit quoque se commorantem in ipsa ignota noticia, *et defluctuatum per ipsam adhesivam unionis sensionem in unitatem, et per omnes mortes in dei vivacitatem:* ibique se sentit unam vitam cum deo.
> (*De calculo* 12/10–14/1)

29 So far I have been able to find one mistake in the Latin as edited by Muller. *De calculo* 32/5: 'ad suam *unitatem* vocat et invitat' translates Middle Dutch 'roept ende noot te sijnre *eeningen*'. Whether any Middle English texts distinguish between 'oned', 'unioun', 'knyttynge', 'oning', 'unicioun' and 'unite' as different moments of the contemplative experience merits further investigation.

In general the Middle English simplifies the Latin. The play of words with the spatial terms height, depth, width and length to express the dynamic nature of union has not at all been rendered by the translator. It is telling that the translator does not translate the sentence that introduces the concept of unity as flowing from the experience of union. (This is the sentence italicized in the Latin passage last quoted.)[30] Because he left out the sentence introducing 'unitas', the next reference to this 'unitas' is translated as being the same thing as the 'unio', 'oned' defined before.

> For the *oned* of god, whiche euere contemplatyfe spiritte pretendys, in loue it is euerlastynglye drawynge yn, and in hymselfe askynge dyuyne persones and alle louynge spyrrytys. And this drawynge in felys euere louer owthere more or lesse, for aftyr mesure of his loue and the manere of his exercyse is his felynge.
> (*Treatise* 232/15–20)

There is only one passage in which the translator introduces the noun 'vnyte' as a translation for Latin 'unitas', only to replace it immediately by the usual 'oned'.

> Bot that at thay synglerly taste and knowe the blyssede trynyte in *vnyte* and the *oned* in the trinyte, is vnto thame moste excellente mete, fedynge and in hymselfe makynge to ryst. (*Treatise* 253/6–9)

The translator does come up with a word that he could have used to distinguish between the 'unio' and 'unitas' of his source text. That he has only used 'vnyte' once suggests that he was unaware of the need to distinguish in terminology between union and unity, between the two aspects of the being one of the soul and God.

The *Treatise* is by no means a very polished text. On the contrary, it very often exhibits the unevenness of a draft version. When, in the short prologue, the translator asks any future reader of the text to 'withdrawe the defawte and gyffe stede to the trowthe' (*Treatise* 229/7–10), it seems an honest request rather than a humility topos. It can be argued that a text like this would only have made its way into a purpose-built and consciously organised anthology such as Amherst if it had been translated in the same environment in which the anthology was put together. The Amherst anthologist included the *Treatise* in the anthology for the obvious merits of its message, and even of the translator's rendering of it, but probably also because he had it close at hand.

Unlike the *Treatise*-translator, who seems baffled and overwhelmed by some aspects of *De calculo*, the compiler of the *Chastising* is in control of his text and handles the *Ornatus* and his other sources deftly. He selects passages with confidence and fits them into his overall plan with great skill. Apart from regularly dropping the name of an *auctor* he borrows a story from,[31] he does not attribute

30 This sentence can also be found in Heneage, but in a slightly different reading: '& defluit natum id est vltra adhesuram vnionis adhesionem in vnitatem & vltra per omnes mortes in dei viuacitatem'. Sargent, 'The Heneage Manuscript', p. 540.

31 For instance 'seint gregori' (*Chastising* 148/3), 'anoþer clerk, ysodorus' (*Chastising*

the passages he selects to their authors or mention his source texts.[32] He is writing a treatise on temptation, intending to teach the 'religious sister' he addresses in the prologue how she can resist temptation with equanimity:

> medeful it were to ȝou, pacientli and gladli to suffre such gostli chastisynges wiþ ful feiþ and sad hope, and abide his ordenance til he sende comfort bi grace and mercy. (95/5–7)

Whereas the *Treatise* is a speculative text, the *Chastising* is very practical in its intentions. Many of the chapters are enumerations intended as checklists, easy to remember: 'six principal causes whi oure lord wiþdrawiþ his comfortis fro his children' (100/18–19), 'sixe general temptacions' (115/20), 'foure goostli infirmytees, whiche bien likned to foure dyuers feuers' (126/4–5). In addition, the compiler understands the beneficial effects of storytelling, frequently using material from Cassian's *Collationes* and evidently savouring it.

> Also abbot secundus, an hooli man and of hiȝ perfeccioun, whiche dwellide in wildirnesse, þis man bicause of an opynion þat he hielde stifli bi sharpe wordis in disputacion aȝens þat hooli man macharium, anon he was so feruentli taken wiþ þe wicked spirit þat he delyuerd at his mowþ kyndeli defieng of mete and drynke. Þis chastisyng he hadde bi grace for purgynge of þe soule, þat no þing schuld abide vnclensid. But anon as macharius preiede for hym, þe wicked spirit fledde awei. (165/10–18)

He wants to inform his audience about how they can expect to be tempted to the profit of their souls, yet at the same time he also recognizes the dangers of saying too much – too colourful descriptions of 'dredeful þouȝtis' could actually trigger them in people who would otherwise never be tried by them:

> it is perilouse to specifie suche þouȝtes, for sum bien traueiled wiþ oo þouȝt þat anoþer man or womman wold neuer, ne parauenture shul neuer imagyne suche a þouȝt, but bi oþer mannys tellynge. Þerfore I wil nat shewe suche þouȝtis in special; also, þouȝ I wold, I may nat ne kan nat, for þer was neuer man ne womman þat herde or assaied hem alle. (119/6–11)

Let us now turn to the compiler's use of fragments from the *Ornatus*. The *Ornatus'* Middle Dutch original, the *Brulocht*, is a mystical treatise of such beauty and structural splendour that it has been likened to a Gothic cathedral. Each of the three books describes a stage in the contemplative life (active, inner or yearning, contemplative), expounding Matthew 25:6, 'See,/ the Bridegroom cometh,/ go out/ to meet him', with each phrase of the verse initiating a discussion of another aspect of the contemplative's experience. If we were to extend the architectural metaphor to the *Chastising*, we would have to liken it to a row of houses, some looking better-kept than others, not built to reach the skies, but with the more practical purpose of being lived in comfortably and safely. The

148/5), 'þe apostle poule' (*Chastising* 156/15–16) and 'An hooli clerk bonauenture' (*Chastising* 158/14–15).

32 He also borrows from, amongst others, the *Ancrene Wisse*, Suso's *Horologium Sapientiae*, Alphonse of Pecha's *Epistola solitarii* and Cassian's *Collationes*.

compiler elaborates on the theme of temptation for the comfort of his reader's soul. This makes the *Chastising* a one-theme text rather than a comprehensive account of a phenomenon in all its aspects, and makes it a text that aims to guard the foundations of the reader's religious life.

In what follows, I will focus on the compiler's response to the concepts of union and unity and Ruusbroec's descriptions of the partnership of God and the soul in contemplation. Like the *Treatise*-translator, he leaves out references to the unity between God and the soul. In Chapter 2, he borrows Ruusbroec's description of spiritual drunkenness, but does not translate the following reference to deification.

> Aliquando miratur de hoc quod non omnes homines diuini efficiuntur
> (*Ornatus* II 502–3)
>
> [Sometimes he is amazed that all people do not become divine.][33]

His translation of another passage/sentence might reflect his unease with the idea of the contemplative's utter and complete belonging to God:

> omnem terrenam consolationem et spem relinquunt et postponunt, ut toti et integri dei sint et deo uiuant. (*Ornatus* II 524–5)[34]
>
> þei forsaken al worldli comfort and put her hope fulli in god. (103/22–104/1)

Again, we encounter Ruusbroec's ideas in a toned-down version, as the compiler has adapted the text to his own purposes. We see the same tendency to drop the exclusively mystical bent of the text in Chapter 3 of the *Chastising*, where a religious person is compared to a bee. '[A bee] is so wise in kynde þat whan it wole abide stille, it wole abide and reste in an hyue wiþ his felawis' (107/11–12). When the weather is quiet, the bee flies out diligently to gather the sweetness of many flowers. She does not rest on flower or sweetness, but draws out honey and wax, 'whiche she berith to the hyue þat she cam fro' (107/17–18). Whenever she goes out in calm weather, 'euermore þe fruyt of swetnesse she beriþ to the hyue' (107/20–1).

The compiler has substituted the more realistic 'hyue' for Latin 'unio' or 'unitas', thereby toning down the contemplative meaning Ruusbroec more clearly inscribes into this passage.

> Fac ergo sicut sapiens apis que cum congregatione sue societatis in *unione* habitat. . . . super nullo flore uel propter pulchritudinem uel propter dulcedinem

33 Trans. Helen Rolfson, *Espousals* (English translation printed on the facing page of the edition of the *Brulocht* referred to above, n. 6), b350–1. This sentence is also missing in Darmstadt, Hessische Landes- und Hahschulbibliothek MS 400. The provenance of this manuscript is the Charterhouse of Wesel, but there is no way of telling whether the compiler's source text agreed with this manuscript, or whether the scribe of the Darmstadt manuscript and the compiler, in the same response to the sentence, both omitted it.

34 Grote's translation is already less pronounced here than the Middle Dutch original, which has an additional 'in eewicheit' (*Brulocht* b457), 'in eternity', at the end of the sentence.

conquiescit, sed propriam utilitatem seriose peragit extrahens mel et ceram, que ad *unitam* illam congregationem defert. (*Ornatus* 544–5; 547–50)[35]

In the reading of the *Ornatus*, the wise man leaves the abundance of God's outward gifts and returns to rest in the loving embrace of God, which is contemplative union with him.

Ille tunc sapiens homo more apis ad dona cuncta et ad omnes dulcedines, que uel quas umquam sentiit, cum consideratione, cum ratione et cum discretione uolabit, et ad omne bonum quod deus sibi umquam largitus est. Et cum sagitta caritatis et intime considerationis debet notare et probare omnem ipsius consolationis et ipsorum bonorum multiplicitatem. Et super nullo flore donorum debet quiescere, sed totus oneratus cum gratiarum actione et laude in illam unionem ubi cum deo quiescere et habitare in unione desiderat, reuolare. (*Ornatus* 554–62)

In the *Chastising*'s reading, the wise man is as the wise bee, who offers all the results of its works to God. I quote the translator's adaptive translation of this passage in full, in order to illustrate how his elaboration of the original at the same time shifts its focus.

Þus schal eche wise man doo þat is in goostli lyuenge: he shal wiþ al mekenesse and gladnesse of spirit, whanne oure lord iesu liȝtned his hert inward, receyue his ȝiftis and taste his swetnesse wiþ reason and discrecion, and biholde wiseli the þe quantite of his benefettis, and take hem as comfort as of goostli likyng. But he shal nat abide and reste upon suche comfortis, be þei neuer so faire, ne sauour þei neuer so swete; but wiþ þat comfort and swetnesse, and wiþ al oþer benefetis, he shal tourne and flee aȝen to þe hyue, þat is to oure lord, wiþ worshippes and þankynges, and þer abide and reste til þe sunne shyne aȝen, þat is to seie, til crist iesu liȝtne his herte and ordeyneþ hym bi grace to flee aboute, while tyme is mery, to taste of his benefetis. But euer, as I seide, þe comfort and þe swetnesse þat he findeþ he shal lowli bere aȝen to oure lord, in whos worship he receyued and gadered al suche swetnesse. (107/22–108/14)

The concept of 'unio' cannot be found in the Middle English text. The closest the *Chastising* approaches the *Ornatus* is in its careful identification of the hive as 'our lord'. The bee abides and rests with the lord, but not in union with him. This seems a minor change, but it has a marked effect on the text. Because the compiler does not translate the *Ornatus* closely here, the mystical meaning of the text is only obliquely rendered, and further weakened in the repetitive paraphrase of this idea at the end of the passage. The wise man should humbly offer all the comfort and sweetness to the Lord, who is the source of these gifts. In the *Ornatus*, the wise man is urged to go beyond the gifts, and fly back to the union with God. The 'beyond-the-gifts-in-union' of the *Ornatus* is not expressed in the *Chastising*.

The cautious reading of Ruusbroec we find in the *Chastising* has sometimes been inscribed in the text at an earlier stage in its transmission than the compiler's activity. The *Chastising* lists four kinds of false contemplation in long passages borrowed from the *Ornatus*. In a passage on true contemplation, the

35 'Unio' and 'unitas' both translate Middle Dutch *eenicheit* (*Brulocht* b440 and b446).

Middle Dutch describes the union of God and the soul as reciprocal. The truncated translation in the *Chastising*, in this instance, originates in Grote's Latin.

> Want de karitate es een minne bant die ons overvoert, ende daer wij ons selves in verloechenen ende met gode vereenicht werden *ende god met ons*.
> (*Brulocht* 2387–9; italics mine)

> Quia caritas est quoddam amoris uinculum, quod nos transvehit et in quo nos ipsos abnegamus et quo deo unimur. (*Ornatus* II 3091–3)

> For charite is a bond of loue, whiche drawiþ us to god, in whiche loue we forsaken ouresilf, and þerwiþ we bien ooned to god. (136/6–8)

It is difficult to say whether the caution in the *Treatise* and the *Chastising* is an echo of Gerson's rejection of Book III of the *Brulocht* as unorthodox. Gerson judged that Ruusbroec's description of contemplative union of God and the soul 'without difference' amounts to a kind of pantheistic union.[36] A marginal annotation next to the passage on Ruusbroec in the *Confirmacio* proves that the English Carthusians knew of Gerson's criticism,[37] but it is likely that this annotation was made long after the *Treatise* and the *Chastising* were translated and compiled. If Gerson's criticism did have its impact, this could explain why it was *De calculo* and not the *Ornatus* that was translated in full, and why the passages selected for the *Chastising* were taken from Book II, and not Book III of the *Ornatus*.[38] It is significant, however, that the English Carthusians did translate Ruusbroec, even if the translated material suggests that both *De calculo* and the *Ornatus* were approached with criticism as well as admiration. The Carthusians of Herne, who played an important role in the preservation of Ruusbroec's works, collected all the documents in the Gerson–Schoonhoven debate about Ruusbroec and the *Brulocht*. Indeed, Gerson first offered his criticism of the *Brulocht* in response to a question of Bartholomeus Clantier, one of the Herne brethren.[39] That Gerson's criticism was not taken – by the Carthusians of Herne and their English brethren – to be a condemnation of Ruusbroec's works, but as a possible reading of them, testifies to the Carthusians' spiritual independence. This inclusive attitude may well be typical of the Carthusians. It signals the openness paradoxically possible in strongly controlled environments.[40]

The cautious attitude towards the equality of God and the soul in the reciprocal play of contemplative love also did not keep the English Carthusians from reading and disseminating Ruusbroec's texts, if the Middle English Ruusbroec texts were indeed translated in Carthusian circles. Yet perhaps more than to their

36 Verdeyen, *Ruusbroec*, pp. 90–1 and Warnar, *Ruusbroec*, pp. 7–14.

37 Colledge, '*The Treatise*', p. 52.

38 Of course, the narrow focus of the *Chastising* is a more immediate argument in favour of the compiler's decision to select from Book II.

39 Warnar, *Ruusbroec*, pp. 260–3.

40 Paraphrasing Smalley, it would indeed seem to have been the case that 'the restriction of texts to a narrow circle made for tolerance within that circle'. Beryl Smalley, *The Study of the Bible in the Middle Ages* (Oxford, 1984), p. xxxvi.

awareness of Gerson's criticism and their perceived need to act on it themselves, the added caution with which certain themes in Ruusbroec's texts are approached testifies to the pastoral concern the translators would have felt for their brethren and for religious or lay readers outside the walls of their enclosure. Like Ruusbroec in his more sober moments, they would have felt that the greatest error for a contemplative was to think that he had reached contemplation when he had not, and the toning down of Ruusbroec's optimistic assertions of the equal partnership of God and the soul may have been a subtle acknowledgment of the humility necessary for the healthy contemplative life.

> Wherefore thay erre, alle thoo that trowes þame to be contemplatyfe and wyrschyps inordynatlye any creature or hase in affeccioun. And also thay erre that trowe thame to hafe contemplacioun or the tyme thay be frome alle the forme and the schappe of alle thynge clensed and put in reste. (*Treatise* 257/25–30)

THE STRUCTURE OF THE SOUL AND THE 'GODLY WYLLE' IN JULIAN OF NORWICH'S *SHOWINGS*

DENISE N. BAKER

MORE THAN FOUR DECADES AGO, Thomas Merton, the foremost contemplative of the twentieth century, acknowledged Julian of Norwich's preeminence as a mystic and a theologian.

> There can be no doubt that Lady Julian is the greatest of the English mystics. Not only that, but she is one of the greatest English theologians. . . . Actually, in Julian of Norwich, we find an admirable synthesis of mystical experience and theological reflection . . . In a word, Julian of Norwich gives a coherent and indeed systematically constructed corpus of doctrine, which has only recently begun to be studied as it deserves.[1]

Since Merton made this assertion in 1961, numerous studies of her *Book of Showings* have revealed that, despite Julian's description of herself as 'a symple creature vnlettyrde', she is extraordinarily learned. However, because she is writing theology in the vernacular and often chooses commonplace English words to translate their Latin equivalents, the erudition and subtlety of her thought is not yet fully appreciated. Although Julian's particular method of acquiring knowledge or her actual sources may not be discernible, her assimilation and augmentation of concepts from Latin theological discourse can be demonstrated. Two terms that Julian uses as metaphors for the structure of the soul provide especially important clues to her familiarity with this discourse: *point* and *ground*. As I shall demonstrate, Julian's topography of the soul not only proves her awareness of mystical theology, but also explains her concept of the 'godly wylle'.[2]

Julian of Norwich subscribes to the paradigm of introspective mysticism derived from Augustine. In *On the Trinity* Augustine seeks an understanding of the transcendent Trinity by looking to the *imago Dei* immanent in his higher

1 Thomas Merton, 'The English Mystics', *Mystics and Zen Masters* (New York, 1961), pp. 140–1.

2 Critics whose discussions of Julian's views on the soul are informative include Joan W. Nuth, *Wisdom's Daughter: The Theology of Julian of Norwich* (New York, 1991), pp. 104–16; Grace Jantzen, *Julian of Norwich: Mystic and Theologian* (New York, 1987), pp. 137–49; Frederick Christian Bauerschmidt, *Julian of Norwich and the Mystical Body Politic of Christ*, Studies in Spirituality and Theology V (Notre Dame, Indiana, 1999), pp. 144–61; and Christopher Abbott, *Julian of Norwich: Autobiography and Theology* (Cambridge, 1999), pp. 105–15.

reason. Julian likewise finds the image of the triune God in the soul: 'oure soule is a made trynyte lyke to the vnmade blessyd trynyte, knowyn and lovyd fro with out begynnyng'.[3] At the same time that she claims that God dwells in the soul, she also insists that the soul dwells in God.

> Oure soule is made to be goddys dwelling place, and the dwellyng of oure soule is god, whych is vnmade. A hye vnderstandying it is inwardly to se and to know that god, whych is oure maker, dwellyth in oure soule, and a hygher vnderstandyng it is and more, inwardly to se and to know oure soule that is made dwellyth in god in substance, of whych substance by god we be that we be'. (pp. 561–2)

This mutual enclosing of God in the soul and the soul in God accounts for Julian's apparently contradictory claims about the priority of self knowledge and knowledge of God. On the one hand, she asserts 'that it is redyer to vs and more esy to come to þe knowyng of god then to know oure owne soule' (p. 570). Later in the same chapter, however, she contends, 'we may nevyr come to the full knowyng of god tylle we knowe furst clerely oure owne soule' (p. 573). These two diverse paths to knowledge of God correspond to the two ways in which the soul coheres to the deity. Julian's topography of the soul identifies these connections using the metaphors of the point and the ground of the soul. A vernacular rendering of the Latin *apex mentis*, Julian uses *point* to refer to the locus of the *imago Dei* enclosed within the soul. She uses *ground* to translate the Latin *fundus* or *profundus* and to identify the subsistence of the soul in the deity, the source of all existence.

As with any commonplace word, *point* has several different meanings for Julian. Her most memorable use of the term comes at the beginning of the Third Revelation in the Long Text, which corresponds to chapter viii in the Short Text: 'And after this I saw god in a poynte, that is to say in my vnderstandyng, by which syght I saw that he is in althyng' (p. 336). Editors Colledge and Walsh provide an explication of 'in a poynt':

> it has been suggested that Julian meant that she saw God as the centre of a circle, the universe, that the image is geometrical and the idea philosophical. This may be so; but it seems more probably that she meant 'in an instant of time'.

Colledge and Walsh's temporal interpretation is supported by the fact that Julian employs *point* on occasion to refer to an instant of time. In chapter 64, for example, she uses the word twice to indicate the moment of death: 'And also god wylle that whyle the soule is in the body, it seeme to it selfe þat it is evyr at þe poynte to be takyn. For alle this lyfe and thys longyng that we haue here is but a poynt' (p. 622). However, her cross-references to the Third Revelation later in the Long Text clarify that *point* in Revelation Three is a spatial rather than a temporal term. Explaining the three ways God is with us, Julian writes, 'And he is with vs

3 *A Book of Showings to the Anchoress Julian of Norwich*, ed. Edmund Colledge O. S. A. and James Walsh S. J. (Toronto, 1978), Part Two, p. 568. Subsequent page references to this edition will be given in the text.

in erth, vs ledyng; and that was shewde in þe thyrde, wher I saw god in a poynt' (p. 549). This location becomes even clearer when she states:

> Owre good lorde shewde hym to his creature in dyverse manner both in hevyn and in erth; but I saw hym take no place but in mannes soule . . . . he shewde hym in erth, where I seyde I saw god in a poynt. (pp. 713–14)

Colledge and Walsh's preferred explication of *point* in Revelation Three as 'an instant of time' must thus be rejected.

The first explication, which Colledge and Walsh dismiss, was originally offered by Sister Anna Maria Reynolds. She regards *point* as a spatial term and attributes Julian's use of it in the Third Revelation to a passage in chapter five of Pseudo-Dionysius's *Divine Names*.

> It is hard to believe that [Julian's] statement owes nothing to the following utterance of the Areopagite, in which, after remarking that Existence belongs to the 'Absolute and Transcendent Goodness', in an incomprehensible and concentrated oneness, he goes on: 'All the radii of a circle are concentrated into a single unity in the centre, and this point contains all the straight lines brought together within itself to one another, and to the one starting-point from which they began.'[4]

Identifying the Pseudo-Dionysian circle with a 'very old image for describing the infiniteness of God', Wolfgang Riehle elucidates the similarities between the Areopagite's statement and Julian's by connecting several passages from the Long Text:

> Among the English mystics it is only Julian who draws on this tradition in her famous image 'I saw god in a poynte', which she interprets as meaning that God is 'in the myd poynt of allthynges', and that creation is being led back by divine grace 'in to the blessyd poynt from thens it cam, that is god'.[5]

Commenting on these and Julian's other uses of *point* throughout the Long Text, Masson further elucidates its apophatic nuance:

> In the case of God being in the 'myd point' of all things, Julian suggests a space within the created where the Creator resides; likewise, in the case of seeing 'god in a poynte', Julian suggests a space in which she, a human being, can locate God, the divinity. In each instance, Julian's 'poynt(e)' acts as a point of access to the divine . . . as a point of access to the apophatic realm.[6]

These interpretations of *point* in the context of Pseudo-Dionysian apophatic mysticism certainly underscore the term's significance in Julian's vocabulary.

4 Sister Anna Maria Reynolds, C. P., 'Some Literary Influences in the *Revelations* of Julian of Norwich (c. 1342–post-1416)', *Leeds Studies in English and Kindred Languages* vii and viii (1952), pp. 18–28 at p. 18.

5 Wolfgang Riehle, *The Middle English Mystics*, trans. Bernard Standring (London, 1981), p. 83.

6 Cynthea Masson, 'The Point of Coincidence: Rhetoric and the Apophatic in Julian of Norwich's *Showings*', *Julian of Norwich: A Book of Essays*, ed. Sandra J. McEntire (New York, 1998), p. 163. Vincent Gillespie and Maggie Ross also associate the *point* of Revelation Three with apophatic consciousness in 'The Apophatic Image: The Poetics of Effacement in Julian of Norwich', *MMT* V, pp. 53–77 at p. 72.

Julian's own Long Text, however, provides even more clarification of her meaning. In the Third Revelation she indicates that this point is not only 'the myd point of all thynges', but also 'in my vnderstandyng'. God resides in the human soul just as God does in all creation. The locus of the deity's presence in the soul is the point at which its two parts, substance and sensuality, are fused together.

> For I saw full surely that oure substannce is in god, and also I saw that in oure sensualyte god is, for in the same poynt that oure soule is made sensuall, in the same poynt is the cytte of god, ordeyned to hym fro without begynnyng. In which cytte he comyth, and nevyr shall remeve it, for god is nevyr out of the soule, in whych he shalle dwell blessydly without end. (pp. 566–7)

God's immanence in the soul can be situated at the point where the *imago Dei* is embodied as the pre-existing substance of the soul is joined to its sensuality. Julian recognizes this juncture: 'And thus is mannys soule made of god, and in the same poynte knyte to god' (p. 558). Julian explicitly identifies this highest point of the soul with the practice of contemplation in recommending that 'we sett þe poynt of oure thought' on the aural promise of eternal reward in the Fifteenth Revelation (p. 624).

These examples clearly demonstrate that Julian was familiar with the spatial metaphor of the soul's summit or point as the site of God's immanence common to the tradition of introspective mysticism originating with Augustine and reinforced by Thomas Gallus's interpretation of Pseudo-Dionysius. Many different terms are used in this Latin tradition, but among the most popular are *apex mentis*, the summit or highest point of the mind, and *acies mentis*, the edge or sharp point of the mind.[7] Commenting on the *Cloud*-author's use of the phrase, 'þe hiȝest & þe souereynest pointe of þe spirit', Hodgson remarks that this key phrase 'is loaded with meaning'.

> *hiȝest* recalls 'innermost', synonymous with it in unitive prayer; it can also connote a degree or quality besides that of elevation; *hiȝest pointe* brings to mind the Latin *summus (supremus) apex*, the 'summit' of the figurative mount of perfection and the peak of the spiritual ascent. But *pointe* itself could translate *acies* 'point or weapon', a common alternative to *apex* in Latin descriptions of the mystic's goal. The innermost depth of the spirit, the soul's unitive faculty, the single-pointedness of approach are all present in 'pointe'.[8]

7 For a survey of the concept of the *apex* or *acies mentis*, see *Dict. spir.* s.v. 'Ame'. See also Denys Turner, *The Darkness of God: Negativity in Christian Mysticism* (Cambridge, 1995), p. 99 n. 40.

8 Phyllis Hodgson, ed., Introduction, *The Cloud of Unknowing and Related Treatises on Contemplative Prayer*, Analecta Cartusiana III (Exeter, 1982), p. lv; Hodgson is referring to the *Cloud*-author's use of this phrase in chapter 41, lines 12–13. See also Patrick J. Gallacher, ed., Introduction, *The Cloud of Unknowing*, TEAMS (Kalamazoo, Michigan, 1997), 2–3; and Rosemary Ann Lees, *The Negative Language of the Dionysian School of Mystical Theology: An Approach to the Cloud of Unknowing*, Analecta Cartusiana CVII, 2 vols (Salzburg, 1983), II, pp. 270–4.

Theorists of contemplation agreed that, as the site of God's immanence in the soul, this *apex* or point was the locus of union with the divine. The fact that Julian is referring to the point of the soul in the Third Revelation is substantiated by the explanation she provides: 'I saw god in a poynte, that is to say in my vnderstandyng.' Understanding in this context is a synonym for Augustine's higher reason and the Scholastics' *ratio superior*, the site of the *imago Dei* in the soul.

A second metaphor that Julian employs to describe the structure of the soul provides further evidence of her familiarity with mystical theology. While she locates God within the soul in its point, she situates the soul within God on its ground. 'God is more nerer to vs than oure owne soule, for he is grounde in whome oure soule standyth' (p. 571). She further explains the nature of this relationship between the soul and God: 'oure reson is groundyd in god, whych is substanncyally kindnesse' (p. 574); 'for verily I saw that oure substannce is in god' (p. 581). *Ground* is an English translation of the Latin *fundus*, bottom, base, foundation, or *profundum*, depth.

Derived from Augustine, these terms are used throughout the Middle Ages to indicate the most interior depth of the soul, the locus of union with God.[9] This metaphor expresses Augustine's doctrine of participation, adapted from Neoplatonic thought and passed on to his medieval successors. 'The centrality of this doctrine', according to Bell, 'lies in the fact that if a thing *is*, then it *is* not by virtue of its own being, but simply because it participates in True Being, which is God.'[10] Thus, to exist means to exist in God: all of creation shares in God's being without being God. Julian's assertion that the substance or higher part of the soul remains connected to the divine substance is the basis of her claim that to know God is to know the self:

> And thus I saw full suerly that it is redyer to vs and more esy to come to þe knowyng of god then to know oure owne soule. For oure soule is so depe growndyd in god and so endlesly tresoryd that we may nott come to the knowyng ther of tylle we haue furst knowyng of god, whych is the maker to whome it is onyd. (p. 570)

According to Julian, then, the metaphor of the ground of the soul indicates that the substance of the soul subsists in God, while the metaphor of the point refers to God's presence in the soul.

Paradoxically, in medieval mystical theology, the point and the ground coincide. The *Cloud*-author sums up this paradox in his oxymoron, 'þe hiȝest & þe souereynest pointe of þe spirit', for, as Hodgson explains, '*souereynest* . . . [defines] that depth of the soul in which God latently dwells' while, as mentioned earlier, *hiȝest* refers to its opposite, the apex.[11] Augustine, for example, contends

9 See *Dict. spir.* s.v. 'Ame' and 'Fond de l'ame', and Riehle, *The Middle English Mystics*, pp. 152–64.

10 David N. Bell, *The Image and Likeness: The Augustinian Spirituality of William of St. Thierry* (Kalamazoo, Michigan, 1984), p. 23.

11 Hodgson, Introduction, *The Cloud of Unknowing and Related Treatises*, p. lv.

that the soul coincides with God at the point of its greatest height and depth. As he phrases it in the *Confessions*, 'Thou wert deeper within me than my innermost depths and higher than my highest parts.'[12] Because this highest point of the soul is also its deepest recess, the metaphors of ascent and depth are interchangeable; the summit or point of the soul is also its foundation or ground. As Turner remarks,

> The *intinerarium intus* is also an *ascensio superius*. The two metaphors of inwardness and ascent themselves intersect at the point where God and the self intersect, so that which is most interior to me is also that which is above and beyond me; so that the God who is within me is also the God I am in.[13]

On several occasions, Augustine explicitly acknowledges this mutual indwelling. 'What place is in me, into which My God may come?' he asks in the *Confesions*.

> Where can God come into me, the God who made heaven and earth? Is there anything in me, O Lord my God, which can encompass Thee? . . . Or, since without Thee nothing that is could be, is it that whatever is contains Thee? . . . Hence I would not be, my God, I would not be at all, unless Thou were in me. Rather, is it not that I would not be unless I were in Thee, 'from whom, through whom, and in whom are all things'? Into what can I invoke Thee, since I am in that Thee?[14]

Thus, the mutual indwelling of God in the soul and the soul in God is a concept that Julian could have derived from the Augustinian tradition, though it is not emphasized as much as the notion of God's immanence in the soul as the *imago Dei*.

Although the idea that the soul subsists in God is implicit in the Augustinian tradition, it becomes most pronounced in the mystical writings of the late Middle Ages. Julian's references to the ground of the soul reveal the same concern with 'the exemplary or virtual preexistence of the soul in God' that McGinn identifies as 'an important theme of the new mysticism of the thirteenth century . . . a notion that served as at least part of the foundation for new modes of conceiving *unio mystica*'.[15] As he explains, this new conception of union draws on the tradition of Christian exemplarism derived from the Neoplatonism of Philo, the first-century Jewish philosopher, who situated the Platonic ideas in the mind of God. Origen and, most importantly, Augustine incorporate this 'intradeical' view into Christian exemplarism by insisting that the Logos contains eternally the forms for all phenomena and acts as the agent of their creation in time. In Book Four of *On the Trinity*, Augustine explicates the first verses of John's Gospel according to this exemplarist theory.

12 Augustine, *Confessions*, trans. Vernon Bourke, The Fathers of the Church XXI (1953; repr. Washington, D. C., 1966), III.6, p. 60.

13 Turner, *The Darkness of God*, p. 99.

14 Augustine, *Confessions*, I.2, pp. 4–5.

15 Bernard McGinn, *The Flowering of Mysticism: Men and Women in the New Mysticism (1200–1350)*, vol. III of *The Presence of God: A History of Western Mysticism* (New York, 1998), p. 214.

> Hence, because there is the One Word of God, through which all things were made, which is the unchangeable truth, all things in it are originally and unchangeably simultaneous, not only the things which are now in this whole creation, but also those which have been and are to be. In it, however, these things have not been, nor are they to be, but they only are; and all things are life, and all things are one, and are rather one being and one life.[16]

This influence of Neoplatonic exemplarism also appears in the writings of later medieval theologians such as John Scottus Eriugena and William of St Thierry. However, as McGinn points out, the Beguine mystics of the thirteenth century, Hadewijch of Antwerp, Mechthild of Magdeburg, and Marguerite of Porete, were the first to refer explicitly to the soul's preexistence in God as the basis of mystical union.[17] The most controversial proponent of this new concept of union was, of course, Meister Eckhart.

Julian's articulation of the essential or ontological union between God and the soul entails the same exemplarist theory that McGinn identifies as characteristic of the new mysticism of the thirteenth century. The soul's virtual preexistence in Christ is the basis of her conception of God as its ground. 'And by the endlesse entent and assent and the full acorde of all the trynyte', Julian explains,

> þe myd person wolde be grounde and hed of this feyer kynde out of whom we be all come, in whom we be alle enclosyd, in to whom we shall all goo, in hym fyndyng oure full hevyn in everlastyng joy by the forseyeng purpose of alle the blessyd trynyte fro without begynnyng. . . . And thus is mannys soule made of god, and in the same poynte knyte to god. (pp. 557–8)

The final sentence sums up Julian's theme of mutual enclosure. Since Christ as Logos is the ground of the soul, man's soul subsists in God for all eternity; but this substance is united to its other part, sensuality, at the moment of embodiment as the *imago Dei* is infused at the point or apex of the soul.

Although there is no evidence that Julian knew the works of the Beguines or their German successors, her emphasis on the preexistence of the soul in the Logos for all eternity and the substantial union between the human and the divine resembles theirs. Like Julian, Eckhart uses the metaphor of the ground to describe this ontological link between God and the soul. 'There is something in the soul', he writes,

> which is so akin to God that it is one [with God] and not [merely] united with Him. It is one; it has nothing in common with anything; nor does anything which is created have something in common with it. Everything which is created is nothing. But this ground of the soul is distant and alien from all created things. Were a man wholly like this, he would be completely uncreated and uncreatable.[18]

16 Augustine, *On the Trinity*, trans. Stephen McKenna, C. SS. R., The Fathers of the Church XLV (Washington, D. C., 1963), IV.1, p. 132.

17 McGinn, *The Flowering of Mysticism*, p. 214.

18 Cited from sermon 225 by John D. Caputo, *The Mystical Element in Heidegger's Thought* (Athens, Ohio, 1978), p. 113. See also Robert K. C. Forman, 'Eckhart, Gezucken, and the Ground of the Soul', in *Studia Mystica* xi (1988), pp. 3–30

Although Julian and Eckhart both locate the ontological union between God and the soul on this ground, there is a crucial difference between them. As McGinn explains,

> Eckhart's formula that 'God's ground and the soul's ground are one ground', that is, that there is in the soul a 'spark' (*vünkelîn*), 'castle' (*bürgelîn*), or 'ground' (*grunt*) that is identical with God . . . is the foundation for Eckhart's claim that the deepest reality of intellectual being is its *indistinct union* with God.[19]

Eckhart's controversial notion of the union of indistinction, his assertion that the ground of the soul is uncreated and identical to God, was, of course, condemned as unorthodox. In contrast, Julian does not contend, as Eckhart and his female predecessors seem to, that the substantial union is a union of identity or indistinction. Rather, although she goes to the brink of such a statement, Julian backs off from that radical assertion and remains within the orthodox Augustinian tradition.

> And I sawe no dyfference betwen god and oure substance, but as it were all god; and yett my vnderstandyng toke that oure substance is in god, that is to sey that god is god and oure substance is a creature in god. (p. 562)

In this first stage of its being, then, as the substance of the soul is ontologically united to the Logos, Julian acknowledges a distinction between the creator and the created. As Turner observes,

> Julian can confidently play with formulas little short of Eckhart's in audacity while remaining firmly within the common Neoplatonic tradition, while Eckhart's version of them departs from that tradition. At any rate, the precise point of divergence between them is now clear: If, for Julian, the only way in which God and I can be said to be distinct is as the uncreated and created are distinct, then for Eckhart that is the one way in which God and I are *not* distinct.[20]

Thus, even though she uses the metaphor of the ground of the soul to emphasize the essential ontological union between the substance of the soul and Christ, she stops short of the radical denial of difference which proved so controversial for Eckhart.

Although Eckhart's conception of the ground of the soul is not the source for Julian's notion, his discussion does provide a crucial clue to her idea about the 'godly wylle'. Sister Anna Maria Reynolds notes a remarkable similarity between Julian's concept of the 'godly wylle' and Eckhart's spark of the soul, as demonstrated in her citation of these passages. Julian claims that

> in ech a soule that shall be safe is a godly wylle that nevyr assentyd to synne ne nevyr shal; whych wyll is so good that it may nevyr wylle evyll but evyr more contynuly it wyllyth good and werkyth good in the sight of god.

19 Bernard McGinn, 'Love, Knowledge and Unio Mystica in the Western Christian Tradition', *Mystical Union and Monothesitic Faith: An Ecumenical Dialogue*, ed. Moshe Idel and Bernard McGinn (New York, 1989), p. 75.

20 Turner, *The Darkness of God*, p. 162.

Eckhart attributes this same indefectibility to the spark of the soul, a phrase he often interchanges with ground of the soul:

> the soul has a spark in her which has been in God eternally, life and light. And this spark is conveyed into every man together with the soul. It is pure light in itself and is always censuring sin and urging to virtue . . . The spark of the soul cannot be extinguished either in hell or heaven.[21]

Wolfgang Riehle also recognizes this resemblance between Julian's conception of the 'godly wylle' and Eckhart's spark of the soul in relation to the metaphor of the ground of the soul. Riehle dismisses any influence of the German on the English mystic, however, because Eckhart 'inclines towards an intellectual rather than an affective knowledge of God'.[22] I do not dispute Riehle's conclusion that Julian is not indebted to Eckhart for her ideas about the ground of the soul. I hope to demonstrate, however, that she derives her conception of the 'godly wylle' from the same discussions about synderesis and the related *scintilla* in the Augustinian and Pseudo-Dionysian mystical theology which influenced Eckhart.

Julian's choice of *point* and *ground* as metaphors indicates that she was aware of the mystical discourse on the soul. Two other terms associated with these metaphors are synderesis and the *scintilla* or spark. These two concepts are derived from Jerome's commentary on Ezekiel, their earliest surviving mention.[23] *Synderesis* is either a Greek word now lost or an erroneous transcription of the word Jerome used. An analysis of his explanation and its medieval interpretations clarifies the complex process by which the *scintilla* was identified with the point and ground of the soul.

Jerome explains that most readers interpret three of the four creatures who support the throne of God in Ezekiel's vision with Plato's division of the soul into rational, emotional and appetitive parts.

> And they posit a fourth part which is above and beyond these three, and which the Greeks call *synteresin*: that spark of conscience which was not even extinguished in the breast of Cain after he was turned out of Paradise, and by which we discern that we sin, when we are overcome by pleasures or frenzy and meanwhile are misled by an imitation of reason. . . . and of which we read in Scripture as the spirit 'which

21 Both quotations cited by Reynolds, 'Some Literary Influences', p. 27.

22 Riehle, *The Middle English Mystics*, pp. 158–9; he attributes Julian's conception of the ground of the soul to the influence of the *Cloud*-author, but the passages he cites from the *Book of Privy Counselling* are not persuasive.

23 For discussion of the complex medieval developments of these terms, see Robert A. Greene, 'Synderesis, the Spark of Conscience, in the English Renaissance', *Journal of the History of Ideas* lii (1991), pp. 195–202, and 'Instinct of Nature: Natural Law, Synderesis, and the Moral Sense', *Journal of the History of Ideas* lviii (1997), pp. 173–90. See also Robert W. Mulligan, S. J., '*Ratio Superior* and *Ratio Inferior*: the Historical Background', *The New Scholasticism* xxix (1955), pp. 23–32; M. B. Crowe, 'The Term *Synderesis* and the Scholastics', *Irish Theological Quarterly* xxiii (1956), pp. 151–64, 228–45; and O. Lottin, *Psychologie et morale aux XII et XIII siècle* (Louvain, 1942–49), II, pp. 103–349.

> intercedes for us with ineffable groaning' (Romans 8:26). 'For no one knows what a man is really like, except the spirit which is in him' (I Corinthians 2:11).[24]

As Greene observes in his masterful survey of the history of *synderesis* in medieval theology,

> In identifying synderesis as a fourth, independent, and superintendent part of the soul, in placing it in apposition with the metaphoric 'spark of conscience' (*scintilla conscientiae*), in citing the story of Cain to exemplify its inextinguishability, and in explicating it by referring to the biblical 'spirit of man', as he proceeds to do, Jerome established a frame of discourse that dominated subsequent discussion.[25]

The definitions of synderesis and the *scintilla conscientiae* were further complicated by Peter Lombard's influential citation of Jerome's commentary in his discussion of the propensity of the will towards good in the *Sentences*:

> Man is therefore rightly said naturally to want what is good, because he was constructed with a good and righteous will. For the higher spark of reason, which, as Jerome says, could not even be extinguished in Cain, always wants what is good and hates what is bad.[26]

Lombard's paraphrase of Jerome is not exact; he omits *synteresin* and substitutes Augustine's phrase 'superior . . . scintilla rationis' from the *City of God* 22, 24.2 for Jerome's 'scintilla conscientiae', thus equating synderesis and the spark with reason. As a result, 'some medieval writers immediately concluded that it was very likely the same as the higher part of the reason described by St Augustine, the part which is turned towards God and the eternal truths'.[27] The ambiguities of Jerome's remarks as well as the changes that Lombard made led medieval theologians to develop two distinct conceptions of synderesis and the *scintilla* or spark.

On the one hand, synderesis is identified in moral theology as the infallible faculty or *habitus* of reason or will which apprehends the principles of the natural law and guides conscience.[28] On the other hand, synderesis was identified in mystical theology with the highest stage of the soul's ascent to God. In this first case, synderesis is synonymous with the *scintilla conscientiae* which, Jerome claims, 'was not even extinguished in the breast of Cain after he was turned out of Paradise, and by which we discern that we sin'.

> Medieval theologians commonly assumed that an inextinguishable spark of goodness existed in man's reason and will (*synteresis rationis et voluntatis*), a natural point at which every person, even if he did not consciously choose to be such, was conformed to God. Each person experienced this residue of prefallen and even

24 Translated in Timothy C. Potts, *Conscience in Medieval Philosophy* (Cambridge, 1980), pp. 79–80.

25 Greene, 'Synderesis, the Spark of Conscience', p. 197.

26 Translated in Potts, *Conscience in Medieval Philosophy*, p. 93.

27 Mulligan, '*Ratio Superior* and *Ratio Inferior*', p. 25.

28 Greene, 'Natural Law, Synderesis and the Moral Sense', pp. 173–89; Crowe, 'The Term *Synderesis* and the Scholastics', pp. 151–64, 228–45; Lottin, *Psychologie et morale*, II, pp. 103–349; Mulligan, '*Ratio Superior* and *Ratio Inferior*', pp. 24–8.

> precreated purity as pangs of conscience and an irrepressible desire for truth and goodness – a permanent reminder of man's eternal and original unity with God.[29]

In the second case, which regards synderesis and the *scintilla* as distinct from conscience, these terms come to play a crucial role in mystical theology. Because mystical experiences exceed the soul's cognitive and volitional powers,

> mystical writers [sought] to designate a special faculty of the soul more profound than reason or will, . . . something deep within the human soul that constantly reminds it of its eternal origin in God. Some medieval authorities described this inner inclination as a 'spark of the soul' (*scintilla animae* or *synteresis*) and, depending on the writer's bias, it was interpreted as a depth dimension of reason, will, or both.[30]

In both moral and mystical theology, synderesis and the *scintilla*, whether as the spark of conscience or of the soul, were often situated in the higher reason. These two terms thus became identified, especially in mystical theology, with the point and the ground of the soul and referred to as the *acies mentis*, the *apex intellectus* or *mentis* (Thomas Aquinas), the *apex amoris* or *affectus* (Thomas Gallus, Bonaventure), the *acies intellectus* (Bonaventure), the *grund* or spark in the soul (Eckhart, Tauler).[31]

Julian's concept of the 'godly wylle' bears a strong resemblance to these two different notions of synderesis and the *scintilla*. She locates the 'godly wyll in the higher party' of the soul and insists that it 'is so good that it may nevyr wylle evylle, but evyr good' (p. 443). Likewise, the moral theologians situate synderesis or the spark of conscience in the higher part of the soul, associating it either with the reason or the will, and contend that it is indefectible. William of Auxerre, for example, identifies synderesis with the *pars superior* and asserts that 'as long as a man follows the dictates of this part of reason, he will never sin'.[32] Other theologians, including Hugh of St Cher, similarly connect synderesis with the higher reason's resistance to sin. Philip the Chancellor, whose discussion proved influential, contrasts the infallibility of synderesis's inherent knowledge of natural law with the fallibility of conscience in applying that law to a particular situation. Alexander of Hales claims that natural law regulates the reason through conscience and the will through synderesis.[33] Bonaventure in his *Breviloquium* defines synderesis as the will's orientation toward good. As Greene observes,

> In attributing synderesis to the natural will Bonaventure was confirming a position that had been implicit in Peter Lombard's citation of Jerome's original use of the term synderesis in his commentary on Ezekiel. Peter had quoted Jerome's passage

29 Steven Ozment, *The Age of Reform 1250–1550* (New Haven, 1980), p. 243.
30 Ozment, *The Age of Reform*, p. 117.
31 Greene, 'Synderesis, the Spark of Conscience', pp. 199–200; Steven Ozment, *Mysticism and Dissent* (New Haven, 1973), pp. 5–8; Mulligan, '*Ratio Superior* and *Ratio Inferior*', pp. 24–8; Crowe, 'The Term *Synderesis*', pp. 151–64.
32 Cited by Mulligan, '*Ratio Superior* and *Ratio Inferior*', p. 26.
33 Crowe, 'The Term *Synderesis*', pp. 151–61.

> in his *Sentences* to support his assertion that 'Man is therefore rightly said naturally to want what is good because he was constructed with a good and righteous will.'[34]

By the end of the thirteenth century, the concept of synderesis in moral theology indicated the inextinguishable portion of the reason or will which retained an infallible apprehension of and attraction to the good. It bears remarkable resemblance to Julian's claim that 'in every soule that shalle be savyd is a godly wylle that nevyr assentyth to synne, nor nevyr shalle' (p. 443).

Julian's concept of the 'godly wylle' may also have been influenced by the mystical theology of Thomas Gallus and Bonaventue, both of whom identify the *scintilla* with the *apex affectus* or *apex amoris* and emphasize the importance of the will rather than the intellect in mystical union. Writing in the first half of the thirteenth century, Thomas Gallus, Abbot of the Victorine house in Vercelli, articulated an 'affective Dionysianism' that influenced many Fransciscans, including Bonaventure, as well as a variety of other late medieval mystics. As McGinn explains,

> Gallus's Dionysianism rests on two significant innovations: a reinterpretation of the ascent to the unknown God which places the experience of affective love above all cognition, and a process whereby the angelic hierarchies are treated primarily as the inner powers of the soul to be energized and set in order to achieve loving union.[35]

The highest stage of this nine-fold internal ascent is the union with God initiated by grace that occurs in the *apex affectus* or *scintilla synderesis*.[36] In the second half of the thirteenth century, Bonaventure borrows these two terms from Gallus and uses them, as well as *apex mentis*, to refer to the part of the soul where the highest of the six successive stages of illumination takes place. Following Augustine and other mystics, Bonaventure claims that this point and ground of the soul are one.

> In the human soul the inmost part and the highest part are the same. This is evident because it is according to both its highest and its inmost part that it especially draws near to God, so that the more that it returns to its interior, the more it ascends and is united to things eternal.[37]

In mystical theology, then, synderesis and the *scintilla* are identified with the point and ground of the soul; these four terms are, to a great extent, interchangeable.

Although Julian does not refer to synderesis or the spark, her erudite use of the metaphors of the point and ground indicates her familiarity with the concept of the soul in mystical discourse. She contends that the 'godly wylle' of one predestined for salvation is substantially united to Christ as the ground of the soul.

[34] Greene, 'Instinct of Nature', p. 186.
[35] McGinn, *The Flowering of Mysticism*, pp. 79, 80.
[36] McGinn, *The Flowering of Mysticism*, p. 85. See also Lees, *The Negative Language of the Dionysian School*, II, pp. 275–88, p. 326 n. 186.
[37] Cited by McGinn, *The Flowering of Mysticism*, p. 105.

> We have all this blessyd wyll hoole and safe in oure lorde Jhesu Crist, for that ech kynde that hevyn shall be fulfyllyd with behovyd nedys of goddys rygh(t)fulnes so to be knytt and onyd in hym that there in were kepte a substannce whych might nevyr nor shulde be partyd from hym, and that thorow his awne good wyll in his endlesse forse(ing) purpose. (pp. 555–6)

Julian's notion of the 'godly wylle' depends on the exemplarist idea of virtual preexistence of the elect in the Christ that is characteristic of the new mysticism of the thirteenth century. This substantial union between the 'godly wylle' and the Logos can be identified with the mystical concept of synderesis or the *scintilla animae*, the highest point of the soul where mystical union occurs. Because God remains in the souls of the elect and their souls remain in God, the portion of the will residing in the higher part or substance of the soul is incapable of sin.

Julian's emphasis on the preexistence of the 'godly wylle', its location in the higher part of the soul, and its indefectibility from good bear a remarkable resemblance to the moral and mystical conceptions of synderesis or the *scintilla* in medieval theology. Although her use of the vernacular obscures her theological erudition, Julian's metaphors of point and ground reveal her familiarity with the mystical discourse on the soul and her concept of the 'godly wylle', a consolidation of ideas about synderesis in these two traditions, manifests her deep learning and her brilliant originality.

'NEB . . . SUMDEAL ILICH WUMMON & NEDDRE IS BEHINDEN': READING THE MONSTROUS IN THE ANCHORITIC TEXT

LIZ HERBERT MCAVOY

> [A] body is always a substance for inscription . . . [T]he flesh writes and is given to be read; and to be written.[1]

IN AN ESSAY EXAMINING the relationship between the female author, reading and writing, French feminist Hélène Cixous interprets the Genesis narrative and Eve's transgression in terms of its providing a fundamental lesson for women about the politics of reading. For Cixous, the primal Edenic location provides the '[s]cene of the meal in which desire and prohibition coexist'.[2] The 'meal' in question here, of course, is that of the 'forbidden' fruit, which provides and remains a primary symbol of humankind's problematic relationship with its own innate desires and its cultural systems of taboo. Faced with the primal prohibition of God's law and her own desire to move beyond its boundaries, Eve chooses to read the apple as symbol of satiation rather than one of transgression or disobedience. Although aware of the rhetoric of death as punishment for indulgence of desire ('For in what day soever thou shalt eat of it, thou shalt die the death'),[3] within an economy where death does not yet exist, its meaning, paradoxically, is devoid of anything meaningful. In its non-existence, death fails to signify, whereas the apple – tactile, mysterious and inviting investigation of its luscious interior – is present in all its multiplicity of potential significations. The contest between law and desire, therefore, turns out to be no contest at all. Thus, Eve's reading of the apple, not as a 'fruit-not-to'[4] but as means towards a 'libidinal education',[5] transforms this first act of female reading into a negotiation of the competing discourses of desire and taboo which are first inscribed upon the apple and subsequently upon her own body as woman. In so doing, she offers up this body to a cultural inscription of both desire and taboo which will forever render her subject to bodily duplicity. In their duality of meaning, therefore, and their susceptibility to contesting readings, the fruit of the forbidden tree

1 Hélène Cixous, 'Coming to Writing', in *Coming to Writing and Other Essays*, ed. Deborah Jenson (Cambridge, Mass. and London, 1991), pp. 1–58 at p. 26.
2 Cixous, 'The Author in Truth', in ibid., pp. 136–81 at p. 149.
3 Genesis 2:17.
4 Cixous, 'Author in Truth', p. 151.
5 Ibid., p. 148.

and the body of the first woman both constitute a foundational monstrous text produced under the proscriptive hegemony of the Law of the Father.

One late medieval tradition, however, offers up the opportunity of a more nuanced reading of such foundational texts. Within this tradition, the agent of Eve's awakening – that is to say the duplicitous serpent – is itself transformed into multivalent monstrous text. The serpent, of course, had long been associated with diabolic incarnation in medieval consciousness and was most often gendered unproblematically male, in keeping with its phallic appearance and diabolic associations. A second tradition, however, inscribes a specifically *female* ontology upon its Edenic incarnation, resulting in the creation of a feminised and monstrous hybrid which surfaces in texts such as *Piers Plowman*, *Ancrene Wisse* and the *Chester Mystery Cycle*. Within this tradition, as cogently demonstrated in the Chester 'Adam' play, for example, not only is Satan himself already essentially hybridic in his fluctuating transition from angel to demon ('The brightest angel I was or this,/ that ever was or yet is'),[6] but he takes on further hybrid status moulded specifically to exploit the traditional link drawn in the Middle Ages between women and uncontrollable monstrous appetite:

> A manner of an edder is in this place
> that wynges like a bryde shee hase –
> feete as an edder, a maydens face –
> hir kynde I will take.
> And of the tree of paradice
> shee shall eate through my contyse;
> for wemen they be full licourouse,
> that wil shee not forsake.[7]

Here, the Chester playwright both rereads and rewrites the traditional Genesis representation, exploiting a complex web of association and hybridising Satan, woman and serpent in the form of the multiple signifier, 'edder'. This creature, possessor of female face, legs and wings, points towards some type of monstrous and ontological miscegenation as lying at the heart of humanity – and female humanity, in particular.[8] It is just such a discourse which frequently raises its head in the religious literature aimed specifically at women during the later Middle Ages – and particularly that directed at the female recluse. On the other hand, the literature of a similar kind written specifically for the male anchorite is almost wholly devoid of this problematic monstrous discourse, as I shall demonstrate. However, just as the inscription of womanhood upon the ambiguous serpent serves to imbue it with monstrous hybridity, so those texts written specifically for enclosed women take on a similar hybridity which, like the monstrous body itself, is always open to contested readings, as I shall demonstrate.

6 *The Chester Mystery Cycle*, ed. R. M. Lumiansky and David Mills, EETS SS III (London, New York and Toronto, 1974), p. 20.

7 Ibid., p. 21.

8 Dyan Elliott examines such links in *Fallen Bodies: Pollution, Sexuality, and Demonology in the Middle Ages* (Philadelphia, 1999).

In her recent book examining literary constructs of hybridity as a source of monstrous discourse, Caroline Walker Bynum concludes that the hybrid is essentially a dialogic entity; as inherently two bodies within a single corporeal boundary, it is neither one thing nor the other, and its 'contraries and . . . simultaneous are in perpetual conversation with each other'.[9] Like the dualistic serpent-woman of the Edenic setting, the hybrid can both destabilise and reveal the world. Thus, in her quest to gain knowledge and to ingest and assimilate it, Eve forever sets herself apart from the Law and the social order. She is, in fact, a type of monstrous *mixtura*, paradigmatic of woman – and the enclosed woman in particular – who is also rendered marginal whilst simultaneously occupying a central discursive space within socio-religious culture. I shall therefore argue that, although functioning as a key metaphor for the dangerous female body, the concept of monstrous hybridity was able to open up for the medieval woman reader a bifurcated text which, like that of the Edenic serpent, could be read in a number of more affirming ways than that for which it was originally designed by its male author. Ultimately, such a hybrid body becomes a fitting symbol for both the anchoritic experience and the anchoritic text in which both meanings and identities ultimately refuse to be pinned down and which, chameleon-like, shift and change according to the gendered perspectives and reading strategies employed by a widening audience.

I

The so-called Katherine Group of texts,[10] along with the popular *Ancrene Wisse*, comprises a collection of works originally written specifically for women either aspiring to, or already living, a holy life of chastity and enclosure and, as I have suggested, within these writings monstrous discourse takes up a position at centre stage. *Seinte Margarete*, an account of the virgin martyrdom of Saint Margaret, for example (a text which the *Ancrene Wisse* author presumes his anchoresses will be reading alongside his own text)[11] graphically delineates a fierce combat with a hellish dragon undertaken by the young virgin.[12] During the

9 Caroline Walker Bynum, *Metamorphosis and Identity* (New York, 2001), p. 160.

10 The editions of the Katherine Group texts examined here (*Seinte Margarete, Sawles Warde, Hali Meiðhad*) will be from Bella Millet and Jocelyn Wogan-Browne, eds, *Medieval English Prose for Women: Selections from the Katherine Group and Ancrene Wisse* (Oxford, 1990). All references to *Ancrene Wisse* will be from the revised Cambridge, Corpus Christi College, MS 402 version: J. R. R. Tolkien, ed., *Ancrene Wisse*, EETS OS CCXLIX (Oxford, 1962), unless otherwise stated. The translations are taken from Hugh White, ed. and trans., *Ancrene Wisse: Guide for Anchoresses* (Harmondsworth, 1993), the page numbers to which will appear parenthetically in the notes.

11 '. . . ower englische boc of seinte Margarete'. *Ancrene Wisse*, p. 125.

12 Within medieval bestiaries, the dragon is often conflated with the serpent and imbued with diabolic associations accordingly. See, for example, *The Book of Beasts*, ed. and trans. T. H. White (London, 1954, repr. 1956), pp. 165–7.

battle, the fearless Margaret is ingested by this demonic beast within her prison cell, an act of monstrous consumption which covertly makes manifest the potential of the female to herself turn monster and assimilate her flesh with that of her monstrous *doppleganger.* Resisting this traditional paradigm of womanhood, however, Saint Margaret feminises the struggle for individuation on her own terms, breaking free of such enforced assimilation and bringing about a type of recontextualised 'monstrous birth' in which her own body bursts free of the monstrous (m)other. Such an act of female resistance forever afterwards renders her the patron saint of childbirth and vanquisher of the diabolic.

Such discourses of the monstrous are equally emphatic in the other texts within the Katherine Group. *Sawles Warde*, an allegory concerning the custody of the soul, for example, contains an even more graphically affective account of the horrors of hell – horrors which are characterised by monstrous cannibalistic hybrids which are 'grisliche ase deoflen, þe forswolheð ham ihal ant speoweð ham eft ut biuoren ant bihinden' [dreadful as devils, which swallow them whole and vomit them out again before and behind].[13] Other acts of consumption also dominate the punishments of the damned – who are also implicitly the text's constructed audience of inherently sinful women. Not only are they endlessly pursued by all manner of 'laðe helle-wurmes' [hideous creeping-things of hell],[14] but these predatory monsters also proceed to gnaw off and ingest an assortment of bodily protuberances, followed by the rest of the dismembered body. Subsequent to this act of bodily incorporation, the ingested bodies are endlessly made whole again and endlessly spewed forth and re-consumed in a type of never-ending process of hybrid union and monstrous re-birth.[15]

A further text within the Katherine Group is the equally emotive *Hali Meiðhad*. Written to extol the 'horrors' of female sexuality and child-bearing and to promote a life of holy virginity, this text similarly constructs the female body as a site of monstrous hybridity. Presuming upon a reading of the female body as 'flesliche fulðen' [carnal filthiness][16] and as the site of ontological corruption, only perpetual virginity can protect the female religious against penetration by the fiend:

> Ant ʒef hit eaver timeð þet ti licomes lust, þurh þe false feont, leadðie þe towart flesliche fulðen, ontswere i þi þoht þus: 'Ne geineð þe nawt, sweoke! Þullich Ich chulle beon in meidenes liflade, ilich heovene engel.'[17]

> [And if it happens that your physical desire, through the false fiend, should ever incite you towards carnal filthiness, answer mentally in this way: 'It does you no good, traitor! In my way of life as a virgin, I shall be like an angel in heaven.]

13 *Sawles Warde*, p. 90.
14 Ibid., p. 92.
15 Ibid., pp. 90–2.
16 *Hali Meiðhad*, p. 2.
17 Ibid., p. 40.

In this text, chastity is not presented simply as a desirable alternative to concupiscence, however; implicit to its discourse is that concupiscence is always engaged in some kind of *dialogue* with the chaste body, articulating its desire relentlessly from the shadows and margins, waiting to assert its own pre-eminence and inscribe itself as text both within and upon the body of the holy woman. As the author reminds his audience, 'euch sunne þet me deð is wiðute þe bodi bute þis ane' [every sin that is committed is outside the body except this one alone].[18] For the author of this text, the woman is not a site occupied by *either* chastity *or* concupiscence but as the ambiguous and monstrous embodiment of *both at the same time*. In effect, the woman always inclines towards the Edenic serpent, within whose hybrid body she disports her ambiguous 'maydens face'.

Central to my argument, however, is that, in spite of the warnings embedded within this text, there is nevertheless also present an alternative discourse which focuses on the chaste female body as the site of potential transcension and apotheosis and which attempts to transform hybridity into unity:

> [The virgin is] Iesu Cristes brude, þe Lauerdes leofmon þet alle þinges buheð, of al þe worlt leafdi, as he is of al lauerd; ilich him in halschipe, unwemmet as he is, ant þet eadi meiden his deorrewurðe moder; ilich his hali engles ant his heste halhen; se freo of hireseoluen ha nawiht ne þearf of oðer þing þenchen bute ane of hire leofmon wið treowe luue cwemen.[19]
>
> [. . . the bride of Jesus Christ, the lover of the Lord to whom all things do homage, lady of all the world as he is lord of all; like him in integrity, spotless as he is, and that blessed virgin his beloved mother; like his holy angels and his highest saints; with such freedom for herself that she need not think about anything at all apart from pleasing her beloved with true love.]

The image here depicted of the virgin as the bride of Christ is, of course, equally as dependent upon narratives of female eroticism as is the image of the concupiscent woman and, as such, simultaneously reinforces and contests the type of monstrous discourse we have just been examining. The impulse towards virginity is in continual contest with the desires of the flesh ('Forþi her is aa feht, ant mot beon aa need' [for here there is always conflict, and must always be of necessity]);[20] each enters into dialogue with the other in true hybridic fashion, vying for pre-eminence within the same corporeal and textual boundaries and thus allowing for alternative readings of both the bodies and the text which contains them.

Such a discursive contest within an essentially hybrid textual body is fully borne out when we turn to *Ancrene Wisse*. A guide written initially for a group of three female recluses by an anonymous male author in the first quarter of the thirteenth century,[21] this text was soon subject to major revision by its author in

18 Ibid., p. 30.
19 Ibid., p. 4.
20 Ibid., p. 14.
21 On this see Bella Millett, 'The Origins of *Ancrene Wisse*: New Answers, New Questions', *Medium Aevum* lxi (1992), pp. 206–28.

order to accommodate a much larger group of women living together as recluses. Similarly, over the course of the next three centuries it would be translated into Latin, French and Anglo-Norman, with one copy even being adapted and interpolated for a Lollard audience.[22] For purposes of this present essay, it is the version edited from the revised Corpus Christi manuscript upon which I will focus because of its relative proximity to the original text and because, although addressing a widening audience, this audience was still envisaged as female and anchoritic.

Within this text – which, like those others previously examined, was clearly constructed to reflect contemporary perceptions about a corrupt female ontology[23] – we find a complex combination of monstrous discourse being engaged with. Moreover, much of this discourse is attached to the body of the anchoress herself which, like that of Eve, is identified as a primary site of sin and hybrid combination of seductive beauty and 'pit' of abjection. Here we find again the female-faced serpent making an honorary appearance, this time in the guise of a scorpion devised to warn its female audience against the sin of lechery:

> Scorpiun is a cunnes wurm þe haueð neb as me seið sumdeal ilich wummon & neddre is bihinden. Makeð feier semblant fikeð mid te heaueð & stingeð mid te teile. Þis is leccherie þis is þe deofles beast.[24]

> [The scorpion is a kind of snake which has a face, so they say, somewhat like a woman's and is a snake behind. It makes a fair show and fawns with its head – and stings with its tail. This is lechery, this is the devil's beast.]

In medieval animal lore, the scorpion was closely associated with the Edenic serpent[25] and the *Ancrene Wisse* author now begins to entangle himself within a complex web of association in order to construct his own hybrid monster. This scorpion, for example, comprises a fatal admixture of desirability ('neb . . . sumdeal ilich wummon') and poison ('stingeð mid te teile') whose power rests on the fact that it is simultaneously phallic and female, devil and diva, same and other.[26] Moreover, the threat it poses rests firmly upon its co-mingling of the

22 This is a version which is extant in Cambridge, Magdalene College, MS Pepys 2498 and has been edited by A. Zettersten, *The English Text of the Ancrene Riwle*, EETS OS CCLXXIV (London, 1976).

23 A consideration of the origins of the misogynistic discourse in the *Ancrene Wisse* lies beyond the scope of this essay. However, for an earlier examination of how the female anchorite may have responded more positively to such discourse see my essay, ' "And neos he himself reclus i maries wombe?": Julian of Norwich, The Anchorhold and Redemption of the Monstrous Female Body', in Liz Herbert McAvoy and Teresa Walters, eds, *Consuming Narratives: Gender and Monstrous Appetite in the Middle Ages and the Renaissance* (Cardiff, 2000), pp. 128–43.

24 *Ancrene Wisse*, p. 107 (99).

25 For a codification of the tangle of association between worm, serpent, snake and scorpion, see MED s.v. 'worm' 2 (a) and (b).

26 For an account of the scorpion's phallic associations see Debra Hassig, ed., *The Mark of the Beast: The Medieval Bestiary in Art, Life and Literature* (New York and London, 1999), p. 171.

familiar and the alien, in keeping with Jeffrey Jerome Cohen's recognition of the 'intimate stranger' who lies at the heart of monstrous representation.[27] According to Cohen, the monster is the 'cultural, linguistic, sexual other who seems to be intimate . . . but in fact brutally converts an identity familiar and secure into an alien thing, into a subject estranged from its own body'.[28] No doubt, such a representation in *Ancrene Wisse* was devised to have just the same effect upon its female audience; not only does the author identify the female anchorite as the site of the alien other but, more crucially, clearly attempts to make familiar that same locus of alienation. In effect, he is demanding of her that, as part of her own 'libidinous education', she read the text of her own body in terms of its being *per se* the 'intimate stranger' which lies at the heart of the monstrous, or, to adopt the words of Bynum, a 'mixed thing(s) with no name(s)'.[29] In effect, she is being asked to read her own body as hybrid and monstrous text.

Viewed within an arena of philosophical debate which still validated a traditional Aristotelean notion of the one-sex model of gender difference and which, on occasion, queried whether woman was, in fact, human at all, the body of the woman becomes infinitely malleable for this type of hybrid representation. Woman, 'being as it were a deformity [*ἀναπηρία*]'[30] is rendered by Aristotle as a type of external, apophatic statement of what man is not, nor could ever be, allowing for an infinite corporeal ambiguity to be written upon her monstrous body. Thus in *Ancrene Wisse* we see the unstable flesh of the female anchorite potentially subject to penetration by and co-mingling with a whole host of bestial partners amongst whom appear the hen, the jackdaw, the raven, the magpie, not to mention the Devil whose 'whore' she is always in danger of becoming.[31] At one point, too – in a frenzy of hybridisation which results in an explosion of almost formless monstrosity within the text – her tongue becomes 'slubbri' [slippery], and she spits out venom with 'meaðelinde muð(es)' and 'ȝeoniende tuteles' [jabbering lips and gaping mouths]. She 'wadeð i wete' [wades in wetness] and with her backbiting she 'cheoweð monnes flesch' [chews men's flesh] and 'culcheð al ut somet þat te attri heorte sent up to þe tunge' [vomits all

27 Jeffrey Jerome Cohen, *Of Giants: Sex, Monsters and the Middle Ages* (Minneapolis and London, 1999).

28 Ibid., p. 2.

29 Bynum, *Metamorphosis*, p. 118.

30 Aristotle, *Generation of Animals*, ed. and trans. A. L. Peck (London, 1963), p. 775a, lines 15–16 (Book 4, Chapter 6). The noun *ἀναπηρία* can also be translated as 'lameness', 'mutilation' or 'stunted development', all of which are classified as pollutants in Leviticus 21 and therefore prohibit access to God's altar. Aristotle uses it on a number of occasions in the context of women and it is significant in this instance that his use seems to stimulate a passage in which he deals in some detail with monstrous pregnancy brought about by corruption within the womb. For a useful overview of Aristotelean theory in this context see Ian Maclean, *The Renaissance Notion of Woman: A Study in the Fortunes of Scholasticism and Medical Science in European Intellectual Life* (Cambridge, 1980).

31 *Ancrene Wisse*, pp. 36 (36), 48 (46), 150 (136).

out together what the poisonous heart sends up to the tongue].[32] Here the female anchorite and her simultaneously familiar yet alien body is rendered a text which articulates the miscegenation which is the dangerous end-point to such ontological monstrosity. She is, quite simply, being asked to read onto the hybrid text of her own permeable body a narrative of similitude *and* otherness.

Permeability, of course, incorporates the notion of violation and a penetration of boundaries which denies the contiguity of the external and internal as separate regions. Like the lady within her castle which is locked up against enemy hordes, like the sealed and protected household of *Sawles Warde* and like the anchorhold which walls up its occupant away from the world, within anchoritic discourse the body of the female anchorite – like that of Eve – is considered to be an internal space open to penetration and contamination by sin entering from the outside:

> [A]se deað com . . . into þe worlde þuruh sunne also þuruh eie þurles deað haueð hire ingong into þe soule . . . & mid gode rihte muwen eiþurles beon ihoten eilþurles vor heo habbeð idon muchel eil to monion ancre.[33]

> [Just as death came . . . into the world through sin, so through eye-windows death has its entry into the soul . . . And quite rightly may eye-windows be called harm-windows, for they have done much harm to many an anchoress.]

Here, death is personified as entering the world in the same way as sin can enter through the eye's opening, rendering an external fear an internal reality and thus breaking down the barriers of an inside–outside conceptualisation. For this reason the anchoress is ubiquitously exhorted to seal up the doorways of her body because of the threat posed to its desired integrity.[34] The concept of penetration in this text therefore takes on an intensely sexual – and gendered – connotation, as does the teleology of those boundaries which are to be penetrated and, in the case of *Ancrene Wisse*, these boundaries are primarily corporeal and female, as we have seen.

32 Ibid., pp. 40 (39), 43 (42), 40 (39), 45 (43), 47 (45).

33 This section is missing from Corpus Christi College, MS 402. It does, however, appear in Cotton Nero MS A. XIV (*The English Text of the Ancrene Riwle*, ed. Mabel Day, EETS OS CCXXV (London, 1952), p. 27, from which edition this extract is taken) and Merton College MS 44, a Latin text of the *Ancrene Riwle*, which has been edited along with British Library, MS Cotton Vitellius E vii by Charlotte D'Evelyn, *The Latin Text of the Ancrene Riwle*, EETS OS CCXVI (Oxford, 1944), p. 15. The translation is from White, p. 33.

34 For an examination of the dangers attached to women's bodies and the construction of gender differences in the Middle Ages see Joan Cadden, *Meanings of Sex Difference in the Middle Ages* (Cambridge, 1993), especially pp. 167, 185, 223.

II

In his study of the function of the monstrous in the Middle Ages, David Williams has identified the monstrous as a 'symbolic language that . . . expressed the inadequacy of human cognition in containing the limitlessness of the real'.[35] According to Williams, as an external reification of 'what-is-not', the figure of the monster in the Middle Ages served apophatically as a negative figure of deformity, offering itself as a template up against which its cataphatic counterpart – that is to say the 'what-is' – could be defined and measured. In this sense, it tended to externalise and (true to its etymology)[36] demonstrate those cultural fears which lay beyond the bounds of human comprehension. In other words, they lay at the same intersection of the internal and the external as does the penetrable body of the female anchorite. Thus, the monstrous served to define and police the culturally normative, raising itself to the level of a conceptual sign. Within the Middle Ages, of course, the culturally normative tended to be the paradigmatic male, as we have seen, and in this context it is possible to recognise the purpose of the *Ancrene Wisse* author in his deployment of monstrous discourse as a means of dictating and policing the spirituality of his female audience.

How this female audience read and interpreted this discourse remains another matter, but before I address the possibilities within such monstrous discourse to provide alternative reading strategies, it may be useful at this point to turn to an anchoritic guide which was written for a specifically male audience during the early fifteenth century. In the light of Williams' theory of the apophatic signification of the monstrous, and the fact that both male and female anchorites were expected to fulfil a similar spiritual function outside that of the priesthood, we could well expect to find such discourse also predominating here. In fact, however, the opposite remains the case. The text in question, the *Speculum Inclusorum*,[37] was written at a time when *Ancrene Wisse* was being more widely

[35] David Williams, *Deformed Discourse: The Function of the Monster in Mediaeval Thought and Literature* (Exeter, 1996), p. 6.

[36] The term is derived from the Latin *monstrum* (unnatural thing or event), *monstrare* (to show or demonstrate) and *monere* (to warn).

[37] The Latin text is extant in two versions, one of which has been edited by Livarius Oliger in 'Speculum Inclusorum Auctore Anonymo Anglico Saeculi XIV', *Lateranum*, n.s. iv (Rome, 1938); the other manuscript, Oxford, St John's College, MS 177, has been reproduced in facsimile form in J. Hogg, ed., *The Speculum Inclusorum, Vol. 2: St John's College Oxford, Ms. 177 of the Speculativum Clausorum*, Analecta Cartusiana LIX:2 (1981). A third manuscript contains an incomplete Middle English translation: Marta Powell Harley, ed., *The Myrour of Recluses: A Middle English Translation of Speculum Inclusorum* (Madison and London, 1995). References will be to the *Myrour*, with the equivalent pages from *Speculum* appearing parenthetically in the notes. For a reappraisal of Oliger's dating of this text as late fourteenth century and the presentation of evidence to suggest it was composed sometime in the first decades of the

disseminated in a number of different hybrid forms amongst the laity of both sexes.[38] Written initially in Latin, the guide was translated anonymously into English as *The Myrour of Recluses* in the late fifteenth century[39] and probably targeted a wider mixed audience, as did later versions of *Ancrene Wisse*.[40] Nowhere in either the Latin or English text, however, do we find the discourse of monstrosity or bodily penetration being used in any significant way in connection with the anchoritic body – nor in the context of sensuality and the five bodily wits. Instead, we find that, rather than being rendered passive and open to contamination or monstrous insemination via the five senses as is the case with the female body in *Ancrene Wisse*, the male anchoritic body tends to be inherently and ontologically proactive and sealed. For example, the primary danger posed to this body is an active 'enclynynge vnto synne' ('inclinata ad peccatum')[41] rather than being penetrated by it. Elsewhere we find that temptation 'induceþ ['inducit'] a man into deedly synne',[42] or the anchorite might 'falle & . . . slyppe into deedly synne' ('labendum in mortale peccatum').[43] On every occasion, sin is something which the anchorite actively moves towards and engages with, rather than having the boundaries of his own body broken down by it. This is entirely in keeping with both texts' primary representation of the anchorite as proactive and empowered *miles Christi* who, unlike his female counterpart, is fully equipped to 'fyȝt continuely . . . again al possible temptacions' ('pugnandum continue . . . contra temptaciones possibiles').[44] Even when the discourse of enclosure *is* specifically introduced, it tends to identify its audience as 'gentil knyȝtes of Ihesu Crist' ('generosi milites Ihesu Christi')[45] who are actively – and successfully – defending a castle-like body so that it remains 'schyt & spered agayn þe voluptuous or lusty melodyes of the world' ('contra voluptuosas seculi melodies clauditur').[46]

fifteenth century, see E. A. Jones, 'A New Look into the *Speculum Inclusorum*', in *MMT* VI, pp. 123–45.

38 For an account of this, see Elizabeth Robertson, ' "This Living Hand": Thirteenth-Century Female Literacy, Material Immanence, and the Reader of the *Ancrene Wisse*', *Speculum* lxxviii (2003), pp. 1–36.

39 *Myrour*, Introduction, p. xxviii.

40 In the second chapter of her unpublished thesis, 'Solitude and Sociability: Constructions of Anchoritism and the Anchoritic Ideal in Late-Medieval England' the Centre for Medieval Studies, University of York), Mari Hughes-Edwards argues that both the *Speculum* and the *Myrour's* sophisticated treatment of contemplative material 'implies that both audiences are groups of considerable spiritual experience and ability'. Jones goes further to suggest that the *Myrour* is not intent on reaching a wider audience outside the reclusory and that the translator 'had in mind an equally restricted readership' as did the original *Speculum* author. Jones, 'New Look', p. 141.

41 *Myrour*, p. 12 (77).

42 Ibid., p. 14 (79).

43 Ibid., p. 12 (78).

44 Ibid., p. 8 (72–3).

45 Ibid., p. 6 (70).

46 Ibid., p. 13 (79).

At this point in the Middle English translation, the author sees it fit to add his own interpolation and focus directly on the female anchorite in an attempt to regender the exhortation, and it is highly likely that it is the discussion of the dangers of sensuality which has incited him to make this addition:[47]

> (& naamly of anchoresses, þat bien more streytly closed þan oþir religious men & women, enclosed in her houses be leue of her souereyns and in alle tymes at her souereyns wyl).[48]

Here, the self-evident implication is that women are more in need of being kept away from the temptations of the world's sensuality and, more importantly, being dangerously sensual beings themselves, the world must be kept away from them. This anti-feminist bias betrayed by the translator is soon compounded by the fact that the Latin text at this point begins to focus specifically on the sense of touch which, we are told, can often invoke lustful thoughts ('in quo contingit voluptas venerea mulitplex').[49] Now the translator proceeds to manipulate the connotations of the verb *contingit* in order to include an image of bodily penetration more suited to hermeneutics of the unsealed female body, simultaneously eradicating the notion of intact male boundaries invoked by the Latin word:[50] 'by the which *entriþ* þe lust of lecherie in sundry wyse'.[51]

The reason for this becomes clear a little further on in the Latin text when the *Speculum* author proceeds to quote I Corinthians 6:10 in order to identify the 'spices of lecherie' to which the anchorite may be most inclined: 'neque molles, neque masculorum concubitores regnum Dei possidebunt'.[52] Here the author identifies both masturbation (*molles*) and sodomy (*masculorum concubitores)* as the most dangerous sins to which the male anchorite can incline. The translation, however, not only drops entirely the reference to sodomy but paraphrastically dilutes the impact of the passage thus:

> Þan ys þer doon a manere or spice of 'lecherie again kynde', which is callyd in Latyn of þe apostyl 'molicies'.[53]

Not only that, but the translator also proceeds to regender the Latin noun *reclusus* at this point, rendering it specifically 'ancresse' (rather than 'recluse' or 'ancres

47 The regendering of this passage is something also addressed by Jones, 'New Look', pp. 139–40. My own interpretation of this passage, however, is dependent upon the punctuation within Harley's edition rather than that of Jones' own reading which closes the parenthesis after 'anchoresses'.

48 Ibid., p. 13.

49 *Speculum*, p. 79.

50 The Lewis and Short Latin dictionary definitions for *contingo* are 'to touch' (I), 'to touch impurely' (IB: 2), 'to border upon' (IB:3), 'to stain' or 'defile' (IIB:1). See *A Latin Dictionary*, ed. Charlton C. Lewis and Charles Short (Oxford, 1879). It would seem that the translator has seized upon those meanings which are related to sinful touching and altered the connotation to include penetration.

51 *Myrour*, p. 13 (my emphasis).

52 *Speculum*, pp. 79–80.

53 *Myrour*, p. 14.

& ankeresses' which he has used on other occasions), telling us 'Alle suych spices of lecherie ben fer from an ancresse, but ȝif it happe percaas of a voluptuous or lusty delectacion'.[54] It would seem that the Middle English translator was unable to countenance a penetrated male body within a text which prefers to present it as sealed and intact and has transferred intimations of penetration to its appropriate site – that is to say, the feminine. Although these changes can also be read as a rather clumsy attempt at making the original material more relevant to a wider audience of both sexes, it is nevertheless very likely that such a slippage also constitutes a subliminal betrayal of the widespread belief that sodomitic practices served to feminise the male body. As a result, the masturbatory and sodomitic anchorite is caused to metamorphose *literally* into his wholly female counterpart in the gulf established between the Latin and the English texts.

There then follows what is offered as a 'true' story ('vera . . . historia')[55] about a hermit who was party to this type of lechery, and again we witness a manipulation of the original meaning within the translation in order to serve a new agenda. Whereas the Latin suggests that the offending hermit was suddenly spirited away by devils during the night ('subito raptus a demonibus'),[56] the Middle English text renders him 'sodeynly ravyssched & taken wiþ a feend'.[57] The Latin term *raptus*, of course, is one which is wholly appropriate within the context of the solitary as *miles Christi*, being originally a term commonly associated with warfare and other militaristic activity.[58] The Middle English term 'ravyssched', however, is one which develops the possibilites of *raptus* drawing on, firstly, connotations of rape and, secondly, a lesser-known usage which refers to the devil's carrying off of souls to hell.[59] Its appearance here, therefore, alongside the reduction of the offending devils to a single entity, not only conjures up inferences of diabolic rape but again, by means of these inferences of penetration, serves to feminise the body of the 'hermyte', transforming him into a hybrid *mixtura* of both male and female.

In accounting for the omission of the reference to sodomy and its absence from the tale, Marta Powell Harley suggests that rather than being a sign of reticence on the part of the translator, he is, in fact, demonstrating an awareness of the distinction made between the two practices, adding that 'the category "masculorum concubitores" is irrelevant to the exemplum of the hermit', and is

54 Ibid., p. 14.
55 *Speculum*, p. 80.
56 Ibid., p. 80.
57 *Myrour*, p. 14.
58 The primary definition of *rapio* is 'seize' or 'lay waste'. See Lewis and Short, *Latin Dictionary*, s.v. An alternative meaning, however, is 'to be carried away by passion' (B2: ci). *The Dictionary of Ecclesiastical Latin*, ed. Leo F. Stelton (Peabody, Mass., 1995), defines it as 'to abduct'. However, in the *Revised Medieval Latin Wordlist*, ed. R. E. Latham (London, 1965), its past participle *raptus* is defined as 'rapt in an ecstasy'.
59 MED 'ravishen', 2 (a) and 2 (d).

therefore omitted.[60] Presumably, however, a hermit would have had greater opportunity for contact with the outside world than his anchorite equivalent, so Harley's explanation appears to fall down at the first hurdle. It is more likely that the omission results from the attempt to regender the material for a mixed audience and to the fact that this sexual practice was primarily regarded as male-on-male penetration during the Middle Ages. Even more important, however, is that a penetrated *male* body would constitute a major distraction within a text which can only envisage the *female* as penetrable and will later rely upon the open and permeable body of a traditionally feminised Christ to provide its primary image and hermeneutic. [61]

III

In the light of this evidence, we can perhaps begin to draw the conclusion that there is a distinct difference between the ways in which monstrous discourses connected with penetration and hybrid assimilation are employed in anchoritic texts directed specifically at men or at women. These preliminary findings suggest that the monstrous was far more likely to be utilised in those texts written for women and, even when it does make an appearance in male-directed texts, it is usually in the context of the feminine. Far from being an environment in which a man or a woman could transcend culturally transmitted attitudes towards the body and reach a point of gender neutrality in order to approach the divine, it would seem that the literature they were expected to read aimed at perpetuating those cultural stereotypes which they had supposedly left behind on the outside of the anchorhold. The question that remains, therefore, is how these apparently repressive discourses of monstrosity were received, processed and transformed by the audience of female anchorites whose own bodies were similarly considered to be sites of the monstrous? Useful to approaching this question is the work of Anne Clark Bartlett who has reassessed how a female audience may have responded to the general misogyny inherent within male-authored medieval devotional texts.[62] Bartlett argues that women may well have focused on what she identifies as the more positive discourses often running counter to or contending with the main discursive strands of the narrative – nuptial imagery, for example, or discourses of spiritual or familial friendships between women. By exercising a

60 *Myrour*, Introduction, p. xvi.

61 Discussion of the feminised permeability of Christ's body is beyond this essay. See, however, Caroline Walker Bynum, *Jesus as Mother: Studies in the Spirituality of the High Middle Ages* (Berkeley, 1982) and Sarah Beckwith, *Christ's Body: Identity, Culture and Society in Late Medieval Writings* (London, 1993). For an insightful examination of the 'monstrous' body of Christ see Robert Mills, 'Jesus as Monster', in Bettina Bildhauer and Robert Mills, eds, *The Monstrous Middle Ages* (Cardiff, 2003), pp. 28–54.

62 Anne Clark Bartlett, *Male Authors, Female Readers: Representation and Subjectivity in Middle English Literature* (Ithaca and London, 1995).

type of selective reading practice, or one which 'goes against the grain', the woman reader could emerge with a far more positive sense of her own subjectivity than that offered to her by those mainstream discourses employed by the male author.

Building on this theory, and in the context of the type of texts which I have been examining here, I think the answer lies in several areas. Firstly, those texts aimed at women such as we see in the Katherine Group and *Ancrene Wisse* are clearly designed to address a range of variable literacies within the audience.[63] This variable literacy not only pertains to the initial group of female anchorites and those of the Corpus revision who, as we know, lacked any depth of literacy in Latin, although were evidently able to read in the English and, probably, French vernacular;[64] it also suggests the widely disparate audiences at whom later revisions and translations were directed, be they male religious, mixed laity, or even Lollard. Presumably, this wider audience with its greater variety of interests, concerns and agendas would prioritise the material contained within these works in different ways according to their own specific type of literacy, be it Latinate, vernacular, pragmatic, professional or recreational.[65] Moreover, it is also highly likely that each individual reader may have been called upon to read the text differently at different moments in time – the type of reading undertaken in a private capacity is likely to have differed from the reading aloud of extracts to others, for example.

One useful way of ascertaining how a woman readership may have dealt with the monstrous discourses directed at them within such texts is to consider briefly the extant writing undertaken by those women themselves. Margery Kempe and Julian of Norwich, for example, were women who were evidently well-read and fully acquainted with cultural attitudes towards them and their problematic bodies[66] and an examination of their writing can testify cogently to how the types

63 On the variability of women's literacy see Felicity Riddy, ' "Women Talking About the Things of God": a Late Medieval Sub-Culture', in Carole Meale, ed., *Women and Literature in Britain 1150–1500* (Cambridge and New York, 1993), pp. 104–27. For an examination of the constructions of female literacy as constructed by the male author, see also Linda Olson, 'Reading, Singing and Understanding: Constructions of the Literacy of Women Religious in Late Medieval England', in Sarah Rees Jones, ed., *Learning and Literacy in Medieval England and Abroad* (Turnhout, 2003), pp. 97–120. See also Robertson, ' "This Living Hand" '.

64 Ibid., p. 10.

65 On late medieval literacies see M. B. Parkes, 'The Literacy of the Laity', in David Daiches and Anthony Thorby, eds, *Literacy and Western Civilization: The Mediaeval World* (London, 1973), pp. 555–77.

66 In asserting that these writers were well-read I use the term advisedly. Whereas there is much internal evidence to suggest that Julian was deeply acquainted with sophisticated philosophical and theological concepts, as well as medical lore, we have no concrete proof of her own reading practices. Margery Kempe, however, demonstrates that, for her, 'reading' was frequently a matter of listening to a priest reading aloud to her. On another occasion, however, she appears to be in possession of a book whilst in church, suggesting that her own reading practices were also more varied than they appear. Ref-

of monstrous discourses we have been examining here could have been received and filtered by the woman reader. By means of highly individualistic and selective reading practices based on their variable literacies, both of these women were able to convert such discourse into a comment on the monstrous masculine and in so doing demonstrate the feasibility – indeed, desirability – of the feminine principle as an equally valid means of accessing the divine.

Margery Kempe, of course, was not an anchorite.[67] She did, however, forge firm anchoritic links, both by means of her long-term and much beloved anchorite confessor, Alan of Lynne, and her well-documented contact with Julian of Norwich. What is significant about her text is the way in which she frequently parries and reflects back upon the masculine traditional discourses of the monstrous body in order to critique those abuses of power and the constraints placed upon her by patriarchal hegemony – the proscriptive and judgemental language of an early confessor, for example, or the insistent sexual advances of her husband and his later descent into senility and incontinence. Similarly, a series of abusive priests, both actual and visionary, are also allied with the monstrous by means of their sexual innuendoes and threats of rape.[68] Thus, Margery brings into the spotlight traditional notions of masculine integrity and redefines them as frequently representative of the socially and spiritually aberrant. This, in turn, tends to throw into firm relief what *is* desirable – and that is the gently feminised Christ of Margery's visionary experiences as seen from the feminine perspective.

Even a more effective – and far more subtle – reversal of those monstrous paradigms everywhere apparent in the anchoritic texts aimed specifically at women is undertaken by the anchorite Julian of Norwich. In Julian we have a woman reader and writer who was probably familiar with *Ancrene Wisse*, as well as a range of other texts which define the female body as a site of monstrosity.[69] Rather than accepting and internalising this discourse the way male authors seem to have done, however, what we find is a similar removal of the monstrous away

erences will be to *The Book of Margery Kempe*, ed. Sanford Brown Meech and Hope Emily Allen, EETS OS CCXII (London, 1940).

67 A later redaction printed by Henry Pepwell in 1521 designates Margery Kempe as 'deuoute ancres . . . of Lynne'. This redaction is published as an appendix in the aforementioned edition, pp. 353–7 (for this quotation, p. 357 n. 11).

68 For a much more detailed account of this treatment of the monstrous in both these texts see my essay, 'Monstrous Masculinities in Julian of Norwich's *A Revelation of Love* and *The Book of Margery Kempe*', in Bildhauer and Mills, eds, *The Monstrous Middle Ages*, pp. 55–74.

69 On this, again see my essay 'Redemption', in McAvoy and Walters, eds, *Consuming Narratives*, especially pp. 129–34. See also Elizabeth Robertson, 'Medieval Medical Views of Women and Female Spirituality in *Ancrene Wisse* and Julian of Norwich's *Showings*', in Linda Lomperis and Sarah Stanbury, eds, *Feminist Approaches to the Body in Medieval Literature* (New York and London, 1993), pp. 142–67, and Alexandra Barratt, ' "In the lowest part of our need": Julian and Medieval Gynecological Writing', in Sandra McEntire, ed., *Julian of Norwich: A Book of Essays* (New York and London, 1998), pp. 240–56.

from the female body and, as we saw in the case of Margery Kempe, its transference to that of the male – and, in particular that of the male devil. In a lengthy and detailed description of Julian's own quasi rape by this intensely masculine fiend we find a monstrous parody being constructed of the unitive and mutually accommodating relationship which she enjoys with her own intensely feminine Christ. On every count, this fiend, as overdetermined representative of the masculine in this text, embodies all its most threatening and destructive attributes, whereas Christ, like the author herself, is the site of a suffering permeability which leads ultimately to salvation. In this sense, the discursive monstrosity within cultural constructs of the feminine is transformed into apt precursor to the fully realised depiction of God as Mother which forms the climactic point of Julian's writing.

Such a treatment of the monstrous in both these texts, therefore, would suggest two things: firstly that female readers of male-authored texts were able to process, filter and reinterpret traditional discourses of the monstrous female in order to forge an alternative route through a text – and their own intellectual and spiritual lives. Secondly, this could facilitate a realignment of such discourse as a means towards gaining authority for themselves and their own religious and literary practices. In this way, the anchoritic text can be seen as being in itself ultimately hybrid or 'monstrous'. Experienced in a number of different ways by a number of different audiences during separate diachronic reading moments, within disparate geographical and socio-religious situations, it could offer an opportunity for both traditional and subversive readings, both of which could lead ultimately to the same destination which was to learn the best, most appropriate way of approaching the divine. Thus, in his exhortation to his female audience to choose the 'right' path the author unwittingly invites them to develop a reading strategy which will allow them to trace a route for themselves, absorbing along the way those more positive discourses whilst rendering subaltern the negative ones which contend for pre-eminence.

Finally, in the same way as Eve's transgressive reading of the apple constituted part of her own 'libidinous education', so the female reader's response to the male-authored text is not necessarily an ideologically 'obedient' one in which she adheres unquestioningly to those parameters laid down for her by the male perspective. As herself a culturally hybrid body, she was able to read and respond to the hybrid text in a multiplicity of different ways and search out its more positive and empowering discursive pathways. As Cixous has asserted about her own reading practices within the cultural hegemony of our own era:

> But I know how to read with my eyes closed. To you, who have eyes with which not to read, I have nothing to reveal. Woman is one of the things that you are in no position to understand.[70]

Instead of reading the texts into themselves, then, Cixous suggests that it is possible for women to read themselves into the text, and in so doing fully respond

70 Cixous, 'Coming to Writing', p. 35.

to the resultant interplay of textual and corporeal hybridity inscribed upon and within each body. The monstrous hybrids of text and body, however, remain ultimately resistant to the imposition of unity upon them, either from within or without. Just as the hybrid body is simultaneously both same and other, so the text – and particularly the unity-minded anchoritic text – defies definition and meaning. With hybridity at the core of the anchoritic text directed at the woman reader, it is the imaginative and ultimately individualistic reading strategies undertaken by those who knew how to read with their eyes closed which provided a means of controlling – or else releasing – its monsters.

REFLECTIONS ON ASPECTS OF THE SPIRITUAL IMPACT OF ST BIRGITTA, THE *REVELATIONS* AND THE BRIDGETTINE ORDER IN LATE MEDIEVAL ENGLAND

ANN M. HUTCHISON

THROUGH HER VISIONARY WRITINGS, some of which arrived in England early in Birgitta's career,[1] and later from her *vita* which became well known as material in support of her canonization was being gathered, Birgitta came to exercise a profound influence on English spirituality, both of the laity and the religious. Her own pattern of living, her design for a new religious order, and her vision of how the Church should function came at a time when religious renewal was desperately needed. In England, she was seen as a beacon of orthodoxy in the crucial period when religious controversy was rife and the established Church was weak. Birgitta's vision of the role of the Church was an inclusive one,[2] and it came to England as members of the lay world, particularly – but not exclusively – women, were struggling to find a place and a voice for the expression of their faith. In addition, because Birgitta was a married woman who managed a large estate, gave birth to eight children, acted as an advisor to the Queen, and then later, with her husband, took a vow of chastity and turned to a more devout life while remaining in the world, English women and men engaged in secular affairs found someone not impossibly removed from this world whom they could emulate.

Today studies of the spirituality of the fifteenth and early sixteenth centuries are turning up more and more devotional material related to Birgitta and the *Revelations* which is providing scholars with a new awareness of just how pervasive her influence in England was. To give a comprehensive picture within the scope of a short essay is, therefore, an unrealistic task, and so I have chosen to look at three particular aspects in an attempt to demonstrate some of the ways in which individuals responded to Birgitta. First, I will discuss an edition of her *vita* printed in 1516. Secondly, I will consider the Middle English poem of a man

1 F. R. Johnston discusses this in 'The English Cult of St Bridget of Sweden', *Acta Bollandiana* ciii (1985), pp. 75–93 at p. 78. His claim that Birgitta 'had become English by adoption' (p. 81) is well founded, but the Latin lines he quotes from the *Nova Legenda* do not actually refer to her *vita*.

2 Alf Härdelin, formerly Professor of Theology at the University of Uppsala has written and spoken extensively on this theme and a former student, Stephan Borgehammar, has published an eloquent piece on this theme in English: 'St. Birgitta, an Architect of Spiritual Reform', *Birgittiana* v (1998), pp. 23–47.

desperately looking to Birgitta for succour. Finally, I will investigate manuscript evidence which suggests that Birgitta and her spirituality became linked to the cult of the Holy Name, a devotion which was growing more and more prominent in late medieval England. Linking all three is the figure of Margery Kempe, a married townswoman from Lynn, the busy port in East Anglia with the closest links to Sweden.[3] Margery, who lived roughly from 1373 to about 1439, embraced the mystical life, but like Birgitta, whom she made every effort to model herself on, she chose to remain in the world and became one of the most notable of Birgitta's English followers in the early fifteenth century.

My first example is Richard Pynson, an active printer in London and, from 1506 until his death in 1529, the King's Printer. In 1516 he published an English summary of a Latin collection of English saints' lives by the Augustinian canon, John Capgrave. In the same volume, following *The Kalendre of the Newe Legende of Englande*, as the translation of the *Nova Legenda Anglie* was called, Pynson observed that it was 'ryght expedyent' to include 'the lyfe of seynt Byrget shortlye abrygged'. To round off the volume, he chose 'a lytell draught of Mayster water [*sic*] Hylton of the medled lyfe' (Prologe).[4] The second and third items are a short Middle English version – not a translation of the actual *Vita Abbreviata* – of the life of St Birgitta[5] and Walter Hilton's *On Mixed Life*, a work with close affinities to, but much shorter than, his more widely known devotional work, *The Scale of Perfection*. What is interesting about this edition is the positioning of the *vita* of the Swedish saint in the midst of texts solely English in both content and authorship without apparent need for explanation or apology, thus suggesting how much a part of the English devotional scene Birgitta had become.

Pynson's putting together of such a volume in the early sixteenth century also reveals the continuing appeal, well into the age of print, of works with devotional and exemplary potential. As he explains, the *vita* of St Birgitta is 'ryght expedyent for euery maner of persone to loke vpon', adding, 'moost in especiall for them that lyue in matrymony or in the estate of wydowhod'. The aims, as Pynson sees them are: first, to enable readers to 'se what grace and vertue was in this blessyd woman which lyued in the same degre as they do'; and secondly, to encourage them 'to desyre to haue lyke grace and vertue'. As a commercial printer, he must of course have had at least one eye on the book trade. This is

3 Lynn was the port at which the delegation sent from Vadstena to help establish the English Bridgettine house, Syon Abbey, arrived on 26 August 1415; see Neil Beckett, 'St. Bridget, Henry V and Syon Abbey', *Studies in St. Birgitta and the Brigittine Order*, Analecta Cartusiana XXXV:19, 2 vols (Salzburg, 1993), II, pp. 125–50 at p. 133 and n. 86.

4 STC 4602; 'The lyfe of seynte Brygette' is on folios CXXVIIIv–CXXIX.

5 Roger Ellis has noted three sources of the *vita* printed by Pynson: the *Vita Abbreviata*, the Bull of canonization by Pope Boniface IX, and chapter three of the *Epistola Solitarii* written by Alphonse of Jaen as Prologue to his edition of Rev. VIII. This information has been taken from a typescript which Dr Ellis kindly gave me, 'Notes on Some Latin and Middle English Lives of St. Bridget of Sweden', pp. 48–54.

more obvious with regard to Hilton, for he admits that he is aware that the *Mixed Life* has been printed before, but is ready with the justification that 'þe more a good thynge is knowen the better it is', and, tellingly, that 'parcase [perhaps] by this occasyon it may come to the knowlege of some men [i.e. people] that otherwyse shulde neuer haue harde speke of it' (Prologe). This particular work, as Marion Glasscoe has pointed out, is 'a cultural document of prime importance for understanding the sensibilities of the lay audience for whom the mystical writers in the vernacular were providing texts'. In initially directing this epistle to a nobleman who feels torn between the demands of his worldly duties and his desire to serve God, Hilton is attempting, Glasscoe suggests, to direct him toward a state of '*discretion* in which self-knowledge and the love of God are the means of integrating what seem like opposites in the equilibrium'.[6] The fact that Pynson's volume was a successful venture – indeed it survives in a number of copies – also reveals an important reason why Birgitta became and continued to be such a key figure in the spirituality of late medieval England. She had a living reality that very few early saints possessed, for as a married woman and later a widow she inhabited the world of real people and shared their experiences – for example, the *vita* details some of the every-day problems Birgitta encountered in the rearing of her children and so forth, which would certainly resonate with many readers; at the same time this woman had been especially chosen by Christ to be his spouse and to receive and pass on his messages and those of his mother.

Pynson was by no means an innovator; rather he could be characterized, to borrow his own words in reprinting Hilton's *Mixed Life*, as one who knew how to capitalize on 'a good thynge'. In this particular case, not only did he choose his texts with care, but he also selected a woodcut that he knew would immediately attract attention, that of Birgitta receiving and writing down the divinely inspired revelations, once again attesting to the central role she played in late medieval English spirituality.[7] More than a century before this, however, one of the early

6 Marion Glasscoe, *English Medieval Mystics. Games of Faith* (London, 1993), pp. 119–20.

7 S. H. Johnston's suggestion that the *Vita* may have been printed for Syon because of the woodcut of St Bridget with the initials 'E. G.' for Elizabeth Gibbs, Abbess of Syon from 1461 to 1518 (E. Hodnett, *English Woodcuts, 1480–1535*, corr. repr. (Oxford, 1973), no. 1349), is unlikely given that it is directed to an audience of married women and widows; see S. H. Johnston, Jr., 'A Study of the Career and Literary Publications of Richard Pynson' (unpublished Ph. D. dissertation, University of Western Ontario, 1977), p. 101. Martha Driver in her studies of early woodcuts has suggested that woodcuts are often reused to indicate provenance or association. In this case, Pynson must surely have intended to emphasize the association with Birgitta and with the house of the Order she founded; see, for example, 'Pictures in Print: Late Fifteenth- and Early Sixteenth-Century English Religious Books for Lay Readers', *De Cella in Seculum: Religious and Secular Life and Devotion in Late Medieval England*, ed. Michael G. Sargent (Cambridge, 1989), pp. 229–44, especially pp. 243–4. The same woodcut is used in Richard Fawkes' 1530 print of *The Myroure of oure Ladye*, a text with clear Syon connections. It is reproduced in John Henry Blunt's edition, EETS ES XIX (London, 1873), following p. lx.

people to recognize 'a good thynge' was Margery Kempe, as we learn from her *Book* and as has, in recent years particularly, been thoroughly documented.[8] For Margery, herself a married woman and mother of fourteen children, Birgitta provided a crucial model, particularly in showing how the roles of mother and wife could be combined with a life of devotion, how one could be spiritually renewed through a vow of chastity, but even more particularly how Christ himself and his mother might communicate with a woman who had lived an 'ordinary' life. Moreover, Margery seems to have adopted a number of devotional practices based on what she knew of Birgitta and the way of life she advocated, a matter to which I shall return. Throughout the fifteenth century, there are many other English women like Margery whose lives Birgitta deeply touched, ranging from the members of the royal households to the bourgeoisie.

From this early period there is another figure who celebrated Birgitta for a number of the same reasons as Margery. This was not, however, a married woman, but an unmarried priest, John Audelay. Audelay was chaplain to Richard Lestrange, Lord of Knockin (1397–1449), who lived in Shropshire in the West-Midlands, across the country from the Lynn of Margery Kempe. Probably exactly contemporary to Margery, Audelay is an important early witness to the significance of Birgitta, and in particular of the new house of her order established by King Henry V near his royal palace at Sheen. We learn of Audelay's devotion to Birgitta from a Middle English poem, written toward the end of his life when he was blind, and therefore probably dictated. The heading in Latin, with a Middle English attribution, reads: 'Hic incipit salutacio Sancte Brigitte virginis et quomodo Dominus Ihesus Christus apparuit illi corporaliter et dedit ill[i] suam benedictionem. quod Awdelay'.[9] The poem begins with the arresting and, I think, deeply felt salutation, 'Hayle! maydyn and wyfe, h[ayle]! wedow Brygytt', a salutation with strong Marian overtones. This is the twenty-third work in a single manuscript, Oxford, Bodleian Library, MS Douce 302 (of the second quarter of the fifteenth century), containing fifty-five poems, fifty-three of

8 In her 'Prefatory Note' to the first edition of the *Book*, Hope Emily Allen discusses how Margery would be aware of Birgitta from ongoing discussions of her canonization; see *The Book of Margery Kempe*, ed. Sanford Brown Meech and Hope Emily Allen, EETS OS CCXII (London, 1940; repr. 1997), p. lvii. See also *The Book of Margery Kempe*, ed. Barry Windeatt (Harlow, 2000), p. 13, and especially the references in the index on p. 468; other scholars too have noted similarities, for example, Clarissa Atkinson, *Mystic and Pilgrim: The Book and the World of Margery Kempe* (Ithaca, 1983), or Gunnel Cleve, 'Margery Kempe: A Scandinavian Influence in Medieval England?', *MMT* V, pp. 163–78.

9 The poem is found in *The Poems of John Audelay*, ed. Ella Keats Whiting, EETS OS CLXXXIV (London, 1931), pp. 164–7. It has also been edited by William Patterson Cumming and appears in the Introduction to his edition of *The Revelations of Saint Birgitta edited from the Fifteenth-Century MS. in the Garrett Collection in the Library of Princeton University*, EETS OS CLXXVIII (London, 1929), pp. xxxi–xxxvii.

which are definitely attributed to Audelay.[10] Through incidental remarks of the poet and from two colophons, it is possible to piece together some details of his life. A colophon after poem 55 asks the members of a religious house to pray for his soul and mentions that Audelay was 'furst prest to the lord Strange' who had founded a chantry 'in this place'. In 1424, Lestrange founded a chantry in Haughmond Abbey, a house of Augustinian canons near Shrewsbury in Shropshire, thus the colophon must have been written sometime after that date. Earlier in the manuscript, after the eighteenth poem, is another colophon dated 1426, and it has recently been shown that this colophon too was written after Audelay's death, so that all the poems in the manuscript must have been composed earlier.[11] These dates are compatible with Audelay's request in poem 23 for prayers for 'ȝong K[yn]g Herre' (line 195). Since Henry V died on 31 August 1422, the poem must have been written after that date; thus its composition must fall between 1422 and 1426.

Although the border country was his home, during his life Audelay was not confined to Shropshire. There is independent evidence that he was in London with Lestrange in 1417,[12] and it must have been during this time that he first became familiar with the Bridgettine house, Syon Abbey. Syon had been established two years earlier by Henry V, and, in the prologue of the foundation charter dated 3 March 1415, Henry, who had a particular devotion to Birgitta, stated that the new foundation was 'especially in honour of the most holy St. Bridget'. A little further on, Henry decreed that it be called 'The Monastery of St. Saviour and St. Bridget of Syon, of the order of St. Augustine, through all successive ages'.[13] Although later under Henry VI, 'St Mary' was added between 'St Saviour' and 'St Bridget' in keeping with the stipulations of the *Regula Salvatoris*,[14] the name given by his father is reflected in Audelay's poem. Audelay notes that 'Our gracious Kyng Herre þe v wes founder of þat place' and that he 'callid hit Bregitsion' (lines 138, 139; i.e. Bridget of Syon), an indication

10 See the introduction to Whiting's edition. There has been much recent interest in Audelay and in this manuscript; see, for example, Richard Firth Green, 'Marcolf the Fool and Blind John Audelay' in *Speaking Images: Essays in Honor of V. A. Kolve*, ed. Robert F. Yeager and Charlotte C. Morse (Asheville, NC, 2001), pp. 559–76; James Simpson, 'Saving Satire after Arundel's Constitutions: John Audelay's "Marcol and Solomon"', *Text and Controversy from Wyclif to Bale. Essays in Honour of Anne Hudson*, ed. Helen Barr and Ann M. Hutchison, Medieval Church Studies IV (forthcoming: Turnhout), and Ad Putter, 'The Language and Metre of *Pater Noster* and *Three Dead Kings*', *Review of English Studies* (forthcoming).

11 Green, 'Marcolf the Fool and Blind John Audelay', pp. 565–6.

12 The relevant documents were discovered by Michael Bennett and are discussed in his article, 'John Audelay: Some New Evidence on his Life and Work', *The Chaucer Review* xvi (1982), pp. 344–55.

13 A translation of the charter appears in George James Aungier, *The History and Antiquities of Syon Monastery, the Parish of Isleworth, and the Chapelry of Hounslow* (London, 1840), pp. 25–30, at pp. 26, 27. See also Beckett, 'St. Bridget, Henry V and Syon Abbey', p. 127.

14 See Beckett, p. 127 and n. 28.

of how closely Birgitta was associated with her foundation in its early days. In addition to this, Audelay locates 'Bregitsion' fairly precisely: 'Beside þe Chene, . . . seuen myle fro Lundun' (line 136), which could indicate that he visited the house himself. Whether or not he actually went to Syon Abbey, Audelay knew the key features that characterized the Order and its Rule: the poem shows that he was aware that the Order was enclosed and that times of speaking were regulated (lines 156ff); it mentions the reverent devotion with which the daily offices are sung and said (lines 163ff); and, with particular emphasis, notes the strict observance of 'þat spiritual plas' (lines 172ff), the practice that gives the prayers of its members special intercessory efficacy. As he states: 'Fore þay may throȝ here precious prayoure purches here oure grace,/ Haue we neuer in þis word [world] wroȝt so moche wo' (lines 183–4).

It is with this profoundly felt statement that we are led back to 1417 and the documents that indicate that Audelay was definitely in London that year.[15] Although he was certainly not the instigator of the incidents that occurred in the Church of St Dunstan's-in-the-East on Easter Sunday of 1417, in his role as chaplain to Lestrange he was present and was charged with aiding and abetting.[16] The troubles began after Easter morning mass when, as Lestrange was leaving the church, he stopped to accost a knight, Sir John Trussell, with whom he seems to have had a running feud. A fierce exchange erupted, but to forestall any violence, parishoners intervened and the two men were escorted to their respective lodgings where pledges to keep the peace were given by each in the presence of three aldermen. By the time of vespers, however, when the rival was back at the church, Lord Lestrange, with an armed group of followers, returned. This time there was considerable violence, resulting in severe injuries to the defenceless knight and his son, and the death of a parishioner who had tried to intervene. Both royal and ecclesiastical courts passed judgement, for not only was this a malicious crime, but occurring in a church and on Easter Sunday, it was the most grave act of sacrilege. That Audelay was present is clear from the records of the King's Bench.[17] Even though he is not mentioned in the inquest of the Archdeacon of London, he was, nevertheless, guilty by association and, as the family priest, he would have been to some extent responsible for those he served. The incident seems to have become a *cause célèbre* and is mentioned in a number of contemporary chronicles.[18]

It is little wonder, then, that Audelay in his old age – and undoubtedly even before – felt a desperate need to atone in every possible way for such a great sacrilege, especially as he believed that his later loss of sight, and eventually of

15 See Bennett, 'John Audelay: Some New Evidence', pp. 346f.

16 Bennett, p. 348.

17 In his plea of mayhem, Sir John Trussell, the injured knight, specifically mentions that Richard Lestrange and his wife, Joan, were with 'John Audley, chaplain' and that the three 'had assisted and abetted' (London, Public Record Office, KB 27/624, m. 76; see Bennett, p. 348 and n. 14).

18 Bennett, pp. 346–8 and n. 9.

hearing too, came upon him as a direct result.[19] What better place to turn than to King Henry V's new foundation known for the efficacy of its prayer, and also – as Audelay mentions more than once in his poem – for the Pardon it offered to pilgrims to Syon Abbey at Lammastide, that is for the octave of the feast of St Peter (1st August), and at one or two other times including, as he also notes, 'mydlenten Sunday'. Although Syon had a number of pardons,[20] the Pardon in the poem refers chiefly to the indulgence that Birgitta herself, acting on instructions from Christ, sought on behalf of her Order, the important *ad Vincula* indulgence available at the church of St Peter ad Vincula in Rome, and Audelay salutes her for this (lines 57–63). In due course this Pardon became available at Syon Abbey, as Audelay recounts:

> Þe pope conferme þer-to his bul þroȝ his special grace,
> In þe worchip of Saint Bregit,
> To al here pilgrems an Lammes-day,
> And also mydlentyn Sunday,
> Þis pardon to last fore ȝeuer and ay;
> God graunt vs part of hit. (lines 139–144)

We can only infer, especially from the last line quoted above, that Audelay must have sought, or considered seeking, this Pardon – or perhaps he left it too late. On the other hand, we know from her *Book* that his contemporary, Margery Kempe, toward the end of her life (probably in 1434[21]), visited 'Shene, a iii days beforn Lammes Day, for to purchasyn hir pardon thorw the mercy of owr Lord' (p. 418/lines 8269–70). In the church itself Margery had one of her, by now famous, fits of weeping brought on by, first, her awareness of 'hir gret unke[n]dnes ayens hir maker', times at which, as she saw it, she 'offendyd hys goodnes'; secondly, the realization of 'the gret abhominacyon [i.e. loathing] that sche had of hir synnys (p. 419/lines 8295–6), and finally, in contrast, because of 'the gret excellent charite of hir redemptowr' (8296–7). In view of the far greater 'abhominacyon' of his sins, Audelay may have felt he could only seek such a pardon at second hand and from afar. As both these cases show, nevertheless, Syon Abbey almost immediately began filling spiritual needs not only of the laity, but of those associated with the Church as well.

19 Derek Pearsall is one of several critics to note that the first eighteen poems form an independent unit, and he describes how in response to a dream Audelay had of God's coming vengeance he felt a pressing need to 'improve both clergy and laity, to provide a "cownsel of conseans" or "ladder of heuen" ' (18.417–18). *Old English and Middle English Poetry*, The Routledge History of English Poetry I (London, 1977), pp. 249–50. This need to reform and make reparation is in keeping with the tone of poem 23 and of others in the manuscript.

20 In an Appendix, Aungier gives two versions of the indulgences granted by Syon cited from manuscript sources, pp. 421–6.

21 See the 'Chronology of the Life of Margery Kempe' (p. viii) and the note to line 8269 (p. 418) in Windeatt's edition (cited above, n. 8). Citations from Margery's *Book* are from the Windeatt edition, and given in parentheses within the text.

Knowledge of Audelay's earlier unreformed life also provides an explanation for the strength of his devotion to Birgitta herself. She was especially 'e-blest' (line 8), he says, because she chose to be chaste (after her motherhood), and encouraged her earthly husband to follow her example; it was as a result of this that the 'moder of God' appeared to her (10). Mary talked to her about Christ's Passion and his pain, and the two women wept together for a time; then, as Audelay reports, Mary spoke to Birgitta again:

> Hayle! blessid Bregit, let be þe tere,
> And þonke my Sun fore His deþ dere,
> Þat has e-ȝeuen þe powere,
> To be wyfe, wedow, and may. (15–18)

Audelay also celebrates Birgitta for her chaste life of poverty: detached from worldly desires and prepared in 'word, wil, dede, and þoȝt, to obey Godis bidyng' (38), she received Christ himself, 'þe perles Prynce to þe con apere' (47). Birgitta, he hopes, will intercede for him (108), will pray for his soul on the day of his death (112), and meantime help him make amends here on earth for his misdeeds (113–14). Thus, in his own weakness, Audelay seeks out the divinely given 'powere' (17) of Birgitta herself as intercessor; he also seeks the 'precious prayoure' (183) of 'þat spiritual plas' (181), that is, 'Bregitsion', or Syon Abbey, for, as he firmly believes, its members 'han þat pouere' (185) to 'purches here our grace' (183).

Although Birgitta's intercessory powers and those of her Order are of foremost importance to Audelay and receive a great deal of emphasis in his poem, Audelay indicates other ways in which Birgitta's spirituality illuminates and supports contemporary English devotional practice. At the end of the first stanza, for example, Audelay clearly links the giving up of 'fleschele lust' (7) for the love of Jesus Christ on the part of both Birgitta and her husband to their being blessed 'in þe name of *swete Ihesus*' (9, italics mine). In the context of the poem, this may be no more than a passing reference to a cult which had been accumulating followers in England throughout the fourteenth century and into the fifteenth, and which, by the end of the fifteenth century, finally achieved official recognition as an established feast.[22] This is the cult of the Holy Name which was celebrated on 7th August, within the octave of Lammas Day.

Some recent discoveries of the association of this cult with Birgitta, especially evident in manuscripts of English provenance containing her *Revelations*, and also – although this connection has long been known – with the English Bridgettine Order, form the final part of this investigation of the role and influence of Birgitta in late medieval England. While the feast was a late develop-

[22] In 1488 the feast day was proclaimed by the Convocation of Canterbury and, in 1489, by the Convocation of York; see R. W. Pfaff, 'The Feast of the Name of Jesus', *New Liturgical Feasts in Later Medieval England* (Oxford, 1970), p. 77; this work is the standard authority on the feast itself.

ment, the cult itself seems to have been present in varying degrees over a longer period, though by the fifteenth century observance intensified at almost every level of the social scale.[23] Henry V was a prominent example among those who had a special devotion to the Holy Name, as reflected, for example, in the name he gave the Carthusian house he founded across the river from Syon Abbey, 'The House of Jesus of Bethlehem'.[24] Syon Abbey too became influential in promoting this cult through particular devotions, such as its famous 'pardon beads', a string of five beads, the first of which betokened the name of Jesus as indicated in the opening line of the accompanying verse prayer, 'Ihu for thy holy name'. The beads match the lines of the verse to be said on them; the verse contains thirty-three words, mystically representing the life of Jesus on earth, concluding with the line: 'Swete Ihu amen'.[25]

As the cult developed in England in the fourteenth century, it seems to have formed 'two major strands':[26] a mystical strand, of which Richard Rolle was the chief exponent, though it was later tempered by Walter Hilton; and a popular strand, a more simple and pragmatic devotion which expressed itself in a public manner with Jesus altars, the name 'Jesus', or the sacred monogram – either 'ihc' or 'ihs' – painted on walls, impressed on seals, written in books, and so forth. Such a bifurcation, however, needs to be approached with caution, since, particularly in cases in which the Holy Name or sacred monogram is written in books, there is some overlap in the two traditions. For the strict mystic, the Holy Name, as Rolle demonstrated in many of his writings, was an aid to contemplation, much in the same way the Jesus Prayer functions in the eastern tradition. In popular hands, the kind of use Rolle was promoting could easily be misunderstood, especially as untrained readers seemed to fail to grasp the metaphorical force of Rolle's utterance, and took terms such as 'heat' or 'the fire of love' literally; this resulted in some 'unusual', and hardly 'spiritual', experiences.

In support of the popular tradition, however, 'the salvific power of the Holy Name is evident in the New Testament', as Eamon Duffy points out in his impressive overview of the period, and indeed the daily Offices began 'Our help is in

23 Recent and ongoing work by Elizabeth New in the historical sphere and Denis Renevey, who has paid particular attention to literary sources, are affording a new understanding of the importance of this cult.

24 Beckett, 'St. Bridget, Henry V and Syon Abbey', p. 130.

25 The verse is found in Oxford, Bodleian Library, MS Douce 54, fol. 35; for a fuller account see, J. T. Rhodes, 'Syon Abbey and its Religious Publications in the Sixteenth Century', *Journal of Ecclesiastical History* xliv (1993), pp. 11–25, especially pp. 12–13 and n. 11. New also refers to the pardon beads and other ways in which Syon Abbey supported the cult in her dissertation, 'The Cult of the Holy Name of Jesus in Late Medieval England, with special reference to the Fraternity in St Paul's Cathedral, London, c. 1450–1558' (unpublished doctoral thesis, University of London, 1999), p. 45 and n. 237.

26 Denis Renevey, 'Name Above Names: The Devotion to the Name of Jesus from Richard Rolle to Walter Hilton's *Scale of Perfection* I', *MMT* VI, pp. 103–21, especially p. 117. This article has guided my thinking in the section which follows.

the Name of the Lord' and Mark 16:17, a passage regularly included in primers and frequently cited elsewhere, promised that 'in my Name they shall cast out devils'.[27] Part of the appeal of the Holy Name in the late Middle Ages was that this was a devotion to which individuals could have immediate access, and as wills and bequests make clear, the laity wished to have more direct involvement in their devotional exercises.[28] The cult emphasized the sweetness,[29] gentleness and accessibility of the human Saviour, and it was this sense of close kinship with the suffering Christ which, Duffy suggests, underlay the popular strand of the English form of the devotion to the Holy Name of Jesus.[30]

Once again, Margery Kempe, the mystic of Lynn and devoted follower and imitator of Birgitta,[31] becomes a useful guide to understanding something of the strength and function of this devotion. The first appearance of Christ to her, following the difficult birth of her first child and the ensuing postpartum psychosis, led to her recovery and to a life-long series of conversations, primarily with Christ and also with his mother. Later, with the permission of Christ himself, these were recorded in Margery's Book written 'to the magnifying of hys holy name, Jhesu' (p. 41/line 11). Margery, a member of the urban elite, felt a need to compete with her more established and noble mentor, and in the *Book* one notices how from time to time Christ or his mother assures her, or she tells the reader, that she is experiencing things not found in '[B]ridis boke' (p. 115/lines 1257–8) or that were also revealed to 'Seynt Bryde' (pp. 129–30/lines 1528–31).

The fact that Christ and the Virgin both spoke to Margery led one of the later Carthusian readers of her *Book* to inscribe the sacred monogram 'ihc' (sometimes 'ihu') in strategic places – usually, but not always, when Christ is named – in the margins and in the rubrics in more than twenty instances throughout the manuscript.[32] Altogether this reader, Windeatt's 'Annotator 4', made more than four hundred notes, and, as Windeatt suggests, he seems especially responsive to 'the account of a soul's enthusiastic devotion'.[33] It is as if, for him, Margery's *Book* itself has become sacred because of the divine words it contained.

27 *The Stripping of the Altars: Traditional Religion in England c.1400–c.1580* (London, 1992), pp. 284–5.

28 Duffy, *The Stripping of the Altars*, pp. 113–16, especially p. 114.

29 Pfaff notes that there is virtually no variation in the text of the Jesus mass as found in missals; the sequence 'Dulcis Jesus nazarenus', like the rest of the mass, is English in origin and is paired with the metrical tract 'Dulce nomen Jesu Christi'; see 'Feast of the Name of Jesus', pp. 67–8. Both Audelay and Syon, as we have seen above, seem to favour this epithet.

30 Duffy, *The Stripping of the Altars*, p. 236.

31 It is also worth noting that the version of her *Book* she successfully dictated was begun in 1436 on 23 July, a date of whose significance Margery was well aware (the feast of the death of St Birgitta is 23 July; see *Book*, p. 204/line 3133).

32 In his edition, Windeatt provides a full list of the four distinct sets of annotations found in the unique manuscript, British Library, Additional MS 61823; see pp. 439–52.

33 *Book*, p. 439.

It was while thinking of this that I examined in another context Oxford, Bodleian Library, MS Rawlinson C41, a manuscript which, as Roger Ellis notes in his authoritative survey of English manuscript versions of the *Revelations*, contains extracts concerning the life of Christ and the Virgin, and also some specifying requirements of the spiritual life.[34] The first set of extracts (fols 2r to 43v) is given the running title 'vita b*ea*te mar*iae*' (except for fols 3v and 4v which read 'vita b*ea*te virg*in*is') and begins with a chapter entitled 'Of the most excellent dignyte of the holy name of the virgin mary'. Here, as seems to be characteristic of the English tradition, it is the Virgin who speaks and her words to Birgitta are reported; Birgitta herself almost disappears. First, the Virgin introduces herself: 'I am qwen of heuyn. & lady of angels. my name is. Maria. as hit is written in the gospel. This name as soon as angells heryth hit. thei joye in ther consciens' (fol. 2r). Toward the end of the Life, a different hand adds in the top margin in black ink 'Ihus maria' (fol. 39r); below Chapter 33, 'Off þe resurrexcon of christ & how he fyrst aperyd to his mother virgyn mari. & of them þat arose with him', begins. At the top of 39v, the same hand writes 'Ihus maria. Laudes deo. Amen.', and below is the beginning of Chapter 34, 'Off the holy lyfe & conuersacon of þe blessyd mother of god after his ascencon'. Two further annotations by the same hand occur on folios 40r and 41v, but neither pertains to the Holy Name.

The second extract begins on folio 44r with the chapter title 'The words of christ to hys spowse of the artyclys of the very trewe feyth. & what be the ornamentis & tokyns. & the wyll þat a spowse ought to haue to her spowse'.[35] The chapter begins with the words of Revelations 1:2, 'I am maker of hevyn. of erth. of þe see. and of all thingis þat be in them.' At the top of this page the same annotating hand seen earlier writes 'Ihus', but this time in red ink. Like the Carthusian reader of Margery, this annotator seems keen to focus attention on the holy words that follow and perhaps to prompt a prayer as well. Here, as in the earlier extract, there are further annotations, but not directly connected to the Holy Name.

One other manuscript among those I have examined, London, British Library, MS Sloane 982, a Latin manuscript of the fifteenth century, contains extracts of the three types described by Ellis: those with a prophetic element, those describing the requirements of the spiritual life, and those providing details of the life of Christ and the Virgin. Especially interesting is its treatment of material from the third category. Here, as Ellis notes, a further division can be made: folios 138r to 149v contain material entirely drawn from the *Revelations*, while folios 121r to 133v present material from the *Revelations* along with material from other traditions. The compiler, in fact, signals his practice of selection in his title: 'libellu[s] centum articulorum dominice passionis extractum et collectum

34 Roger Ellis, ' "Flores ad Fabricandam Coronam": An Investigation into the Uses of the Revelations of St Bridget of Sweden in Fifteenth-Century England', *Medium Aevum* li (1982), pp. 163–86 at pp. 174, 177, 178.

35 Although this chapter begins the extract, it seems to be labelled 'capitulum iij'.

de diuersis libris'.[36] Rather than presenting a continuous narrative, as in Rawlinson C41, the compiler here aimed to create a work of meditation, and therefore the narrative material is arranged so as to allow spaces for meditation and prayer.[37] The devotional use in this case is further enhanced by elegant marginal annotations in red. The top margins contain an elaborate 'ihc', as does the right or left margin, depending on whether it is a recto (where it is on the right) or a verso (where it is on the left). On folio 121r in the lower margin is written 'Virgo maria mater dei', each word separated by a dividing flourish, and on subsequent folios the order is 'maria virgo mater dei'. Thus the contents of each opening are framed with the intention of enhancing the experience of the devout reader. In addition, the top margin of the first recto folio (121r) bears a crest in red and gold which appears to be a representation of the five wounds, suggesting an association – if not a direct connection – with Bridgettine observance.

Following the conclusion of this 'libellus' on folio 133v is added a prayer in Middle English. It is introduced in red by 'her folowes an askynge of our lordes blessynge' and then the petitions follow in black ink, among them one beginning 'Mak me þi broþer. þat I may haf heuenly heritage with þe' and concluding with: 'Mak me þi sponses þat y may haf þi godhed in me'. Added in red in the margin beside this petition are the words 'ora pro holy Nomina'. This seems to be the work of an attentive, but, to judge from the mingling of Latin and Middle English, untrained reader desirous of following the example of one known to have been chosen to be *sponsa Christi*.

The first full opening of the final extract (folios 138v–139r) concerning the life of the Virgin, the Passion of Christ, the mother's sorrow 'et multa alia' has, in the same elegant hand as annotated the previous extracts, in red ink 'A' written over 'M' surrounded by flourishes. This representation of the *Ave Maria* appears only at this first opening, but as in the earlier example, it is in the left margin of the verso and the right of the recto, thus framing the opening. There is also a small tipped-in fragment of paper written on the verso only which reads: 'Dixit mater dei ad sponsa x^{i} . . .' with a finger pointing at the text on folio 139r. Once again a spiritual advisor appears to be directing a keen apprentice reader. The manuscript affords no hint of its provenance, but both spiritual director and reader must certainly have felt a kinship with Birgitta and the devotional tradition she spawned.

Although neither Rawlinson C41 nor Sloane 982 can with any certainty be linked to Syon Abbey, two manuscripts with firm Syon provenance do have discrete indications of devotion to the Holy Name. One is Cambridge, Corpus Christi College MS 141, the *Registrum*, or finding list, of the brothers' library c. 1500 to 1524. In his recent new edition, Vincent Gillespie has pointed out that inside the capital 'H' of 'Hec', the first word of the second of three notes which

36 Ellis, 'Flores ad Fabricandam', p. 177.
37 Ellis, 'Flores ad Fabricandam', p. 178.

appear at the opening of the *Registrum*, is a small 'ihc'.[38] In the right margin of the same folio is a 'now-defaced scroll miniature'[39] – one wonders if there might have been a connection. The second Syon manuscript which bears witness to observance of the Holy Name is British Library, Harley MS 612, the great repository of key Bridgettine texts. Folios 133r to 160v contain the *Celeste Viridarium*, the compilation of Birgitta's revelations pertaining to the life of Christ and the Virgin made by Alphonse of Jaen in response to the request of the sisters of the newly-founded mother-house of the order in Vadstena.[40] This large and beautiful manuscript, whose pages are of parchment of the highest quality, bears almost no annotations apart from 'official' corrections which are entered in elaborate scrolls. Folios 133r to 160v, however, have been carefully read by someone who makes periodic notes in a cramped hand using dark ink. On folio 158v, for example, in the left margin opposite a rubric which begins 'de sancta concepcione & infancia sua . . .' and ends 'de sanctissima morte & assumpcione sua', the hand notes 'non corrigitur'. What appears to be the same hand writes at the top of the opening folio of the *Celeste Viridarium* (fol. 133r) and also at the top of the opposite verso (fol. 132v) a small but clear 'IHC' followed by 'A' written over 'M'. This reader, violating as he did the directive in the Syon Additions not to write in manuscripts,[41] seems to have placed a higher value on ensuring that the revelations concerning the lives of Christ and the Virgin be read correctly and with appropriate reverence.

From the foregoing, it seems clear that some readers of Birgitta's Revelations shared the devotional instincts of the fourth annotator of Margery's *Book*. Knowledge of the Revelations, and perhaps also the *vita*, led others, like Margery herself and the Middle English petitioner of Sloane 982, to see Birgitta as a model and guide, as Pynson was later to advocate. For still others, Birgitta and her Order were important for their 'powere' as intercessors, a power Audelay so fervently desired and, one might add, urgently needed, as Margery and the many who sought succour in making the pilgrimage to Syon also felt they did. There is much more that could be mentioned in considering the significance of Birgitta, her *Revelations* and the Bridgettines in late medieval England. One example that comes to mind is the widely disseminated sequence of prayers attributed to Birgitta, *The Fifteen Oes*. There are also, I suspect, manuscripts and annotations awaiting discovery, or additions to known manuscripts, such as prayers by Birgitta or individual revelations that might have been added by the devout on empty pages or in the spaces between works in devotional compilations, or even

38 *Syon Abbey*, ed. Vincent Gillespie, with *The Libraries of the Carthusians*, ed. A. I. Doyle, Corpus of British Medieval Library Catalogues IX (London, 2001), p. 4.

39 Gillespie, *Syon Abbey*, p. 4.

40 Ellis, 'Flores ad Fabricandam', p. 167.

41 *The Syon Additions for the Brethren* can be found in *The Rewyll of Seynt Sauioure*, III, ed. James Hogg, Salzburger Studien zur Anglistik und Amerikanistik VI (Salzburg, 1980), ch. 2, 'Of lyght defawtes', p. 18.

in the compilations themselves. That Birgitta's influence was strong in England can be attested to by the continuous and continuing existence of her order. Today the nuns of Syon Abbey are in South Brent, Devon, but they are still known for the efficacy of their prayer and they continue to receive pilgrims. The *Revelations* too were read long after the Reformation began – as late as the end of the sixteenth century, an English Jesuit in Brazil wrote to request a copy of the *Revelations* to sustain him in his work.[42]

[42] This is John Yates, *alias* John Vincent, from a family closely associated with the Bridgettine Order. In a letter written to Sir Francis Englefield in the 1590s, he requests certain books, 'and also the Revelations of St. Bridget, wherewith I should be much comforted in this banishment . . .'; see *Records of the English Province of the Society of Jesus*, ed. by Henry Foley, 7 vols in 8 (London, 1875–1883; repr. New York, 1966), I, pp. 284–295 at 295.

HOLY WOMEN IN PRINT: CONTINENTAL FEMALE MYSTICS AND THE ENGLISH MYSTICAL TRADITION

C. ANNETTE GRISÉ

THE INFLUENCE OF continental female mystics was felt in England not only in the late medieval manuscript tradition, but also in the early printed textual tradition. Printers such as William Caxton, Wynkyn de Worde, and Richard Pynson included the lives and works of such mystics as Catherine of Siena, Bridget of Sweden, and Elizabeth of Hungary among their publications. These texts may not represent an overwhelming contribution to the printed mystical tradition in England, but they find their place beside the modest contribution made by Middle English mystics to the print tradition.[1] The late medieval mystical tradition in print evinces a shift toward a more didactic focus, presenting shorter treatises more often, and ones that are more suitable for a general devout audience. Holy women from the continent are represented primarily in lives, extracts and prayers attributed to them rather than in full-length accounts of their mystical experiences. They usually function in two ways: their holy lives act as examples for the readers in how to live virtuous lives and/or their life and works are mined for materials for instructing the audience on good Christian living. Their use from 1491 to the Reformation and beyond demonstrates their continued popularity in a variety of forms.

The incunabula and early printed texts pertaining to continental women mystics concern their lives and revelations, and prayers associated with them. Bridget of Sweden is well represented in the printed tradition,[2] which is not

1 See George R. Keiser, 'The Mystics and the Early English Printers', *MMT* IV, pp. 9–26, for a full analysis of the English mystics in print, as well as discussions of related devotional treatises and the texts associated with continental mystics. He notes that Walter Hilton's *Scale of Perfection* is the only full-length treatise by an English mystic to be printed in late medieval England, but that it ran into multiple editions (p. 9).

2 Little scholarly work has been done on late medieval English editions of Bridget of Sweden's life and works: F. R. Johnston's important article, 'The English Cult of St. Bridget of Sweden', *Analecta Bollandia* ciii (1985), pp. 75–93, provides some details of the printed texts. For information on the manuscript tradition, see Roger Ellis, ' "Flores ad Fabricandam . . . Coronam": An Investigation into the Uses of the Revelations of St Bridget of Sweden in Fifteenth-Century England', *Medium Ævum* li (1982), pp. 163–86. Scholars have paid more attention to the printed versions of the *Fifteen Oes*, especially because they play a significant role in the development of printed Books of Hours and Primers throughout the sixteenth century. See Eamon Duffy, *The Stripping of the Altars: Traditional Religion in England c.1400–c.1580* (New Haven

surprising when we recall that the fifteenth-century Bridgettine house of Syon Abbey maintained an active presence in furthering Bridget's cult in England.[3] The tradition of continental female mystics in early English books begins and ends with the *Fifteen Oes* (attributed to Bridget of Sweden in the Middle Ages),[4] first published in 1491[5] and finally in 1545,[6] and printed many times over in Books of Hours and Primers of this period. Caxton produced the first edition at the request of Lady Margaret Beaufort and her daughter-in-law Elizabeth.[7] A popular text both in manuscript and print, the Caxton edition was reprinted twice on its own and attached to Books of Hours and Primers printed from 1494. *The Lyfe of seynt Birgette* is appended to the *New Legende of Englande* (STC 4602), an abridged translation of Capgrave's *Nova Legenda Anglie* produced by Richard Pynson in 1516, where it is followed by Latin prayers to Bridget. Furthermore, Richard Fawkes issued an edition of *The Myrrour of Oure Ladye* (STC 17542), the Middle English translation of and commentary on the Bridgettine office created for the nuns of Syon Abbey, in 1530.[8] Around the same time (probably 1530), a series of extracts from her revelations is published by Thomas Godfray;

and London, 1992), pp. 249–56; Helen C. White, 'The Fifteen Oes', *The Tudor Books of Private Devotion* (Wisconsin, 1951) pp. 216–29; and, more recently, Jennifer Summit, *Lost Property: The Woman Writer and English Literary History, 1380–1589* (Chicago, 2000), pp. 111–26.

3 See Martha Driver, 'Nuns as Patrons, Artists, Readers: Bridgettine Woodcuts in Printed Books Produced for the English Market', *Art Into Life: Collected Papers from the Kresge Art Museum Medieval Symposia*, ed. Carol Garrett Fisher and Kathleen L. Scott (East Lansing, Michigan, 1995) pp. 237–68, for a discussion of the role of the Bridgettines of Syon Abbey in the early history of printed books in England.

4 Duffy's claim that '[t]he "Fifteen Oes of St Bridget" . . . are English in origin, probably composed either in the devotional world of the Yorkshire hermitages associated with figures like Richard Rolle and his disciples, or in the circle of the English Brigittines' in *Stripping of the Altars*, p. 249, is the closest scholars have come to determining the provenance of these prayers.

5 William Caxton, *The Fifteen Oes* (London, 1491); STC 20195. Further references to STC will be made in the body of the essay, where appropriate.

6 Although my focus is generally to 1535, when the last edition of the *Four Revelations of Saynt Birget* appears, there is a 1540 primer that includes the *Fifteen Oes* (R. Copland, c. 1540, STC 16017.5) and finally R. Wyer's edition of the *Fifteen Oes* in 1545 (STC 20196.5). At that point, the *King's Primer*, published by Marshall in 1545, supercedes the originally Catholic primer tradition, displacing the *Fifteen Oes* and various other popular devotions. For further information on the *Fifteen Oes* in late medieval and early modern Primers, see White, 'Fifteen Oes', pp. 216–29.

7 Keiser in 'Mystics and the Early English Printers' argues that the *Fifteen Oes* was published 'possibly in conjunction with one of two now lost *Horae* issued at about the same time' (p. 11).

8 The modern edition by John Henry Blunt, *The Myroure of oure Ladye*, EETS ES XIX (London, 1873; rpt. Millwood, NY, 1981) makes use of the printed text for the part of the manuscript that was considered lost when Blunt was preparing his edition; Ann M. Hutchison is currently preparing a new edition of the text. See also her essay, '*The Myroure of oure Ladye*: a Medieval Guide for Contemplatives', *Studies in St. Birgitta and the Brigittine Order*, vol. II, ed. James Hogg (Salzburg and New York, 1993), pp. 215–27.

entitled *The Four Revelations of Saynt Birget* (STC 1915), it was printed with Bernard of Clairvaux's *Golden Epistle* in a collection of devotional texts, and was likely published with the *Folowyng of Christ* (STC 23963).[9] Published around the same time, the first edition of the *Werke for Housholders* (STC 25412) by the Bridgettine monk Richard Whytford, the self-titled 'wretch of Syon,' also included the *Four Revelations of Saynt Birget*, although it is omitted from later editions.[10]

Catherine of Siena almost holds her own against Bridget in the printed tradition in a way that she did not in the manuscript tradition in late medieval England.[11] In 1492 (probably one year after the *Fifteen Oes* appeared in print) Wynkyn de Worde published a *Lyf of Saint Katherin of Senis* along with the *Revelations of Saynt Elysabeth of Hungarye* (STC 24766, rpt. in 1500, STC 24766.3), selected extracts from the revelations of Elizabeth of Töss, daughter of King Andreas III of Hungary and great-niece to St Elizabeth, daughter of King Andreas II of Hungary.[12] The most substantial of the incunabula in England from the continental holy women, the Catherine life seems to have been inspired by contemporary Italian editions and is the first edition of Catherine's life and/or works to be published outside of Italy.[13] As well as the *vita*, there is the Middle English version of Catherine's *Dialogo*, *The Orcharde of Syon*, that was origi-

9 After its moment in the sun, the *Four Revelations* appears only once more, when Godfray reissues it in 1535, after which point the text does not appear, possibly because the materials on pagans and pilgrimage to the Holy Land had rendered it too controversial in the face of growing calls for church reform in the period.

10 Johnston distinguishes the Godfray version from that included in Whytford's text, but they are in fact the same text (Johnston, 'English Cult of St. Bridget of Sweden', pp. 87–8). The companion piece to the *Four Revelations*, *The Golden Epistle*, is originally published from the Godfray print in the first edition of Whytford's *Werke*, but in subsequent editions (and at the same time as the Bridget text is omitted) it is replaced by Whytford's new translation of the Bernardine treatise.

11 See my essay, 'Catherine of Siena in Middle English Manuscripts: Transmission, Translation, and Transformation', *The Medieval Translator 8*, ed. Rosalynn Voaden, René Tixier, Teresa Sanchez Roura and Jenny Rebecca Rytting (Turnhout, 2003), pp. 149–59, for further information on Catherine of Siena's inclusion in late medieval English manuscripts. I note that, apart from the Middle English translation of her revelations, *The Orcherd of Syon* (written for the nuns of Syon Abbey), Catherine is best known by a short, popular extract, 'Clennesse of Sowle'.

12 Alexandra Barratt, 'The Revelations of St. Elizabeth of Hungary: Problems of Attribution', *The Library*, 6th series xiv (1992), pp. 1–11, and Sarah McNamer, ed., *The Two Middle English Translations of the Revelations of St. Elizabeth of Hungary* (Heidelberg, 1996), p. 9.

13 Ruth Mortimer, 'St. Catherine of Siena and the Printed Book', *The Papers of the Bibliographical Society of America* lxxxvi (1992), p. 12. I have argued elsewhere that although de Worde follows the Italian version and may have borrowed from contemporary Italian interest in Catherine, he tells us in his preface that he is working from a Latin source ('Catherine of Siena in Middle English Manuscripts', pp. 154–5). The *Legenda major*, Raymond of Capua's authoritative Latin life of Catherine, was not published until 1553 (in Cologne), although there are two abridgements published in Italy in the fifteenth century, a copy of one of which is now at the British Library (Edmund

nally written for the Syon nuns and is printed in 1519 by Wynkyn de Worde (STC 4815).[14] The final Catherine text printed in the first half of the sixteenth century is found in a collection of seven devotional treatises published in 1521 by Henry Pepwell (STC 20972).[15] Among the pamphlets printed is the 'Dyuers doctrynes deuoute & fruytfull taken out of the lyfe of that gloryous vyrgyne & spouse of our lord Saynt Katheryn of Seenes'.[16] The collection is contemplative in nature, as well as being didactic. Other treatises in this collection not related to holy women are Richard of St Victor's *Benjamin Minor*, Walter Hilton's *Angels' Song*, and three texts by the *Cloud*-author: *The Epistle of Prayer*, *The Epistle of Discretion in the Stirrings of the Soul*, and *The Treatise of Discerning of Spirits*. In addition, the Catherine extracts are followed by 'A shorte treatyse of contemplacyon taught by our lorde Ihesu cryst or taken out of the boke of Margery kempe ancresse of Lynne', a reprint of a collection of extracts from the *Book of Margery Kempe* that had previously been published twenty years earlier by Wynkyn de Worde in circa 1501 (STC 14924).

Although selections from Elizabeth of Hungary are published in 1492 with Catherine of Siena's *Lyf* and then reprinted in 1500, materials from her life and revelations are not found elsewhere in the medieval English print tradition. Apart from the texts mentioned above, the only other material that can be linked to continental holy women is a collection of prayers entitled a *Meditation of the Seven Sheddings of Christ's Blood* printed in 1500(?) in Westminster by Wynkyn

G. Gardner, *Saint Catherine of Siena: A Study in Religion, Literature, and History of the Fourteenth Century in Italy* (New York, 1907), pp. viii–xi).

14 Three of the more recent considerations of *The Orcherd of Syon* are Jane Chance, 'St. Catherine of Siena in Late Medieval Britain: Feminizing Literary Reception through Gender and Class', *Annali d'Italianistica* xiii (1995), pp. 163–203; Denise Despres, 'Ecstatic Reading and Missionary Mysticism: *The Orcherd of Syon*', *Prophets Abroad: The Reception of Continental Holy Women in Late Medieval England*, ed. Rosalynn Voaden (Cambridge, 1996), pp. 141–60; and C. Annette Grisé, ' "In the Blessid Vyneȝerd of Oure Holy Saueour": Female Readers in *The Myroure of Oure Ladye* and *The Orcherd of Syon*', *MMT* VI, pp. 193–211.

15 Henry Pepwell, *Here foloweth a veray deuoute treatyse (named Benjamyn) of the myghtes and vertues of mannes soule, & of the way to true contemplacyon, compyled by Rycharde of saynt Vyctore* (London, 1521). There is no modern edition of the work, but Edmund Gardner published a modern English translation of these treatises: Edmund G. Gardner, ed., *The Cell of Self-Knowledge: Seven Early English Mystical Treatises Printed by Henry Pepwell in 1521* (London and New York, 1910). I have examined the British Library copy, Shelfmark C.37.f.19; references will be to this copy.

16 Jennifer Summit incorrectly identifies the Catherine extracts as coming from the *Orcherd of Syon* in *Lost Property*, pp. 128–9, but they instead have links both to manuscript and print traditions of the abridged versions of her *Legenda*: the 'Dyuers doctrynes' is found in British Library, MS Royal 17 D.v, fols 59r–62r and follows almost word-for-word selections from de Worde's *Lyf*. The minor deviations among the three texts suggest that none of the three extant texts is copied directly from each other but that there was a (now missing) source text from which all three versions derive.

de Worde (STC 14546).[17] While this text does not make any mention of continental female holy women,[18] the manuscript version of this meditation, entitled the *Revelation of the Hundred Pater Nosters*, attributes the prayers to Mechtild of Hackeborn.[19] Thus, Mechtild, who was known to some degree in the manuscript tradition in England, is not known explicitly in the Middle English early print tradition.[20]

When one considers an overview of the texts by and about holy women from the continent, one notes that several of the most significant and substantial of the texts are printed only once: the *Lyf of Katherin of Senis*, the *Lyfe of Saint Birgette* published with the *New Legende of Englande*, the *Orcharde of Syon*, and the *Myrrour of Oure Ladye*. The latter two are Syon-commissioned pieces, lengthy texts that target the specific audience of the Syon nuns and therefore would appear to be of limited interest to those outside of Syon Abbey. Since these texts were produced at the request and expense of their audience, the nuns at Syon Abbey for which the materials were originally written in manuscript form, the printer could be assured of a return on his investment and could take certain risks, such as printing longer mystical texts and paraliturgical pieces that might not otherwise appeal to a mass market.[21] The prologue to the *Orcharde* suggests that the neglected and unique manuscript of the text, found languishing in a corner of the Abbey by their steward, Master Richard Sutton, who then commissioned its printing, represents a forgotten gem of the mystical tradition which assured its value for devotional readers outside the Abbey (STC 4815, fol. B

[17] It is identified as 'A Contemplacyon or medytacyon of the shedynge of the blood of our lorde Jhesu Cryste at seuen tymes' in the incipit and in the colophon as 'a medytacyon of the .vij. shedynges of the blood of our lorde Jhesu cryste' (fol. a ii r and b iv v). I will refer to it as the *Meditation of the Seven Sheddings of Christ's Blood*.

[18] Neither Mechtild of Hackeborn, the attributive author of the meditations, nor Bridget of Sweden, who garners a brief mention (along with Bernard, who is also missing in the print version) in the extant manuscript account (London, British Library, MS Lansdowne 379, fols 44v–45r), appears in the printed version.

[19] MS Lansdowne 379, fols 41r–54r.

[20] For details of Mechtild's popularity in late medieval English manuscripts, see T. A. Halligan, ed., *The Book of Ghostly Grace of Mechtild of Hackeborn* (Toronto, 1979), pp. 47–59, and Rosalynn Voaden, 'The Company She Keeps: Mechtild of Hackeborn in Late Medieval Devotional Compilations', *Prophets Abroad: The Reception of Continental Holy Women in Late Medieval England*, ed. Rosalynn Voaden (Cambridge, 1996), pp. 51–70. Moreover, there was a Latin collection of accounts of holy men and women including Mechtild (as well as Hildegard of Bingen and Elizabeth of Schönau) that was available in England: *Liber trium virorum et trium spiritualium virginum*, ed. Jacobus Faber (Paris, 1513). It was in the Syon library (M107, M121; see Vincent Gillespie, 'Dial M for Mystic: Mystical Texts in the Library of Syon Abbey and the Spirituality of the Syon Brethren', *MMT* VI, pp. 241–68 at p. 267).

[21] It is curious that Bridget's revelations, the most popular of the continental female mystical materials in late medieval English manuscripts, is not printed, especially since there was the Ghotan 1492 Lubeck edition of Bridget's works in Latin.

iii v).[22] The *Orcharde* did find an audience outside that of the original, as a copy of the text is known to have been passed on from a Syon nun to a laywoman:[23] although the prologues address the Syon nuns, it is first and foremost a translation of Catherine's revelations and therefore is not limited strictly to a cloistered community. The *Myrrour* does seem more suitable for its original audience rather than a larger lay audience, for in England it is only at Syon that the Bridgettine office was being performed; thus, it is only at Syon that the translation and commentary on the office would be viewed as essential reading. Yet, this argument does not take into account several factors that may have made a text like this one attractive to non-Bridgettine readers, such as the continuing proscriptions against English Biblical materials which helped to foster a growing market for Books of Hours and Primers as instructional tools and devotional reading for pious laypeople, an interest in the mixed life, and the large number of benefactors and patrons of Syon who might wish to possess an English version of the Bridgettine office.[24]

It has furthermore been argued that the *Lyfe of Saynt Birgette* published by Pynson is a Syon text, since Syon is the only place we know of where the source materials could be found.[25] The parameters of the collection are delineated at length in the Prologue: it includes saints from England, Scotland, Ireland, and Wales, and also saints who spent time in any of these countries. Nevertheless, the appended *Lyfe of Saynt Birgette* is justified by the author not because of any English Bridgettine connection to Syon (even though it is possible that that is an implicit reason for its inclusion, if it had been produced at Syon), but because of its applicability to wives and widows: the 'lyfe is ryght expedyent for euery maner of persone to loke vpon moost in especiall for them that lyue in matrymony or in the estate of wydowhod þat they may se what grace and vertu was in this blessyd woman which lyued in the same degre as they do and the

22 See my ' "In the Blessid Vyneȝerd of Oure Holy Saueour" ', pp. 197–8, for a discussion of this prologue.

23 See David N. Bell, *What Nuns Read: Books and Libraries in Medieval English Nunneries* (Kalamazoo, MI, 1995), pp. 192–3 (Syon A.32), where Elizabeth Strickland's copy of the *Orcharde* is discussed: this book was given by Strickland's executor, Sir Richard Assheton of Middleton, to his wife.

24 Jane Fowler, widow of Richard Fowler, late Chancellor to the Duke of Lancaster, bequeathed '[t]o the abbas of Syon and her successors my grete booke that ys of the servyce of their religion'. Her will, proved in 1505, demonstrates her affinity with Syon Abbey, for she asks to be buried there and also leaves 100 marks 'in redy money or in plate' to the Abbess and convent (J. R. H. Weaver and A. Beardwood, *Some Oxfordshire Wills*, Oxfordshire Record Society XXXIX (Oxford, 1958), pp. 84–5). I am grateful to J. Frank Henderson for supplying me with this reference.

25 Most critics support this contention: see Johnston, 'The English Cult of St. Bridget of Sweden', p. 81 and Duffy, *Stripping of the Altars*, p. 79. Julia Bolton Holloway goes so far as to attribute the authorship to Thomas Gascoigne, who is known to have written a Life for the Syon nuns (*The Life of Saint Birgitta* (Toronto, 1991), pp. 8–9).

rather to be encouraged to desyre to haue lyke grace and vertue' (STC 4602).[26] This life illustrates that although we might at first glance expect an overwhelming emphasis on the contemplative life in the texts being considered here, there is a surprising amount of material on combining the contemplative with the active lives. It is not so surprising when we recall that Bridget and Catherine both had significant public roles, and they both dealt with the contradictory pulls of inward devotion and outward service in their lives and works.

It is possible that the *Lyf of Saint Katherin of Senis* printed by de Worde also comes from Syon Abbey for the same reason that the Bridget Life could: Syon is the only place in England where we know that a Latin *vita* of Catherine of Siena existed, although we do know that Cicely Neville, Duchess of York, gave a copy of the English Life of Catherine to her granddaughter Bridget, who was a nun at Dartford.[27] Dartford cannot be discounted as a potential site for de Worde's source, since the female religious audience is not specified and a Dominican Priory like Dartford would be a likely place to find support for the Dominican tertiary Catherine of Siena. This text does not possess a strictly mystical or contemplative focus; rather it, like many of the other texts under discussion, makes use of the mystical experiences and the manner of living of holy women as a means to teach, instruct, and advise the audience. The translator of the *Lyf of Saint Katherine of Senis* explains to his female religious audience that he has provided them with this material so 'that ye may lerne ther-by holy examples and doctrynes the whiche our lorde hath shewed in suche a vessell, by kynde seke and bryttell, but by grace meruaylously made strong and precyous'.[28] This point, repeated throughout the text, stresses the two most important attributes of texts about holy women: they offer good examples of holy living for their audience, and they provide useful teachings to instruct their audience.[29]

The excerpted *Four Revelations of Saynt Birget* is also instructional in purpose, selecting various lessons from them for the edification of its readers

[26] The pages of the prologue are unnumbered; this quotation appears near the conclusion to the prologue, pp. 6–7.

[27] The life of Catherine was known in manuscript in England: Syon Abbey had a copy of her *vita* in the monks' library (Gillespie, 'Dial M for Mystic', p. 266); for Cicely's donation of a copy of the Life of St Catherine of Siena (and a 'boke of Saint Matilda') to her granddaughter Bridget, at the Priory at Dartford see Paul Lee, *Nunneries, Learning and Spirituality in Late Medieval English Society: The Dominican Priory of Dartford* (York and Woodbridge, 2001), p. 169.

[28] C. Horstmann, 'The Lyf of Saint Katherin of Senis', *Archiv für das Studium der Neueren Sprachen und Litteraturen* lxxvi (1886), pp. 33–112, 265–314, 353–91, at p. 72. STC 24766, fol. D ii r.

[29] The *Lyf* is a particularly good place to find evidence about the function such texts played, according to their writers: it is self-conscious about its relationship to its audience, periodically interjecting to provide commentary, clarify a statement or passage, or simply signposting the end of a chapter, for example. The 'Loo, maydens' or 'Loo ye, maydens' that introduces virtually all of these interjections betrays an anxiety about how the text is being read and a desire to shape that reading, while also attempting to provide, in a clumsy manner, a touch of familiarity to the text.

rather than providing a comprehensive survey of Bridget's mystical experiences. The extracts come from Book Six of her *Revelations*[30] and detail the following four points: the Virgin Mary's assertion that one must love God above all else, Christ's teaching on the active and contemplative lives,[31] Christ's comments on the devotion of non-Christians, and Christ's instructions for preparing to visit the Holy Land. Extracts one, three, and four concern themselves with non-Christians (the first extract uses an example of a pagan woman who is converted), while the bulk of the text resides in the second chapter, the lengthy treatment of the active and contemplative lives. This is a significant aspect of popular devotion, and suits the pious lay audience at which such printed texts were aimed; moreover, it allows us to set the discussions of pilgrimage and the state and fate of non-Christians within a larger framework of a devout lay audience actively seeking ways of manifesting their piety within a secular context – if not in any real way, at least by reading about it.

The *Fifteen Oes* also is consistent with a lay interest in popular devotional traditions, in this case, in prayer cycles attributed to holy women such as Bridget. This group of fifteen prayers, each beginning with the invocation 'O Jesu' and based on a revelation given to a holy woman (identified at some point in its history as Bridget) about the seven wounds of Christ,[32] gained such immense popularity in manuscript and print that it became a significant touchstone in the controversy about reforming the Primers in the 1530s, drawing fire from Reformers as an example of suspect devotional practices practised by the 'superstitious' laity but retaining its appeal for the devout audience even into the Marian period.[33] While *The Meditation of the Seven Sheddings of Christ's Blood*[34] never achieved the circulation that the *Fifteen Oes* did (in manuscript or in print), it complements our examination of the latter text because of its similarity in form and context: it too is a series of prayers (seven in this instance, one for every day of the week)[35] that has been associated with a woman mystic from the continent.

30 The *Four Revelations* notes the source for each of the extracts in the colophons: extract one corresponds to chapter fifty of the *Revelations*, extract two to chapter sixty-five, extract three to chapter eighty-three, and extract four to chapter forty-one (STC 1915, fols A v v–A vi r, A viii r, C vii r, and C vii v).

31 See Ellis, ' "Flores ad Fabricandam . . . Coronam" ', p. 185 n. 31 and Joyce Bazire and Eric Colledge, ed., *The Chastising of God's Children and the Treatise of Perfection of the Sons of God* (Oxford, 1957), p. 7 and n. 3 for discussions of the manuscript correlative.

32 See Duffy, *Stripping of the Altars*, pp. 249–56, for a description of the visionary context of these prayers.

33 See White, 'Fifteen Oes', pp. 216–29, and Summit, *Lost Property*, pp. 111–26.

34 On the *Hundred Pater Nosters*, see P. F. Wormald, 'The Revelation of the Hundred Pater Nosters: a Fifteenth-Century Meditation', *Laudate* xiv (1936), pp. 165–82; Voaden, 'The Company She Keeps', pp. 63–4, and Gillespie, 'Dial M for Mystic', p. 249.

35 The annotations to the Huntington Library printed text (used for STC 14546) include assignations of the meditations to specific days of the week, starting with Sunday, which correspond to those incorporated into the manuscript version in Lansdowne 379.

Although we cannot be as certain as we can with the non-attributed examples of the *Fifteen Oes* that the audience would have been aware of the connection between Mechtild and these meditations, it is nevertheless a useful example of the ways in which quasi-mystical materials can make their way into print. Moreover, it suggests one of the significant shifts we find from the manuscript to print traditions of continental female mystics: since Mechtild's *Booke of Ghostlye Grace* was known in late medieval England in manuscript but not in print, we can trace in this one example the movement from an interest in circulating and reading visionary accounts in manuscripts to an interest in gathering, printing and buying meditations and prayers, lives, and extracts that provide instruction on living a devout life.

While devotional instruction can often be a component of visionary accounts, there appears to be a larger proportion of didactic texts and excerpts in the printed tradition than in the manuscript tradition, suggesting that the printers and their audience sought these kinds of materials in greater numbers than they did more traditionally mystical texts. The shift to a more didactic devotional context is evident in the *Meditation* in the instruction offered on saying meditations effectively. The opening chapter performs this function most fully as it describes how to pray devoutly:

> But whan we shall consyder his paynes or whan we shall praye, yf we wyll haue comfortable felynge of deuocyon in our soule. At the begynnynge of our prayer or contemplacyon we must withdrawe our mynde & wyttes fro all outwarde thynges & besynes as moche as we may. And thynke on that thynge that our contemplacyon or prayer is of. (STC 14546, fol. a ii r)

After one has cleared one's mind and put a meditational image in one's mind, the text goes on to describe the next steps of preparation: to incite an emotional response to the image ('haue pyte & compassyon in thy herte'), to participate actively in the meditational scene ('Take hede how pyteously he wepeth . . . and wepe with hym yf þu can'), and by extension to insert oneself into the scene, in this instance by acknowledging one's implication in Christ's suffering ('for thou art the cause of his wepynge') (fol. a ii v). It is at this point that 'thou mayst begynne thy deuocyon' (fol. a ii v), having been conditioned to internalize the meditations and perform them devoutly. Hence, this text does not only offer a series of meditations on Christ's suffering, it also instructs the audience in how to say meditations and prayers. In this way, it follows the kinds of catechetical and didactic programmes undertaken in the Books of Hours and Primers of the period.

Mechtild's omission from the printed tradition does point to a narrowing of the field: Bridget and Catherine are well represented in printed texts, but other mystics do not have the same impact. In fact, the only mystic apart from Bridget and Catherine who enters the printed tradition is Elizabeth of Hungary. De Worde publishes five folios of revelations from Elizabeth of Hungary with the much longer Life of Catherine, and it is primarily the Virgin Mary's accounts of her life and instructions on devotions and how God's grace comes only from prayer, humility, and a commitment to suffering tribulations patiently. A comparison drawn by the Virgin Mary between Elizabeth and the martyrs recommends a figurative martyrdom attainable by all Christians: deny worldly things and earthly garments, suffer tribulations willingly, and bear patiently persecutions from your neighbours in order to gain your heavenly reward with the martyrs.[36] The collection of extracts thus highlights the instructional and didactic over the mystical and contemplative, emphasizing that it is hard work and perseverance that are valued by God. By drawing the close relationship between the Virgin Mary and Elizabeth it both reflects a Marian *imitatio* model and distances Elizabeth from the reader, while at the same time suggesting that, although the audience may not achieve Elizabeth's state of perfection on earth, it is still possible to live a good Christian life by emulating her piety, meekness, patience, and obedience.

Henry Pepwell's 1521 collection of devotional treatises includes extracts from Catherine of Siena's Life. The 'Dyuers doctrynes deuoute & fruytfull taken out of the lyfe of that gloryous vyrgyne & spouse of our lorde Saynt Katheryne of Seenes' presents several lessons cobbled together from the same source from which de Worde's 1492 *Lyf* is derived.[37] Like most of the other texts under examination here this is not a mystical treatise, it is a collection of sayings and teachings from the account of Catherine's life and revelations that are meant to provide guidance and instruction to the devout reader. Many of the doctrines concern themselves with ways of overcoming suffering and temptations but the second and the final doctrine offer advice on how to become closer to God. The last selection describes the importance of prayer in gaining and increasing in virtue, and thus represents a straightforward type of instruction for the reader on how to live a good Christian life through devout prayer. Doctrine Two, in contrast, is a more challenging view of prayer, meditation, and contemplation as the keys to religious perfection. It begins with two comments: 'Thynke on me, and I shall thynke on the' which is expounded by Catherine: 'That a soule whiche is verely unyde to god perceyueth not, seeth not, nor loueth not herself, nor none other soule, nor hath no mynde of no creature but onely on god' (STC 20972, fol. D i v). The rest of the doctrine explains these ideas further, arguing that by gaining an 'inwarde knowledge' (fol. D ii r) of God through annihilating her own will and thinking only of God, Catherine can find a state of perfection that effectively replaces the external world outside the self with an internal, all-encompassing space within the self contained in God. This idea of achieving a union with God as opening up an inner contemplative space that renounces – yet paradoxically contains – everything outside the self is evident in the longer *Lyf of Katherin of Senis* as well. Catherine counsels her confessor Raymond of Capua 'that whan that he sholde walke outward by-cause other-whyle of grete outward besynesse and occupacyon that nedys must be done . . . he sholde make wythin hys sowle a

36 Carl Horstmann, 'The Reuelacions of Saynt Elysabeth', *Archiv für das Studium der Neueren Sprachen und Litteraturen* lxxvi (1886), pp. 392–400 at p. 397. STC 24766, fol. q ii v.

37 Most of the doctrines come from what is Book 1, chapters 10 and 11 of de Worde's *Lyf*.

pryuee celle, of whyche pryue cell he sholde neuer goo out'.[38] This elaboration of the inner space suggests that one can make a pious act out of anything, and that it is in the eye of the beholder – or more correctly, it is in the mind's eye of the beholder.

The *Dyuers Doctrynes* thus offers some insight into the larger themes of Catherine's life and works, distilling it into small lessons the reader can consider individually or together. The *Shorte Treatyse of Contemplacyon*, published by Pepwell at the same time, performs a very similar process on the *Book of Margery Kempe*. I wish to consider here Margery Kempe's place among the continental female mystical tradition in English printed texts for two reasons: Kempe explicitly aligned herself with the tradition of holy women from the continent, and Henry Pepwell's interest suggests that he sees Kempe as a native example of this tradition as well, since she is included in a collection of devotional treatises that also contains selections from Catherine of Siena. In a sense, then, Kempe acts as the English link in this collection between the texts by the male mystical writers Hilton and the *Cloud*-author and the extracts from the continental female mystic Catherine of Siena.

The *Shorte Treatyse of Contemplacyon* offers sound bites of wisdom on living a good Christian life, beginning with Margery's desire for martyrdom (just as Elizabeth of Hungary had desired), which is transmuted into a figurative martyrdom where she can suffer humiliation and persecution in its stead (STC 20972, fol. A iv r). But Christ further asserts here that although asceticism, penitential practices, and alms-giving may be good, 'I haue often tolde þe doughter that thynkynge, wepynge, & hye contemplacyon is þe best lyf in erthe, & thou shalt haue more meryte in heuen for one yere thynkynge in thy mynde than for an hondred yere of prayeng with thy mouth & yet thou wylte not beleue me, for thou wylte byd many bedes' (fol. A i v). This passage demonstrates one of the most significant themes of the *Shorte Treatyse*: intention versus action. Christ several times grants Margery Kempe recognition for what she desires to do, that is, for having the proper will attuned to Christ's desires rather than focusing on her own desires, or for that matter, on her physical body and the ascetical practices that she can impose upon it.[39] In this light, Margery's designation as an anchoress in the incipit holds symbolic value for this treatise (and for the collection as a whole), as she denies the outer world and the body and turns toward an inner knowledge of and communion with God. This inner contemplative space – a theme shared, as we have seen, with the *Dyuers Doctrynes* of Catherine of Siena in the collection – seems remarkable considering the source text *Book of Margery Kempe* and its avowal of both a sprawling geography and the physical body.[40] Nevertheless, *A Shorte Treatyse of Contemplacyon* argues for a conservative

[38] Horstmann, 'Lyf', p. 51. STC 24766, fol. B ii v. See also her imagining that she serves Christ, Mary, and the apostles when she serves her family (pp. 51–2; fol. B iii r).

[39] For example, see fol. A iii r.

[40] Obvious examples of these tendencies are Margery's travels around England, Europe, and Jerusalem, and the emphasis on sexuality in the text, for example, her physical

moderation in devotional practices, since it is religious excess that is at issue at the beginning of the text. While Catherine's treatise has the resistance of temptation at its heart, and for Margery's treatise the matter concerns the rejection of excessive ascetic practices, they both turn to the same end: to pray to Christ and try to conform her will to his. Both women abase themselves, seeking humility, patiently suffering, and striving to emulate Christ.

Critics have argued that *A Shorte Treatyse of Contemplacyon* deliberately misrepresents the *Book of Margery Kempe* in order to sanitize Margery Kempe and her narrative.[41] While it is true that we see a very different Margery in the printed extracts, I want to argue for a different reading of this aspect. When we place Margery Kempe in the context of the Middle English publications on continental holy women, we can argue that Margery Kempe is treated no differently than her continental counterparts, whose long and unwieldy texts are often abridged and extracted, with writers often pulling out materials that would be of interest to their audience and/or to the particular theme or topic within which they were working. From this perspective, Margery Kempe achieves her goal of becoming recognized publicly as a holy woman: she no longer merely emulates Bridget, Catherine, and their sisters, she is placed alongside them and subjected to the same reading and extracting practices that they are. Although I agree that the Margery Kempe we see in the *Short Treatyse* is not the vibrant, unusual one we meet in the longer version of the text, much of the shift can be understood in terms of changing devotional fashions and the adaptations which the texts by and about holy women from the continent underwent in the printed tradition. Instead of long accounts of a woman's mystical experiences – a popular manuscript genre – printers issue lives of holy women, instruction on devotion for laypeople (and female religious) taken from visionary texts, and prayers and meditations derived from or attributed to holy women. The emphasis shifts to shorter texts and accounts, apart from commissioned works like the *Orcherd* and *Myroure*. That they find a place within a printed devotional tradition that prefers use-specific and instructional texts rather than lengthy contemplative treatises argues for the adaptability of female mystical materials. This appears to be a response to a larger European popularization of texts such as devotional treatises, biblical commentaries, lives of saints, and prayer books in the fifteenth and early sixteenth centuries, when the enthusiasm for mystical texts was waning: James Hogg has examined a German instance in which 'the visionary *Revelationes* [of

relationship with Christ, her attempts to extract a vow of celibacy from her husband, and the opening of the text with Margery's post-partum vision of Christ.

41 The Kempe extracts have attracted scholarly attention especially as they provide such a distinctly different perspective on Kempe than we find in the manuscript version. See Sue Ellen Holbrook, 'Margery Kempe and Wynkyn de Worde', *MMT* IV, pp. 27–46; Karma Lochrie, *Margery Kempe and Translations of the Flesh* (Philadelphia, 1991), pp. 203–26, esp. pp. 220–5; Diane Watt, *Secretaries of God: Women Prophets in Late Medieval and Early Modern England* (Cambridge, 1997), pp. 157–8, and Summit, *Lost Property*, pp. 126–38.

St Bridget] became a treatise on leading the Christian life, whereby St Birgitta was held up as an example, offering advice and warnings to her readers'.[42] My study demonstrates that this kind of transformation of mystical to devotional texts was occurring in England at the same time.

The use of printed materials on the continental female mystics demonstrates that there was a taste among printers and their audience for didactic rather than contemplative materials. George R. Keiser suggests that excerpts and devotional treatises could satisfy a demand for printed materials about mystics whose names 'had a certain *cachet*',[43] and it appears that a fuller examination of the continental female mystics in English printed texts supports this argument. The predilection for expensive, lengthy manuscripts containing detailed accounts of visionary experiences was replaced with the popularity of shorter, pithier printed texts outlining how to live a good Christian life and offering holy women as examples. It is a testament to the continuing popularity (and staying power) of these holy women and to the flexibility of their texts that they manage to survive in the printed market, far away – both physically and generically – from their original milieu.[44]

42 James Hogg, 'St Birgitta's *Revelationes* Reduced to a Book of Pious Instruction', *Vox Mystica: Essays on Medieval Mysticism*, ed. Anne Clark Bartlett, et al. (Cambridge, 1995), pp. 201–29 at pp. 225–6.

43 Keiser, 'The Mystics and the Early English Printers', p. 24.

44 I am grateful to the Arts Research Board at McMaster University for support in conducting the research for this essay.

THE RECEPTION OF CONTINENTAL WOMEN MYSTICS IN FIFTEENTH- AND SIXTEENTH-CENTURY ENGLAND: SOME ARTISTIC EVIDENCE

DAVID GRIFFITH

THE RAPID GROWTH IN THE production and circulation of vernacular religious texts from 1400 to 1530 and the sustained investment in church refurbishment and decoration over the same period are rooted in the laity's desire to take greater personal control over its devotional and spiritual life. I have argued elsewhere that the laity's burgeoning sense of itself as a literate community can be explored through depictions of books and readers in the art of the parish church.[1] These links between lay reading habits and artistic patronage can be followed in many other directions, most obviously through the influence of book illustration upon images in other media. One area of particular interest is the relation between the increased availability in English of devotional and contemplative texts in printed books from the early 1490s which included those of a number of Continental women mystics, and the appearance of painted images of these *mulieres sanctae*, especially Bridget of Sweden, Catherine of Siena and Elizabeth of Hungary, on late-medieval church furniture.[2]

The use of devotional images of these women is not of course a late fifteenth-century phenomenon and illustrations of Bridget and Catherine are found in English manuscripts from the early fifteenth century. Naturally enough these kinds of illuminated manuscripts were produced for wealthy patrons for whom Continental mystics represented empowered and empowering feminine religious experience, members of what Denise Despres has called a 'spiritually elite circle of women influenced by the Carthusians or Brigittines'.[3] In both the Middle English version of Bridget of Sweden's *Liber Celestis* (British Library, MS

1 David Griffith, 'A Portrait of the Reader: Secular Donors and their Books in the Art of the English Parish Church', *Imagining the Book*, ed. John Thompson et al. (forthcoming: Turnhout).

2 This essay is closely related to a full-length study of the subject: *Art and Community in Late Medieval England. The Painted Roodscreens of Devon and Cornwall*; in preparation.

3 Denise L. Despres, 'Ecstatic Reading and Missionary Mysticism: *The Orcherd of Syon*', *Prophets Abroad: The Reception of Continental Holy Women in Late-Medieval England*, ed. Rosalynn Voaden (Cambridge, 1996), pp. 141–60 at p. 151. For discussion of the circulation of the works of these Continental women within a framework of English women's literacy see Mary C. Erler, *Women, Reading, and Piety in Late Medieval England* (Cambridge, 2002).

Cotton Claudius B.I) produced c. 1410–20,[4] and the fourteenth-century Carew-Poyntz Hours (Cambridge, Fitzwilliam Museum MS 48) into which a single full-page illustration of Catherine of Siena was added in the mid-fifteenth century,[5] the women are shown in the act of contemplation. As a freestanding icon in the Carew-Poyntz Hours the image of Catherine bears little direct relation to the manuscript's extended sequence of Marian texts, but MS Cotton Claudius B.I includes a visualisation of Bridget's sacred conversations with the Virgin Mary and John the Evangelist that are a central feature of the Middle English text. In both of these manuscripts there is an implicit link between reading and looking during personal devotions and in similar fashion the woodcuts that accompany printed English versions of their texts seek to offer visual representation of the mystical experiences recounted in the accompanying texts. Thus, of the illustrations in de Worde's 1519 edition of *The Orcherde of Syon*, an English translation of a Latin version of *Il Dialogo* made for the Bridgettine nuns at Syon, one shows Catherine in Dominican habit, seated and reading a book and receiving her stigmata during a vision of the Godhead, and the other places her among a community of nuns, a book in her lap, a burning heart representing her mystical fervour in her hand and her feet trampling down a thoroughly miserable devil.[6] In all these cases the element of portraiture establishes a concrete association between text and image. It presents an imaginative reconstruction of parts of the textual narrative and directs the reader's responses to the central issue of contemplation.

When the production of images moves away from the confines of the book, the relation between image and text is necessarily changed and the saintly portrait may have taken on new functions. These altered roles, and the altered perceptions of the spectator, are manifest in the paintings that adorn the lower sections of the English roodscreen, the structure that supported the beam on which stood the rood figures and which marked a physical boundary between the activities of the laity in the nave and of the clergy in the chancel and choir.[7] Points

4 For analysis of the images see Joan Isobel Friedman, 'MS Cotton Claudius B.I: A Middle English Edition of St Bridget of Sweden's *Liber Celestis*', Voaden, *Prophets Abroad*, pp. 91–113.

5 See Lucy Freeman Sandler, *Gothic Manuscripts, 1290–1390*, 2 vols (London, 1986), II, pp. 143–5; and Despres, 'Ecstatic Reading', pp. 150–1.

6 These images are discussed by Martha Driver, 'Pictures in Print: Late Fifteenth- and Early Sixteenth-Century English Religious Books for Lay Readers', *De Cella in Seculum: Religious and Secular Life and Devotion in Late Medieval England*, ed. Michael Sargent (Woodbridge, 1989), pp. 229–44 at pp. 241–4; and Martha Driver, 'Nuns as Patrons, Artists, Readers: Bridgettine Woodcuts in Printed Books for the English Market', *Art into Life*, ed. Carol Garrett Fisher and Kathleen Scott (East Lansing, 1995), pp. 237–67 at pp. 244–5.

7 The standard works are Francis Bond, *Screens and Galleries in English Churches* (London, 1908); F. Bligh Bond and Dom Bede Camm, *Roodscreens and Roodlofts*, 2 vols (London, 1909); and Aymer Vallance, *English Church Screens* (London, 1936). Important recent studies are Simon Cotton, 'Mediaeval Roodscreens in Norfolk – Their Construction and Painting Dates', *Norfolk Archaeology* xl (1989), pp. 44–54;

of contact can still be made between these paintings and illustrations from printed books but in this new setting the images of the holy women are inevitably aligned within iconographical schema more appropriate to a context of parochial or community devotions, one in which a textual ground for the image is no longer explicit and which frames the mystic within a larger conception of sainthood. This in turn leads to a simplified form of composition, an isolation of key features that brings these figures into line with the traditions of English screen painting. In some cases these images merely gesture towards the saint's contemplative experience. Divorced from the text, images may become more generally representative of Christian perfection though still remaining as a type of the independent religious female peculiarly attractive to some literate sections of the parish family.

With its rood figures, loft and bays of open tracery the roodscreen structure dominated the church space and, as Eamon Duffy has demonstrated, was 'a crucial focus of ritual activity and piety, of direct interest to every parishioner'.[8] It presented a physical frame for the activities and responsibilities of the laity, often formed the backdrop for nave altars, and offered a site for extensive display of devotional images that were painted on the dado.[9] Panel paintings, though often expensively produced with lavish use of gilt and gesso, could be made or remade with fewer problems than reglazing or repainting walls and the abundance of examples from the period 1400 to 1530 exemplifies the willingness of the pious laity to spend money on the beautification of the parish church whilst attending to their own devotional interests and spiritual needs – commemorative inscriptions and even family portraits reminded generations of worshippers to pray for the souls of the generous benefactors. In this way screen iconography is a useful measure of changes in reading and devotional practices and offers one way of mapping lay contact with mystical texts.

and Eamon Duffy, 'The Parish, Piety and Patronage in Late Medieval East Anglia: The Evidence of Rood Screens', *The Parish in England 1400–1600*, ed. Katherine L. French, Gary G. Gibbs and Beat A. Kümin (Manchester, 1997), pp. 133–62. Useful general studies include Robert Whiting, *The Blind Devotion of the People. Popular Religion and the English Reformation* (Cambridge, 1991); Eamon Duffy, *The Stripping of the Altars. Traditional Religion in England 1400–1580* (London, 1992), and C. Pamela Graves, *The Form and Fabric of Belief. An Archaeology of the Lay Experience of Religion in Medieval Norfolk and Devon*, British Archaeology Reports, British Series CCCXI (Oxford, 2000).

8 Duffy, 'Parish, Piety and Patronage,' p. 136.

9 See W. G. Constable, 'Some East Anglian Rood Screen Paintings', *The Connoisseur* liv (1929), pp. 141–8, 211–20, 290–4, 358–65; W. W. Lillie, 'Screenwork in the County of Suffolk', *Proceedings of the Suffolk Institute of Archaeology* xx (1930), pp. 214–26, 255–64; xxi (1931–33), pp. 179–201; xxii (1934–36), pp. 120–6; W. W. Lillie, 'Medieval Paintings on the Screens of the Parish Churches of Mid and Southern England', *Journal of the British Archaeological Association* ix (1944), pp. 33–47; and W. W. Williamson, 'Saints on Norfolk Rood-screens and Pulpits', *Norfolk Archaeology* xxxi (1955–57), pp. 299–346.

Though often complex in its sequential arrangement of figures and mini-narratives, screen iconography in essence offers a set of variations upon the standard theme of judgment and forgiveness. As the culminating event of the scheme of redemption the crucifix or rood, placed at the apex of the structure, validates the power of the sacred community depicted on the lower tiers of the screen. The figures on the lower sections act as focal points for supplication and intercession and fall into several established and interdependent groupings – apostles, prophets, Church Doctors, angelic orders, virgin martyrs, and local or contemporary saints. A feature of these groupings, particularly of the female figures, is its homogeneity.[10] Of the women saints biblical figures such as the Virgin, her mother Anne, and Mary Magdalene all feature prominently, as do some of the more popular local and national saints with regional cults such as the Anglo-Saxon Benedictine abbess Etheldreda whose shrine at Ely Cathedral made her popular throughout East Anglia,[11] and Sidwell who was venerated throughout the diocese of Exeter and beyond.[12] But the most common type is the virgin martyr who offers a model of chastity, fidelity and moral and spiritual fortitude. Multiple personal and devotional reasons account for the popularity of these figures but their critical function was as powerful healing or 'helper' saints.[13] Sympathetic association viewed particular saints as intercessors for those with certain afflictions or conditions. Prayers were raised to Apollonia for toothache, to Margaret for safe delivery in childbirth, and so on across the fullest range of disease, misery and misfortune. Even when more contemporary figures were added to this virginal cadre the imagined potency of the intercessor was usually the main factor, as with the thirteenth century Sitha (or Zita) of Lucca, who quickly became the favoured patron saint of the domestic sphere.[14]

These exemplary lives were presented to the laity in the liturgy, in sermons

[10] Eamon Duffy, ' "Holy Maydens, Holy Wyfes": Women Saints in Fifteenth- and Sixteenth-Century England', *Women in the Church*, Studies in Church History XXVII, ed. W. J. Sheils and Diana Wood (Oxford, 1990), pp. 175–96 at p. 180.

[11] The twenty or so screen surviving images are listed in Virginia Blanton-Whetsell, '*Imagines Ætheldredae*: Mapping Hagiographic Representations of Abbatial Power and Religious Patronage', *Studies in Iconography* xxiii (2002), pp. 55–108 at pp. 92–3.

[12] Michael Swanton, *St Sidwell. An Exeter Legend* (Exeter, 1984).

[13] Duffy, *Stripping of the Altars*, pp. 155–205. For an interesting if somewhat random collection of images of saints from English roodscreens see Edward Tasker, *Encyclopaedia of Medieval Church Art* (London, 1994), pp. 95–176.

[14] Zita occurs on screens in Norfolk and Suffolk. See more generally Sebastian Sutcliffe, 'The Cult of St Sitha in England: an Introduction', *Nottingham Medieval Studies* xxxvii (1993), pp. 83–9. The popularity of contemporary male religious figures follows a similar trajectory. The unofficial 'saints' Henry VI and the Buckinghamshire rector Sir John Schorne were highly esteemed for their miracle working – so much so that Schorne was moved to Windsor in 1478 to lie next to the King's shrine – and both appear on screens in Devon and East Anglia. For an overview of these twin cults see G. W. Bernard, 'Vitality and Vulnerability in the Late Medieval Church: Pilgrimage on the Eve Of the Break with Rome', *The End of the Middle Ages? England in the Fifteenth and Sixteenth Centuries*, ed. John L.Watts (Stroud, 1998), pp. 199–238 at pp. 206–9.

and in visual images but the appetite for literary materials in English was met and further fuelled by successive editions of de Voragine's compendious *Legenda Aurea* by Caxton and de Worde from the 1480s, editions of John Mirk's *Liber Festivalis*, and a range of hagiographic collections such as Pynson's 1516 edition of *Kalendre of the Newe Legende of England*, a gathering of lives of native saints from Alban to Winwalloe. Screen paintings sometimes point to personal contact with or even ownership of these textual materials, as in the copying by the early sixteenth-century painters of the Devon screens at Bradninch and Ugborough of images of sibyls found in the borders of early French *horae*, many of which were targeted at the English market.[15] But in general terms the process of inspiration, commission and design follows less navigable routes. In some cases the artists may have based the figures on textual sources not provided by the patron, on comparable visual materials, or on designs in their own pattern books. Stylistic similarities between a number of Norfolk screens indicates the employment of established patterns by at least one East Anglian atelier but as with most aspects of panel painting little is known about the precise methods of execution.[16]

This complex interaction of textual and visual sources governing roodscreen iconography is signalled in the painted images of Elizabeth of Hungary who died in 1231 and was canonised in 1235. Elizabeth's visionary experiences detailing her discussions with Christ and the Virgin enjoyed widespread popularity in Europe giving rise to versions in five vernacular languages including an English text, *The Revelations of Saynt Elysabeth the kynges doughter of hungarye*, which was known to Margery Kempe and others in East Anglia in the 1430s.[17] The visions were in fact probably those of the uncanonised Dominican Elizabeth of Töss (c. 1294–1326) but at a very early stage they became associated with her great-aunt who had become famous for a life of personal austerity and benevolence to the poor. The pronounced form of affective piety described in the *Revelations* – 'contynually prayng daye and nyghte with full brennyng desire, and wepyng with full bytter morning, and euer thynkyng, spekyng, and working that I trowed were most pleasing to my Creatour'[18] – offered a model for Margery Kempe's own contemplative experiences and her invocation of Elizabeth's 'tretys' demonstrates that the pious laity had detailed knowledge of her writings, albeit in Margery's case mediated through her spiritual father.[19]

15 See Félix Soleil, *Les Heures Gothiques et la literature pieuse aux XVe et XVIe siècles* (Rouen, 1882), pp. 87–98; Bond and Camm, *Roodscreens and Roodlofts*, pp. 296–7, 358–9; Tasker, *Encyclopaedia*, pp. 171–6.

16 See, for example, Duffy, 'Parish, Piety and Patronage', p. 155.

17 The surviving manuscript version was probably written by a south Norfolk scribe for the nuns at Bruisyard abbey in Suffolk and is now Cambridge University Library, MS Hh.i.11. For the Middle English versions and their Latin source see Sarah McNamer, ed., *The Two Middle English Translations of the Revelations of St Elizabeth of Hungary*, Middle English Texts XXVIII (Heidelberg, 1996).

18 Wynkyn de Worde's edition (McNamer, *Revelations*, p. 79, lines 1–5).

19 Barry Windeatt, ed., *The Book of Margery Kempe* (Harlow, 2000), p. 296.

Figure 1. Elizabeth of Hungary (right), Barnham Broom, Norfolk, c.1500.

Away from urban environments like Lynn, with their concentration of parish churches and religious houses, access to books for both clerics and layfolk was less extensive. For images produced in these contexts textual sources are more likely to be general and untraceable. The three definitive sightings of Elizabeth on fifteenth-century screens are in rural parishes in the eastern counties: at Barnham Broom (figure 1) and Upton in Norfolk, and at Fulbourn in Cambridgeshire. The Fulbourn Elizabeth is late fifteenth century and the Norfolk figures are probably c. 1500; in all three cases the screens themselves are older than the paintings though there is no evidence to suggest that the surviving images replaced earlier sequences. She is joined at Barnham Broom by Popes Gregory and Clement, an unidentified bishop, a royal male (possibly Edward the Confessor), Etheldreda and her saintly sister Withburga, a third local saint in Walstan of Bawburgh, and the virgin martyrs Dorothy and Ursula.[20] The Upton Elizabeth is part of a more obviously coherent grouping of the Four Doctors, Helena, Etheldreda and Agatha, but at Fulbourn she and John the Apostle are the sole survivors of a now destroyed screen.[21] There is a fourth possible appearance at Torbryan, Devon (figure 2), in paintings roughly contemporary with the Norfolk examples. This is one of the most complete screens in Devon and has forty saints on its dado, including evangelists, apostles, and a notable group of contemporary saints. The figure taken to be Elizabeth stands next to Catherine of Siena, Zita, Victor of Marseilles, and a Cistercian monk who should probably be understood as Bernard of Clairvaux.[22] That Elizabeth's usual emblems of a basket of loaves and a purse as seen on the three East Anglian screens are replaced here by a triple crown is however problematic. This use of a tiara of the type often worn by the Trinity in early woodcuts is perhaps an indirect allusion to her divine conversations but the identification remains uncertain.

No obvious iconographic pattern emerges for any of these screens and the choices may have been determined by personal preference or the atelier's available designs rather than a desire for a unifying devotional theme. Ideally the source of any given image sequence would be clearly discernible in individual book ownership but when so little is known about the patrons, their books, or the processes of donation and commission for screen painting tracing these kinds of connections is rarely possible. Even when names of specific donors are known, as at Upton where an inscription records the screen as the gift of Agnes and

20 Nikolaus Pevsner and Bill Wilson, *Norfolk 2: North-West and South*, 2nd edn (Harmondsworth, 1999), p. 193.

21 For Upton see Nikolaus Pevsner and Bill Wilson, *Norfolk 1: Norwich and North-East*, 2nd edn (Harmondsworth, 1997), pp. 704–5. The figure of Elizabeth is not to be identified as Joan of Valois, daughter of Louis XII of France, as suggested by D. P. Mortlock and C. V. Roberts, *The Popular Guide to Norfolk Churches* (Fakenham, 1981), p. 102. Given that Joan was canonised only in 1505 this would seem to be extraordinarily unlikely. For Fulbourn see Lillie, 'Medieval Paintings', p. 39 and plate.

22 Bond and Camm, *Roodscreens and Roodlofts*, p. 355.

Figure 2. Elizabeth of Hungary (left) and Catherine of Siena, Torbryan, Devon, late fifteenth or early sixteenth century.

William Wynne, both of whom died in 1505,[23] it is still possible that the named donors are merely representatives of communal sponsorship.[24] Indeed, this kind of corporate responsibility may account for the large majority of screen paintings, including those at Barnham Broom, Fulbourn and Torbryan, for which there is no inscriptional or testamentary evidence.[25]

In these circumstances the reasons for Elizabeth's inclusion within such informal groupings, as well as Catherine of Siena's appearance with her at Torbryan, may be determined by general perceptions of the status of the *mulieres sanctae* in relation to that of other saints. In this respect the iconographic details become peculiarly significant. Unlike the printed works of Bridget and Catherine the edition of *The Revelations* was published without woodcuts, nor is there an English tradition of illustrations associated with her mystical experiences. This lack of dialogue between image and text clearly accounts for the development of an iconographic tradition that owes little to the details recorded in Elizabeth's *Revelations*. The juxtaposition of Elizabeth and Catherine at Torbryan is recognition of their status as mystics, which in itself may account for the unusual iconography of the triple crown, but in the East Anglian churches the contemplative dimension of her life that so moved Margery Kempe is painted out. All three instances offer pattern-book iconography: static figures in formal poses holding large, unmistakable emblems that speak of the physical dimensions of the saint's life. The focus rests instead upon Elizabeth's acts of charity that provide the key elements of the standard hagiographic accounts. The Fulbourn figure, nimbed and dressed in voluminous robes, carries a basket of food and a purse, signifying her prodigious alms-giving and disinterest in the royal status and worldly goods to which she had been born. On both Norfolk screens she bears a nimbus and wears a white cloak and veil over a red gown, the dress of a secular woman rather than a tertiary of the Franciscans as the elder Elizabeth had become. At Barnham Broom she carries a large goblet or chalice and a basket of loaves, and at Upton she carries a bowl and a basket. If we assume that these details accord with the patrons' understanding of Elizabeth's story the textual source for the paintings appears to have been something other than *The Revelations*, the most likely witness being the detailed accounts in the *Golden Legend* and its abridgment the

23 Cotton, 'Mediaeval Roodscreens', p. 52.

24 For examples of joint sponsorship in Norfolk see Duffy, 'Parish, Piety, and Patronage', pp. 145–6.

25 The only Barnham Broom parishioners to offer glimpses of themselves are those who made bequests to the fabric fund in the 1430s and 1440s and those for whom there are or once were monumental brasses: see Paul Cattermole and Simon Cotton, 'Medieval Parish Church Building in Norfolk', *Norfolk Archaeology* xxxviii (1983), pp. 235–79 at p. 238; and Mill Stephenson, *A List of Monumental Brasses in the British Isles* (rpt, 1964; London, 1926 & 1938), p. 321. The loss of all relevant Devon probate materials prevents possible identification through bequest and here the only evidence of patronage is the De Bryan and the Wolston heraldic glass in the chancel: see Bridget Cherry and Nikolaus Pevsner, *Devon*, 2nd edn (Harmondsworth, 1989), p. 866.

Figure 3. Catherine of Siena, East Portlemouth, Devon, early sixteenth century.

Gilte Legende.[26] The visions are mentioned briefly but the basic impulse of the narrative is Elizabeth's care for the sick and her own privations, concerns that are also seen in the sole surviving glass panel from a narrative of her life from St Peter Mancroft in Norwich where she is shown distributing alms,[27] and which were as Caroline Bynum has observed especially identified with her across European society.[28]

The standardisation that characterises images of Elizabeth can also be detected in the two surviving screen paintings of Catherine of Siena, at Torbryan and at East Portlemouth, another south Devon church where the paintings can be dated on stylistic grounds to the early sixteenth century. Just as Elizabeth is presented as sainted queen, protector of the sick, and intercessory figure, Catherine's significance is established through her relationship to the other figures on the screen as well as through visual acknowledgement of her own revelatory experiences. At Torbryan she wears a nimbus, a crown of thorns and a white mantle covering a black robe (figure 2). In her right hand she holds a heart and her raised left palm is held outwards. The image at Portlemouth differs only to the extent that in her left hand she holds an open book with a red cover (figure 3). Both images have an obvious correspondence with the illustration in de Worde's 1519 edition of *The Orcharde of Syon* in which Catherine receives the stigmata and holds a heart, her special attribute. The design of this woodcut is easily adaptable to the full frontal, single-figure pose of the screen paintings but the link between the two cannot be made with absolute conviction. Nor can the possibility of the design of one screen influencing the other. In an area like the South West where book ownership appears to have been unusual and where printing and bookselling established themselves slowly, the role of the book in the development of designs is difficult to place.[29] Until we have an accurate chronology for Devon screen painting suggestions of artistic influence and similarities in design and technique are bound to be merely conjectural.

Catherine's appearance at Portlemouth may in fact be down to a more general respect for her religious order rather than an interest in her authorial position. The village's wealth came from shipping and fishing. It provided ships for the early campaigns of the Hundred Years War and for pilgrims travelling to Santiago

26 For a discussion of the English lives see McNamer, *Revelations*, pp. 40–42.

27 Christopher Woodforde, *The Norwich School of Glass-Painting in the Fifteenth Century* (Oxford, 1950), p. 35.

28 Caroline Walker Bynum, *Fragmentation and Redemption. Essays on Gender and the Human Body in Medieval Religion* (New York, 1992), p. 197. An alternative reading of the qualities embodied by Elizabeth and other virgin martyrs is offered by Larissa Tracy, 'Silence and Speech in the Female Lives of the *Gilte Legende* and their Influence on the Lives of Ordinary Medieval Women' in her *Women of the 'Gilte Legende'. A Selection of Middle English Saints' Lives* (Cambridge, 2003), pp. 101–28.

29 The only known press in the region (active 1525–34) was that of Richard Thomas, monk of Tavistock: see H. P. R. Finberg, *Tavistock Abbey*, 2nd edn (Newton Abbot, 1969), pp. 290–3. On literacy and book ownership in the Exeter diocese see Whiting, *Blind Devotion*, pp. 198–9.

de Compostella, and by the early fifteenth century it was prosperous enough to rebuild its church entirely and to install a new and elaborate roodscreen.[30] Only the nave and aisle sections of this structure remain but these carry panel paintings of local and regional significance. The poor state of repair and the absence of inscriptions has left some of the figures obscure, and Victorian and twentieth-century restoration may have upset any original coherence, but here as elsewhere the eclectic gathering of saints appears to have no discernible iconographic pattern.[31] SS Mark, John and Jerome are probably all that remain of quartets of the Evangelists and Church Doctors, just as the two sibyls in the south aisle may be the survivors of a set similar to those at Bradninch and Ugborough. Other figures include the patronal saint Winwalloe, Sir John Schorne, Edward the Confessor, Francis, Sebastian, Lawrence, Dorothy, Pope Cornelius, one or two unknown male and female saints, and the fragments of a Coronation of the Virgin scene that shows one of the screen's donors, probably a member of the local Champernoun family, being ushered into the presence of the deity by flanking angels.[32]

Portlemouth's most intriguing feature is the unique appearance together on a screen of three black robed and nimbed figures. For the Champernoun patron Catherine's status as a Dominican tertiary appears as important as any Bridgettine or Carthusian dimension. A damaged figure of a black robed male holding a book must be Dominic with the Order's Rule while Peter the Martyr (otherwise known as Peter of Milan) stands with a sword through his head, an emblem of his martyrdom at the hands of heretics in 1252. Dominic and Peter appear most famously in English art on the early fourteenth-century Thornham Parva Retable made for the Dominican house at Thetford in Norfolk – by Order of the Dominican Chapter these two saints had to be depicted in their own buildings – but otherwise painted representations are exceedingly rare.[33] This is Dominic's only surviving appearance in screen painting and the figure of Peter the Martyr is one of only two extant examples, the other being at Hennock to the south-west of Exeter.[34] Such an unusual trio implies a strong inclination towards

[30] Cherry and Pevsner, *Devon*, p. 350; and John Stabb, *Some Old Devon Churches*, 3 vols (London, 1911), I, pp. 110–11 and plate 90.

[31] The current arrangement differs from that listed by Bond and Camm (*Roodscreens and Roodlofts*, p. 344) and must have been altered during restoration in the 1960s when the stripping of overpaint revealed hidden figures (my thanks to Hugh Harrison for this information).

[32] The screen was erected during the tenancy of the Champernouns, holders of the advowson during the fifteenth century: see *The Register of Edmund Lacy, Bishop of Exeter, 1420–1455, Registrum Commune, II*, ed. G. R. Dunstan, Devon and Cornwall Record Society, new series X (Torquay, 1966), p. 229.

[33] Christopher Norton, David Park and Paul Binski, *Dominican Painting in East Anglia. The Thornham Parva Retable and the Musée de Cluny Frontal* (Woodbridge, 1987), pp. 42–3.

[34] See Tasker, *Encyclopaedia*, pp. 122, 157. Examples survive in fifteenth-century East Anglian stained glass: see Woodforde, *Norwich School*, pp. 87, 110, 188.

the Black Friars who had two houses in the Exeter diocese, in Exeter itself and at Truro in Cornwall.[35] Though the Dominicans probably did not involve themselves in the affairs of local parishes on the scale of the landed and wealthy Benedictines and Cistercians,[36] the prominence and appeal of the order as preachers and confessors to the laity may account for this appearance of Dominican saints in otherwise unexpected circumstances. Such an interest could well have been nurtured by the *Golden Legend*'s lives of both Dominic and Peter the Martyr, and by some appreciation of Catherine's status as an honoured and learned member of the Order. For the patrons or artists to provide examples of suitable imagery would prove easy enough in a context where the saints were known and respected, even in the absence of specific textual source materials.

The only instance of a portrait of one of the Continental holy women being clearly based upon a printed source is that of Bridget of Sweden, whose appearance on the screens at Horsham St Faith in Norfolk and Kenn in Devon matches the design of one of de Worde's woodcuts.[37] The better preserved of the two is at Horsham St Faith, a parish just north of Norwich that also housed a Benedictine monastery. Here Bridget (figure 4) is one of a dozen neatly executed figures on a screen that appears to have been paid for by one Michael Hay who in 1492 gave five marks to make 'a new perke [screen]'.[38] According to an inscription of 1528 the screen was the gift of William Wulcy (or Wolsey) and his two wives Joan and Alice but this must refer only to the paintings. Attentions of iconoclasts have left the faces badly damaged and all of the identifying labels and emblems have been partially erased. Nonetheless a cautious identification gives, from the north side, a crowned female in red and gold who holds a heart in her left hand and would appear to be Catherine of Siena; Etheldreda; a nun, probably meant for Clare;[39] an armoured male figure, probably Alban; Helen; a bishop, probably Leger; Bridget (inscription *Sca Brigida*); Oswald; Apollonia; Roche; a female, probably Genevieve; and Lucy. Set against a red diapered background Bridget wears a dark, perhaps green cloak over a golden-yellow robe with a belt, ermine cuffs to indicate her royal status, white veil and a wimple. She has a nimbus, is seated on

35 L. F. Snell, *The Suppression of the Religious Foundations of Devon and Cornwall* (Marazion, 1967), p. 129.

36 Whiting, *Blind Devotion*, pp. 52, 119.

37 Neither of the two other possible sightings can be linked to book illustration. A badly worn mid fifteenth-century image inscribed *Sca Brigida* from Ufford, Suffolk, shows her in a black habit, holding a book and crosier. It is also suggested that she appears in an early sixteenth-century painting on the screen at Westhall, also in Suffolk: see Judith Middleton-Stewart, *Inward Purity and Outward Splendour. Death and Remembrance in the Deanery of Dunwich, Suffolk, 1370–1547* (Woodbridge, 2001), pp. 226–8; and Tasker, *Encyclopaedia*, p. 115. The identification here is dubious since Bridget carries what looks to be a heavy chain; the inscription *Sca Beda* is also problematic.

38 Cotton, 'Mediaeval Roodscreens', p. 49.

39 This figure has previously defied identification. Clare also appears on the screen at Trimingham on the north Norfolk coast.

Figure 4. Bridget of Sweden before the Godhead, Horsham St Faith, Norfolk, early sixteenth century

a chair before a slender writing desk, and her gaze is lifted to a figure of God the Father who appears centre-left in the midst of gold rayed clouds.

Duffy argues that the design of this panel is based upon the cut used in the *Dyetary of Ghostly Helthe*, a Syon pamphlet published by Wynkyn de Worde in 1520, and that it both reveals Wulcy's interest in the writings of Bridget (and Catherine) and indicates the extent to which the textual materials were circulating among the pious prosperous laity in England through the agency of the Bridgettine house at Syon.[40] The two images are obviously very closely related and the differences between the two, notably the removal of all peripheral figures in the painting, is clearly the result of the painters working to the constraints of the panel.[41] The source illustration need not however have been taken from the

40 Duffy, *Stripping of the Altars*, pp. 167–8, and plate 61.

41 The unusual iconography of the crowned female figure holding her heart might also be

Dyetary of Ghostly Helthe. It was a popular design and had been used by de Worde in a Book of Hours in 1519 and was to be reused a further seven times in titles published before 1528, the date of the screen painting, and at least as many again before 1534.[42] Popular prints such as this would have been available to well-connected members of the community and to regional painters based in Norwich. Bridget's works and numerous associated texts, sponsored by Syon and its friends and given great impetus by the printed editions, were increasingly popular from the middle of the fifteenth century and circulated widely in East Anglia.[43] The inclusion of an abbreviated life of Bridget in the commonplace book of Robert Reynys, churchwarden of the parish of Acle at the end of the fifteenth century, shows the extent to which devotion to the saint had permeated the lower reaches of Norfolk literate society.[44]

Regardless of the specific source the link between patron, iconography and book ownership is as unusual as it is compelling. As elsewhere, personal preference probably accounts for the range of saints portrayed, perhaps with some degree of negotiation with the parish community. But there is here a much stronger sense of reading habits having influenced these choices. A broad theme of divine visions or inspiration links Bridget to Oswald, Helen and Lucy; alternatively, a monastic connection unites Bridget, Catherine, the Francisan Clare, and the abbess Etheldreda; and other associations are undoubtedly present. The issue of real significance though is the depiction of Bridget in the act of writing. This distinguishes her from all other female figures on English roodscreens for whom the attribute of a book simply indicates a textual narrative that authorises their witness to the Christian faith. Here Bridget proves her own authority both through her vision and through her literacy and she is comparable to the four learned Doctors of the Church, the only other figures on screens or pulpits depicted in the act of writing. If the popularity of the image of St Anne teaching the Virgin to read is to be connected with her promotion as a sacred role-model for the education of children in the domestic sphere,[45] the choice of Bridget of Sweden recording her visions makes explicit the notion of literate secular patrons – male and female – engaged in sophisticated theological discourse. It is as Duffy

explained by the influence of the craftsman working without a precise visual source. Catherine had no royal connections and the figure looks more like an amalgam of Catherine and Elizabeth of Hungary.

42 Edward Hodnett, *English Woodcuts 1480–1535* (1935; rpt. Oxford, 1973), pp. 178–9; and Driver, 'Pictures in print', pp. 242–3.

43 A summary of the circulation and ownership of Bridget's *Revelations* is given by Alexandra Barratt, 'Continental Women Mystics and English Readers', *The Cambridge Companion to Medieval Women's Writing*, ed. Carolyn Dinshaw and David Wallace (Cambridge, 2003), pp. 240–55 at pp. 248–50.

44 C. L. S. Linnell, 'The Commonplace Book of Robert Reynys of Acle', *Norfolk Archaeology* xxxii (1961), pp. 120–1.

45 See Wendy Scase, 'St Anne and the Education of the Virgin: Literary and Artistic Traditions and their Implications', *England in the Fourteenth Century*, ed. Nigel Rogers (Stamford, 1993), pp. 81–96.

argues a reflection of personal devotion to a popular mystical author, but it also provides evidence of an intellectual vitality and confidence amongst the laity that affirms the mutuality of personal and communal forms of devotion.

This manifestation of a patron's interests as a focus for parish piety can also be seen in the Bridget portrait on the screen at Kenn near Exeter, the only surviving depiction in the South West and an important witness to the promotion of Bridget's cult in England in the early sixteenth century. Whereas William Wulcy's choice of image probably stemmed from his ownership of a Bridgettine text, the Kenn painting offers direct links with those responsible for the promotion of Bridget's writings and ultimately takes us to Syon itself. No hard evidence about the patronage of the screen exists although the parish was evidently of significance – it gave its name to the deanery – and had important sponsors. This area around Exeter was a traditional centre of power for the Courtenay family, the Earls of Devon, which owned numerous estates in mid and south Devon, including houses at Tiverton, Colyton and Broadclyst.[46] The Courtenays presented to Kenn church and their arms were recognised by nineteenth-century antiquarians in the east window of the chancel and in the window of the south aisle,[47] which appears to have housed one of the many Devon chantry chapels endowed by the family.[48] The eleven-bay screen retains a sequence of more than thirty figures painted in a distinctly regional style somewhere between 1500 and 1530. Whilst not quite deserving of Cherry and Pevsner's dismissive 'bad painted saints',[49] this is still rather unsophisticated work that produces flat inexpressive faces and harsh black outlines. Apostles, Doctors, virgin martyrs, and St Anne teaching the Virgin to read are all conventional choices, but surprising and subtle features also emerge: a matched pair of Francis and Hubert, each before a vision of the crucifix; Roche and Sebastian, saints called upon to ward off plague; the rare and peculiarly English image of the lily crucifix together with an Annunciation;[50] and Bridget at her desk (figure 5). Once again the combination of standard issue and more fashionable saints implies a general interest in new forms of devotion within the parish community, but the Bridgettine dimension argues for more specific concerns. Shown veiled and wearing a black robe over a white gown Bridget is again seated and in the act of writing. Here though she has a scroll rather than a book, a crown instead of a nimbus and her attention is fixed upon the dove of the Holy Spirit rather than an image of God the Father. The

46 On the Courtenays' position in Devon society see M. Cherry, 'The Courtenay Earls Of Devon: The Formation and Disintegration of a Late Medieval Aristocratic Affinity', *Southern History* i (1979), pp. 71–97; and L. C. Durant, *'Sorrowful Captives': the Tudor Earls of Devon* (Pontypool, 1960).

47 George Oliver, *Ecclesiastical Antiquities in Devon*, 3 vols (Exeter, 1840), I, p. 37.

48 Nicholas Orme, 'The Dissolution of the Chantries in Devon, 1546–48', *Devonshire Association Reports and Transactions* cxi (1979), pp. 75–124 at pp. 96, 109.

49 Pevsner and Cherry, *Devon*, p. 512.

50 On the tradition of this image see E. J. M. Duggan, 'Notes Concerning the "Lily Crucifixion" in the Llanbeblig Hours', *National Library of Wales Journal* xxvii (1991–92), pp. 39–48.

Figure 5. Bridget of Sweden (left), Kenn, Devon, early sixteenth century.

Horsham St Faith painting undoubtedly bears a stronger likeness to the printed illustration but the designs of both panels appear rooted in a common source and key diagnostic features of the saint's iconography – the visionary object and the apparatus of writing – are clearly present. Indeed, the differences in the Kenn version are quite appropriate to the migration of images between media and accord with the ways in which the printed illustrations inspired images in other formats. The active promotion of Bridget's cult that gave rise to the publication of a slew of Bridgettine texts also saw the Order's house at Isleworth become an increasingly popular pilgrimage site from which emanated pewter badges to be worn by those who had made the journey to listen to the brethren preach and to secure the generous 'Pardon of Syon' given at Lammastide.[51] The powerful influence of printed illustrations of Bridget is present even in these cheap and disposable objects, on which she is depicted sitting at her desk receiving her revelations whilst an angel, an element of the woodcut not found in either of the screen paintings, stands in attendance.[52]

The Kenn screen is unlikely to have been paid for by the Courtenays – the figures are not high status work and neither the screen nor the paintings advertise coats of arms or insignia in the fashion demanded by high class patronage and seen in the family's stained glass commissions here and elsewhere in the diocese. The paintings are, however, coeval with the influence of Countess Katherine (1479–1527), daughter of Edward IV and Elizabeth Woodville and widow of the ninth Earl of Devon, William Courtenay, who had died in 1511 leaving her with two young children.[53] The Countess's position within the parish probably manifested itself in a sense of familial patronage rather than regular involvement but it was she who presented the new rector Thomas Michell in 1517 and this unique example in Devon of a painted portrait of Bridget signals her connection with Kenn parish life.[54] During her widowhood Katherine gained a reputation for generosity in alms and religious offerings and for an active participation in the spiritual life of the diocese that included patronage of the religious orders, members of which were invited to preach at her house at Columbjohn near Broadclyst.[55] Her religious interests must also have been influenced by her family's devotion to the monastic life and to the Bridgettines in particular. Edward IV had been a staunch defender of Syon and the renowned piety of his

[51] See F. R. Johnston, 'Syon Abbey', *History of the County of Middlesex*, I, Victoria History of the Counties of England, ed. J. S. Cockburn et al. (London, 1969), pp. 178–91 at p. 180.

[52] Brian Spencer, *Pilgrim Souvenirs and Secular Badges* (London, 1998), pp. 178–9. For possible sources of this design in manuscripts related to Syon see Driver, 'Nuns as Patrons', p. 249.

[53] The following discussion of Katherine relies on Margaret Westcott, 'Katherine Courtenay, Countess of Devon, 1479–1527', *Tudor and Stuart Devon. The Common Estate and Government*, ed. Todd Gray, Margery Rowe and Audrey Erskine (Exeter, 1992), pp. 13–38.

[54] Oliver, *Ecclesiastical Antiquities*, I, p. 39.

[55] George Oliver, *Monasticon Dioecesis Exoniensis* (Exeter, 1846), pp. 330, 334.

mother Cecily, Duchess of York, encompassed a strong devotion to the female mystic saints.[56] It was Cecily who bequeathed a copy of a life of Catherine of Siena to Katherine's youngest sister Bridget who had entered the Dominican house at Dartford, and a volume containing Bridget's revelations to Katherine's cousin Anne de la Pole who had risen to become the abbess of the English Bridgettines at Syon.[57] Katherine also enjoyed close relations with her eldest sister Elizabeth, whose marriage to Henry VII in 1486 had reunited the Houses of York and Lancaster, and who had looked after Katherine and her children in 1503 when William Courtenay had lost his title after having been charged with conspiracy. Elizabeth had developed a particular interest in devotional and mystical texts and with the co-operation of her mother-in-law, Margaret Beaufort, had sponsored Caxton's edition of *The Fifteen Oes* in 1491, a work ascribed to Bridget.[58] An inventory of the books at Katherine's main seat at Tiverton castle taken after her death in 1527 does not reveal an explicit Bridgettine or mystical slant to her devotional life but the collection did include a personal matins book, a copy of the *Legenda Aurea*, and other printed and manuscript books.[59] Thus, while neither Katherine's familial connections nor her own personal piety should be taken as evidence for her direct patronage of the Kenn paintings they seem to offer irresistible evidence for Bridget's presence at Kenn. It would be remarkable indeed if these contacts did not exemplify the ways in which knowledge of the mystics was introduced into the visual and devotional life of the rural parish.

To conclude, even in the face of limited knowledge about the men and women who commissioned screen paintings and the painters who actually carried out the work, screen iconography is a valuable index of the changing nature of lay artistic patronage and especially of the impact of literacy on the choice of devotional imagery. Devon donors do not have such a concern with self-referentiality as their East Anglian counterparts and do not appear so keen to present themselves as purchasers and benefactors. Nor do they appear to have been willing or able to pay for the high-production values characteristic of the East Anglian screens, even if a workshop sufficiently skilled to carry out such a commission could be found. There is nothing in the South West to compete with the elegance and sense

56 Edward's restoration of rights taken away during Henry VI's reign was rewarded with a record in the house's obit roll: see Johnston, 'Syon Abbey', pp. 185, 188. See also C. A. J. Armstrong, 'The Piety of Cecily, Duchess of York: A Study in Late Medieval Culture', in his *England, France and Burgundy in the Fifteenth Century* (London, 1983), pp. 135–56.

57 For a discussion of Cecily's bequests see George Keiser, 'The Mystics and the Early English Printers: the Economics of Devotionalism', *MMT* IV, pp. 9–26 at pp. 23–4. Cecily's devotion to Bridget is further attested by an image of the saint in the now lost glass at Fotheringay church in which she was buried in 1495: see Richard Marks, *The Medieval Stained Glass of Northamptonshire* (Oxford, 1992), p. 73.

58 Felicity Riddy, ' "Women Talking About the Things Of God": A Late Medieval Sub-Culture', *Women and Literature in Britain 1150–1500*, ed. Carol M. Meale, 2nd edn (Cambridge, 1996), pp. 104–27 at p. 108.

59 Public Record Office, SP1/46, 51–6; Westcott, 'Katherine Courtenay', pp. 31–2, 38.

of the numinous of the paintings at Ranworth and Barton Turf, or the quality of craftsmanship of those at Cawston, Southwold and Thornham.[60] There is, however, an inventiveness and sophistication to the iconography that owes much to the enthusiasm with which the county's laity adopted new devotional and liturgical practices. Marion Glasscoe has shown that the late fifteenth-century paintings and texts in the Chudleigh chapel at Ashton church, some five miles from Kenn, were inspired by the Latin text of the newly instituted Feast of the Transfiguration.[61] This and other screens in the county – for example, the biblical scenes at Bradninch, the vices and virtues at Bridford, and the Christ child with *orbus mundi* at Combe Martin[62] – attest to a willingness to embrace innovation. The Bridget painting at Kenn may stem from literate devotional practice but in this new context it transcends the exclusivity of the written page and becomes part of communal worship.

Given the spread of interest in Continental holy women and the ongoing renewal of votive and devotional images from 1450 to 1530 it is perhaps surprising that so few of these figures appear as painted images. Notwithstanding the wholesale destruction of screens a mere dozen surviving examples suggests a rather limited appeal. For other European female mystics such as Mechtild of Hackeborn and Marguerite Porete the very restricted circulation of their works fully explains their failure to move beyond an elite monastic readership to more popular status, but the paucity of images of Bridget, Catherine and Elizabeth, might be thought to indicate a degree of conservatism in the choice of figures. It must be remembered however that they were competing with many other popular and potentially helpful saints and there had to be particular reasons for their inclusion. The combination of interested patron, opportunity for patronage, and access to suitable craftsmen must have occurred only rarely. More tellingly, although the paintings reveal only so much about the reception and use of mystical texts they encourage us to think about the ways in which these holy women were drawn into larger groupings of saints and the ways in which this process both reflects and contributes to the construction of parochial lay identities. If the surviving screen paintings across the country can be said to demonstrate the mass appeal of the apostles and the virgin martyrs, the appearance of more contemporary witnesses to Christ's Resurrection reveals the extent to which the reading habits of the literate laity could influence the devotional life of larger sections of the community through artistic patronage. And whilst firmly

60 Men who were involved in other kinds of work, including glass painting, may have carried out higher quality screen painting in the diocese but where they were based, what kinds of commissions they took on and whether they worked across different media is open to question. A discussion of the geographical range of the Exeter school of glass painters is given by Chris Brooks and David Evans, *The Great East Window of Exeter Cathedral: A Glazing History* (Exeter, 1988), pp. 107–9.

61 Marion Glasscoe, 'Late Medieval Paintings in Ashton Church, Devon', *Journal of the British Archaeological Association* cxl (1987), pp. 182–90.

62 Bond and Camm, *Roodscreens and Roodlofts*, pp. 299–300, 308.

rooted in literate culture this sponsorship of devotional images exposed Bridget and the other Continental women to a much wider community of devotees, both literate and unlettered. The identification of the *mulieres sanctae* amongst standard screen iconography is a great incentive to follow research into other areas of lay devotion and artistic activity.

DISCRETIO SPIRITUUM IN TIME: THE IMPACT OF JULIAN OF NORWICH'S COUNSEL IN THE *BOOK OF MARGERY KEMPE*

NAOË KUKITA YOSHIKAWA

BELIEF IN THE TRINITY, which is manifested as an interplay of the Father as power, the Son as wisdom and the Holy Spirit as the bond of love between the Father and the Son, was a fundamental aspect of the Christian faith in the late Middle Ages, as it is today. Christians understand that God loved them in creating them in his likeness; he loved them more in the costliness of their redemption; but his greatest act of love is the gift of the Holy Spirit, by which they know and love him, and are assured that they are his children chosen for salvation.[1] The love of the Holy Spirit is believed to be manifested in the gifts of the Holy Spirit – wisdom, understanding, knowledge, piety, fortitude, counsel, and fear of the Lord[2] – through which the Holy Spirit can direct the supernatural life of the soul.

The gifts of the Holy Spirit are a key for exploring Margery Kempe's experiential awareness of the life of grace.[3] The process is initiated after her mystical marriage to the Godhead in Rome on her way back from Jerusalem (ch. 35) – marking a threshold in her relationship with the Trinity. From then on the law of charity and obedience orders her life, as the presence of the Holy Spirit in her soul is signalled by the ongoing activity and effects realised through the gifts of the Holy Spirit. But Margery undergoes a series of ordeals in the period following her return to England after her Jerusalem pilgrimage. The ordeals range from poverty, sickness, tears and crying to accusations of heresy – all of which she associates with the suffering of Christ. Yet these events in her life are actually steps in her spiritual progress: through the ordeals she discerns percep-

1 J. P. H. Clark, 'The Trinitarian Theology of Walter Hilton's *Scale of Perfection, Book Two*', in *Langland, the Mystics and the Medieval English Religious Tradition, Essays in Honour of S. S. Hussey*, ed. Helen Phillips (Cambridge, 1990), pp. 125–40 at p. 132.

2 *The New Catholic Encyclopedia*, 18 vols (New York, 1967), 'Gifts of the Holy Spirit', VII, 99–101 at p. 99. Lorens d'Orléans notes that the medieval *figura* of the seven gifts of the Holy Spirit as protection against sin is derived from Isaiah 11:2–3. See *The Book of Vices and Virtues*: *A Fourteenth Century English Translation of the* Somme le Roi *of Lorens D'Orléans*, ed. W. Nelson Francis, EETS OS CCXVII (London, 1942, repr. Millwood, NY, 1968), p. 117.

3 *The Book of Margery Kempe*, ed. Sanford Brown Meech and Hope Emily Allen, vol. I, EETS OS CCXII (London, 1940, repr. 1961), hereafter the *Book* in the text and BMK in footnotes. All citations to Margery Kempe are from this edition and will be followed by chapter, page and line number.

tively the gifts of the Holy Spirit and increases her experiential awareness of the possibility of redemption in this life.

Importantly, *discretio spirituum* is a prerequisite for fully embracing the gifts of the Holy Spirit, for Christian faith takes it for granted that supernatural powers, both divine and diabolic, are present in time and eternity. And it is through the *discretio spirituum* that we might assess the veracity of Margery's spiritual experience. Furthermore, Margery's experience is influenced by the process of intellectual and spiritual development that Julian of Norwich underwent to attain a renewed perception of faith. For, after Margery has persuaded her husband to the vow of chastity, she pursues a new life-style as the bride of Christ. But being not always confident of the veracity of her spiritual experience, Margery visits a group of religious figures for endorsement of the revelations she receives from Christ in her holy meditations. Among the spiritual experts, Julian gives crucial advice on Margery's concern about the counsel of evil spirits. Julian does not directly mention to Margery that *discretio spirituum* is a dynamic process that accompanies internal transformation by the grace of the Holy Spirit. But Julian's counsel, which centres on the love of the Holy Spirit, might have determined the way Margery receives the gifts of the Holy Spirit and makes inner progress through her assiduous efforts.[4]

Discretio spirituum in Medieval Culture

Margery opens her *Book* with her post-partum insanity. She explains the episode of bizarre behaviour as diabolical possession, thereby revealing her experiential awareness of the diabolic power present in her life:[5]

> Sche sey, as hir thowt, deuelys opyn her mowthys al inflaumyd with brenny[n]g lowys of fyr as þei schuld a swalyd hyr in . . . And also þe deuelys cryed up-on hir with greet thretyngys & bodyn hir sche schuld forsake hir Crystendam hir feyth, and denyin hir God, hys Modyr, & alle þe seyntys in Heuyn'.
>
> (ch. 1, p. 7, lines 23–31)

At the same time, Margery's devotion to the Holy Spirit runs throughout the *Book*: in the Proem and elsewhere she invokes the assistance of the Holy Spirit; it is typically shown in the 'Prayers of the creature' which include the hymn *Veni creator spiritus*. This prayer which Margery used for her daily devotions after her

4 Richard Lawes notices that both Margery and Julian had their spiritual experiences in the context of intense sickness and speculates that 'perhaps they discussed this and perhaps Julian's own experiences lead her to stress trust of inner locutions despite their possible intermingling with illness'. See 'The Madness of Margery Kempe', in *MMT* VI, pp. 147–67 at p. 165. Santha Bhattacharji suggests that Julian's advice about the need to trust the guidance of the Holy Spirit influenced Margery. See *God is an Earthquake: The Spirituality of Margery Kempe* (London, 1997), p. 32.

5 Miraculously she is restored to herself by the appearance at her bedside of Christ as a fair young man asking, 'Dowtyr, why hast þow forsakyn me, and I forsoke neuyr þe?' (ch. 1, p. 8, lines 20–1).

return from the Jerusalem pilgrimage[6] shows that she starts with an invocation to the Holy Spirit to enter her soul. She probably knew the teaching of St Paul: 'Likewise the Spirit also helpeth our infirmity. For we know not what we should pray for as we ought; but the Spirit himself asketh for us with unspeakable groanings' (Romans 8:26).

Margery's references both to the Holy Spirit and to an evil spirit indicate her knowledge, at least in retrospect, of *discretio spirituum*: while she desires to find reassurance that her spiritual experience was inspired by God, she is keenly aware of the problem of false discernment. She says, 'so wistly I defye þe Deuyl, & al hys fals cownsel, and al þat euyr I haue don, seyd, er thowt, aftyr þe cownsel of þe Deuyl, wenyng it had be þe cownsel of God & inspiracyon of þe Holy Gost' (Book Two, 'Prayers of the creature', p. 248, lines 28–32). Significantly, *discretio spirituum* is relevant to a theme of her *Book*. Margery writes her book at the request of clerics who believe that she is inspired by the Holy Ghost: 'Summe of these worthy & worshepful clerkys tokyn it in perel of her sowle and as þei wold answer to God þat þis creatur was inspired with þe Holy Gost and bodyn hyr þat sche schuld don hem wryten & makyn a booke of hyr felyngys & hir reuelacyons' (Proem, p. 3, lines 20–5). This implies that *discretio spirituum* is not only important to Margery's life but it also validates her writing on her form of living so that 'hys goodnesse myth be knowyn to alle þe world' (Proem, p. 4, lines 1–2).

The doctrine of *discretio* was listed by Paul in I Corinthians 12:10 as one of the gifts of the Holy Spirit and developed by the Church in the Middle Ages.[7] Although the nature of the doctrine refers to the experience perceived subjectively, a more precise definition that emphasises the external aspects of the recipient was constructed towards the end of the Middle Ages until it became a skill acquired not merely by the gift of the Holy Spirit but through rigorous theological study and ecclesiastical office.[8] It is in this cultural milieu that Margery's experience of *discretio spirituum* can be explored. More specifically her experience can be discussed by employing Alfonso of Jaén's *Epistola solitarii ad reges* as a key text that illuminates her spirituality and shows *discretio spirituum* as a dynamic process through which Margery discerns her whole experience, guided by the Holy Spirit.[9]

6 See Allen, BMK, p. 349 n. 248/1–2 and p. 350 n. 253/23.

7 Major theologians and their works on *discretio spirituum* are cited by Rosalynn Voaden, 'Women's Words, Men's Language: *Discretio Spirituum* as Discourse in the Writing of Medieval Women Visionaries', in *The Medieval Translator* V, ed. Roger Ellis and René Tixier (Turnhout, 1996), pp. 64–83 at p. 79 n. 5.

8 See ibid., p. 66. For the definition and development of *discretio spirituum*, see Rosalynn Voaden, *God's Words, Women's Voices: The Discernment of Spirits in the Writing of Late Medieval Women Visionaries* (Woodbridge, 1999), pp. 46–56.

9 I would like to thank Dr Roger Ellis for confirming that *Epistola* was a standard text of *discretio spirituum* in the early fifteenth century and that Alfonso's criteria were probably known to Margery via Alan of Lynn, who made indexes to the Revelations of St Bridget. Voaden also states that 'Alfonso's treatise profoundly influenced contem-

Drawing on the teachings of theologians like Augustine and Thomas Aquinas, Alfonso formulated a summary of the criteria of *discretio spirituum*; as a spiritual director of St Bridget of Sweden, he used it in constructing Bridget as a visionary in the discourse of *discretio spirituum*.[10] According to Alfonso, this doctrine authenticates subjective visionary experience according to seven signs: the person lives a virtuous life under the supervision of a spiritual director; as a result, the recipient is inflamed by love and charity; the recipient feels a deep inward knowledge of the truth of revelation; the vision is true to Scripture and accepted teachings; a true visionary experience would bear a fruit; the visionary knows the time of her death, and there are posthumous miracles.[11] Importantly, Alfonso insists that 'the ferst most serteyn sygne . is yat ye vision is of god . whan yat persone seing visions is really meke and levis undir obediens of sum spiritual fadir vertuos and expert in spiritual lyff'.[12] His emphasis on meekness and humble obedience is reflected in the way he advocates Bridget as an exemplary visionary: Bridget's willing submission to her spiritual directors was the principal criterion in Alfonso's claim for her authenticity.

The question of discerning spirits is problematic for Margery, whose lack of skill in the discourse of *discretio* affects her judgement by third parties. The *Book* testifies to how difficult it was for a laywoman to justify the validity of her spiritual experience. She is aware of the need for submission and obedience, but it is also the case that her behaviour towards spiritual superiors is inconsistent and even belligerent and that her reputation in this respect adversely affects her claim to be God's mouthpiece.[13] For example, Margery is accused of Lollardy because of her apparent lack of submission to clerical authority.[14]

But we have evidence that at some points Margery conforms to the conventions of *discretio spirituum*. For example, like Bridget, Margery first confides her spiritual experience to a Dominican anchorite who was then her confessor.[15] Margery is shown 'to secure ecclesiastical sanction by giving evidence of divine authorization'.[16] As mentioned above, Margery's submission to the guidance of her spiritual superiors is highlighted in her seeking help from spiritual advisors:

porary and subsequent dissertations on *discretio spirituum*, including Gerson's important treatise, *De probatione spirituum*'. See 'Women's Words, Men's Language', p. 67.

10 For detailed argument on Bridget as an exemplary visionary, see *God's Words, Women's Voices*, pp. 73–108.

11 'Women's Words, Men's Language', p. 67.

12 'The Middle English *Epistola solitarii ad reges* of Alfonso of Jaén: An Edition of the Text in London, British Library, MS Cotton Julius Fii', edited by Rosalynn Voaden, in *God's Words, Women's Voices*, Appendix, fol. 252v, lines 7–9, pp. 176–7.

13 Voaden considers that when Margery is depicted as fearful over her visions and her way of life, her presentation conforms most closely to the discourse of *discretio spirituum* – humility, modesty and submissiveness. When she is attacked, or challenged in her beliefs, then her behaviour tends to deviate from it and she starts to challenge authority. See *God's Words, Women's Voices*, p. 139.

14 See BMK, ch. 52, pp. 123–8.

15 See BMK, ch. 5, p. 18.

16 *God's Words, Women's Voices*, p. 123.

she presents her spiritual experience to Richard Caister,[17] William of Southfield, and Julian, who are all gifted with the charism of *discretio*.[18] William of Southfield, a Carmelite, assures Margery of the working of the Holy Spirit in her soul: ' "dredyth ȝe not of ȝowr maner of leuyng, for it is þe Holy Gost werkyng plentyuowsly hys grace in ȝour sowle"; "put non obstakyl ne obieccyon a-gen þe goodnes of þe Holy Gost" ' (ch. 18, p. 41, lines 13–14 and 24–5). He uses internal criteria for the *discretio* by paraphrasing scriptural passages: 'he dwellyth not in a body soget to syn. He fleth al fals feynyng & falshede';[19] 'he askyth of us a lowe, a meke, & a contryte hert wyth a good wyl';[20] and 'My spyrit schal restyn vp-on a meke man, a contryte man, & dredyng my wordys' (ch. 18, p. 41, lines 29–33).[21]

That the spiritual experts acknowledged Margery as illuminated by the Holy Spirit suggests the credibility of her experience: her occasional failure in meeting the objective external criteria of *discretio spirituum* does not undermine the veracity of her spiritual experience. For although individual discretion can be externally recognised, it cannot simply be externally judged by third parties. As the internal state of the individual cannot be separated from a capacity for discernment, the key to *discretio* is neither the judgement of a third party nor the skill of discerning spirits, but it has to do with the internal and psychological state of the recipient of the grace.[22] In this context, the recipient's life is judged by the extent to which s/he bears spiritual fruit in his/her life. Ultimately, the progress culminates in faith – a state of mind that is stable and steadfast in the right faith. And it is through the gifts of the Holy Spirit that the recipient's inner self is finally transformed into this new state.[23] This transformation accompanies the grace of contrition, sweetness of devotion and acquisition of virtues. Thus, *discretio spirituum* is a dynamic process through which the believer discerns his/her whole experience, as guided by the Holy Spirit.

Through this process we can assess Margery as one who had been in close touch with God and made spiritual progress as the recipient of grace. This spiritual transformation takes place in Margery as she internalises the story of the

17 Ibid., p. 126. Voaden describes Caister as the very model of a medieval spiritual director who initially had doubts about the veracity of women's spiritual experiences.

18 Margery clusters together the scriptural references to the Holy Spirit in chapters 17, 18 and 19 which recount her visits to the spiritual authorities.

19 Cf. Wisdom 1:4.

20 Cf. Psalm 50:19.

21 Cf. Isaiah 66:2.

22 For the argument on internal criteria, see Rebecca Selman, 'Voices and Wisdom: A Study of Henry Suso's *Horologium Sapientiae* in Some Late Medieval English Religious Texts' (unpublished doctoral thesis, University of Exeter, 1998), p. 107.

23 See Oliver Davies, 'Transformational Processes in the Work of Julian of Norwich and Mechthild of Magdeburg', in *MMT* V, pp. 39–52. Ritamary Bradley notices that the transformation is seen as 'an "honorable ennobling" as part of the *asseth*'. See 'Julian of Norwich: Everyone's Mystic', in *Mysticism and Spirituality in Medieval England*, ed. William F. Pollard and Robert Boenig (Cambridge, 1997), pp. 139–58 at p. 145.

Incarnation and is led to participate in the creative work of the Trinity as she overcomes her wretched state of humanity. Through her meditational experience and the events of her life she increases in awareness of its creative and redemptive force – the dynamic working of divine love in time and space.

Julian's Counsel and the *Revelation of Divine Love*

Margery describes to Julian the grace of contrition and compassion and wonderful revelations she received from God, for 'þe ankres was expert in swech thyngys & good cownsel cowd geuyn' (ch. 18, p. 42, lines 16–17). Julian's counsel shows that she is well versed in the Scriptures, spiritual theology and the literature of discernment. Perceiving intuitively the goodness of God in Margery's spiritual experience, Julian gives Margery a sympathetic counsel. In emphasising the impotence and barrenness of the devil, she assures Margery of the indwelling of God in the human soul and demonstrates the centrality of the working of the Holy Spirit in a soul. Julian's counsel is illuminated by the Long Text of *A Revelation of Love*,[24] which shows how she is led into a new awareness of redemption by interpreting the showings and elucidates the psychological dynamic of Julian's struggle to attain faith in the creative work of the Trinity in time.

Julian advises Margery to be obedient to the will of God, for Julian feels that it is not false spirits but the Holy Spirit that mediates between God and Margery. Then she assures Margery that the Holy Spirit is by its nature charity.[25] This belief is seen in her argument on charity in the Long Text:

> Thus charite kepith us in feith and in hope; and hope ledith us in charite. And at the end al shall be charite . . . Charite onmade is God; charite made is our soule in God; charite goven is vertue; and that is a gracious geft of werking in which we loven God for himselfe and ourselves in God and that God loveth, for God.
>
> (LT, ch. 84, p. 133)

With this total faith in charity, she gives the internal criteria for *discretio*: the soul acquires the virtues of chastity and stability in faith and belief through the working of the Holy Spirit.[26] Possession of these virtues indicates the presence of the Holy Spirit.

Julian defines the tears of contrition, devotion or compassion as a sign that the Holy Spirit is in the soul.[27] Julian's emphasis on the nature of tears as the gift of

24 Julian of Norwich, *A Revelation of Love*, ed. Marion Glasscoe, 3rd rev. edn, Exeter Medieval English Texts and Studies (Exeter, 1993). All citations to the Long Text of *A Revelation of Love* (to be abbreviated LT) are from Glasscoe's edition and are followed by the chapter and page number in parentheses.

25 See BMK, ch. 18, p. 42, lines 24–6.

26 See BMK, ch. 18, p. 42, lines 26–8.

27 See BMK, ch. 18, p. 42, line 36–p. 43, line 1.

the Holy Spirit is in accord with the passage Margery quotes from St Jerome: 'terys turmentyn mor þe Devylle þan don þe peynes of Helle' (ch. 18, p. 43, lines 7–8):[28] both Julian and Jerome are ratifying the gift of tears. In a culture where *discretio* is crucial to spiritual life, the devil's influence is most feared by those who receive revelations. Margery must have been relieved to learn from Julian's counsel that tears release the soul from the devil and that 'God & þe Deuyl ben euyrmor contraryows' (ch. 18, p. 43, lines 8–9). The devil has no power in a soul when it is in harmony with God through the working of the Holy Spirit. Julian also expounds that, through the work of the Holy Spirit, one receives the gift of right faith and belief, which prevents the devil from operating his negative power of doubting and deluding:

> & þe Holy Gost makyth a sowle stabyl & stedfast in þe rygth feyth & þe rygth beleue . . . He þat is euyr-mor dowtyng is lyke to þe flood of þe see, þe which is mevyd & born a-bowte wyth þe wynd, & þat man is not lyche to receyuen þe gyftys of God. (ch. 18, p. 42, lines 28–34)

Ultimately, faith produces stability and peace of mind. As Julian aptly explains, 'What creatur þat hath þes tokenys he m[uste] | stedfastlych belevyn þat þe Holy Gost dwellyth in hys sowle' (ch. 18, p. 42, lines 34–6).

Julian concludes her counsel to Margery with the most profound virtue of Christian life. She reveals that: 'Pacyens is necessary vn-to ȝow, for in þat schal ȝe kepyn ȝowr sowle' (ch. 18, p. 43, lines 16–18).[29] In her account of her own fifteenth revelation, Julian explains how God rewards man for his patience in waiting on God's will and God's time, and for extending that patience over the whole span of life.[30] The influence of Julian's counsel is present in Margery's perception of the working of the Holy Spirit. Through the accounts of Margery's life we learn that she is making spiritual progress as she discerns the working of God in her.

Margery's Spiritual Progress

Margery's mystical marriage to the Godhead in Rome (ch. 35) signals a new era for her spiritual progress and the development of her relationship with the Holy Trinity. The mystical marriage enables her to embrace the Holy Trinity in her soul and assures her that 'þis is an holy lyfe & þe tyme is ryth wel spent' (ch. 35, p. 89, lines 18–19). As the events in Rome that follow the mystical marriage show, her life is ordered by the law of charity and obedience – the virtues taught by Christ and elevated by the grace of the Holy Spirit.[31] However, her biograph-

28 For the fear of the devil's counsel, see BMK, ch. 22 where in her deathbed meditation Christ assures her that her weeping torments the devil, thus validating her experience as being of divine origin.

29 Cf. Luke 6:22–3 for the paradoxical merit of contempt and Luke 21:19 for patience.

30 See LT, ch. 64, pp. 104–6.

31 See BMK chapters 36 and 37 for the virtues.

ical narrative concentrates on the ordeals in her life when she settles in Lynn after the pilgrimage. Margery cries loudly when the Lord puts her in mind of his Passion. Though her crying reflects the intensely emotional experience in Jerusalem and a highly visual meditation on Mount Calvary which focuses on Christ's sufferings on the cross, she becomes a target of blame, slander, and contempt for that crying.

Her heresy trial also happened in this period. Although orthodox in her understanding of the Church's doctrine, Margery's eccentric behaviour invites suspicions of Lollardy. But this painful experience not only increases her fortitude and compassionate identification with the suffering Christ but also empowers her as a mouthpiece of God as she discerns the counsel of the Holy Spirit. For example, at the inquisition by the Steward of Leicester she claims that she has received grace from the Holy Spirit and that her speech and conversing come from the Holy Spirit and not from her own knowledge.[32] Arrested as a Lollard, she says: 'þer may no man sey a good worde wyth-owtyn þe ȝyft of þe Holy Gost, for owr Lord Ihesu Crist seyd to hys disciplys, "Stody not what ȝe schal sey, for it schal not be ȝowr spiryt þat schal spekyn in ȝow, but it schal be þe spiryt of þe Holy Gost" ' (ch. 55, p. 135, lines 30–5).[33] On another occasion she is consciously discerning wisdom, understanding and knowledge infused by the Holy Spirit. While being tried on suspicion of Lollard activity in York, she is required to interpret the words: *Crescite et multiplicamini* (Genesis 1:22). Margery's answer is remarkably similar to Julian's counsel which emphasises the virtues of charity, chastity and patience: ' "Ser, þes wordys ben not vndirstondyn only of begetyng of chyldren | bodily, but also be purchasyng of vertu, whech is frute gostly, as be heryng of þe wordys of God, be good exampyl ȝeuyng, be mekenes & paciens, charite & chastite, & swech oþer" ' (ch. 51, p. 121, lines 3–8). In her life of patience under persecutions, Margery deepens her understanding of Julian's counsel to the point of saying: 'pacyens is more worthy þan myraclys werkyng' (ch. 51, p. 121, lines 8–9).

Furthermore, Margery suffers from various illnesses sent by God after the pilgrimage. In her experience of intense pain, she tries to understand the meaning of the Incarnation: 'Why woldist þu be-comyn man & suffyr so meche peyne for my synnes & for alle mennys synnes þat xal be sauyd . . . for thy gret peyn haue mercy on my lityl peyne' (ch. 56, p. 137, lines 29–34). She increasingly goes back to the Passion and identifies her particular imitation of Christ: 'Þe sayd creatur had gret bodily sekenes, ȝet þe Passyon of owr merciful Lord Crist Ihesu wrowt so in hir sowle þat for þe tyme sche felt not hir owyn sekenes but wept & sobbyd in þe mend of owr Lordys Passyon' (ch. 56, p. 138, lines 15–19).

This experiential knowledge of the Passion acquired through physical pain echoes Julian's theology of the Incarnation – her teaching on the redemption of our sensuality. In the Long Text Julian deliberates over the whole dimension of

32 See BMK, ch. 47, p. 113.
33 Cf. Matthew 10:19–20.

sin and pain governed by God's intention of redemption. As she wrestles to articulate the insight that human physicality or sensuality is central to the Incarnation, her psychological understanding of the Passion is deepened. She argues that 'in our substance we arn full, and in our sensualite we faylyn; which faylyng God will restore and fulfill be werkyng mercy and grace plentiously flowand into us of his owne kynd godhede' (LT, ch. 57, p. 91). By accepting the limitations of life in this world of flesh, we are sharing in the Passion of Christ and being restored through the grace of God. Through this psychological process Julian becomes aware that the misery of sensuality can be transformed into joy through the Passion and that this awareness of transcendent love is a part of eternal bliss.[34] Living in this world in the flesh is necessary because it is the way that we learn the meaning of the Passion through bodily identification with Christ Incarnate: 'for all mankynd that shal be savid be the swete incarnation and blisful passion of Criste, al is the manhood of Criste' (LT, ch. 51, p. 79). By undergoing a similar psychological process as Julian did, Margery penetrates the meaning of the Incarnation.

Significantly, in the darkest period of her life, God reveals to Margery that through these ordeals, she is following the true way to heaven:

> 'Dowtyr, I must nedys comfortyn þe, for now þu hast þe ryth wey to Heuyn. Be þis wey cam I to Heuyn & alle my disciplys, for now þu xalt knowe þe bettyr what sorwe & schame I suffyrd for thy lofe, and þu schalt haue þe mor compassyon whan þu thynkyst on my Passyon'. (ch. 63, p. 156, lines 9–14)

After this revelation, when she has fled from the accusations by her fellow Christians into the Prior's chapel in Lynn, Margery has an intensified recollection of the Passion and of the suffering mother, which causes her to say in her crying, ' "Lord, I am not þi modir. Take a-wey þis peyn fro me, for I may not beryn it. Þi Passyon wil sle me" ' (ch. 67, p. 164, lines 25–7). Her compassion for the suffering of Christ increases and she responds deeply to the Good Friday preaching: 'Ihesu is ded' (ch. 69, p. 167, line 18). She is rescued from spiritual suffering by meditating on the Passion.

However, her spiritual crisis comes when she starts to doubt the counsel of God, when he reveals to her the fate of the damned souls.[35] God blames her for not believing his secret counsels, which he confides to her out of his high mercy for her. Then he chastises her by sending a sexual temptation: the abhominable sights that threaten her chastity make her suspect God has forsaken her.[36] She believes some evil spirit is deceiving her. Then, for her forwardness and her unbe-

[34] For Julian's doctrine of substance and sensuality, see LT, ch. 54, pp. 86–7. Tugwell argues that 'sensuality means our whole life, as lived within the terms of the body, the terms of this world'. See Simon Tugwell, *Ways of Imperfection: An Exploration of Christian Spirituality* (London, 1984), p. 197.

[35] Margery mentions in chapter 23 that her revelations of the damnation of souls drove her to the verge of fear and despair. See BMK, pp. 54–5.

[36] See BMK, ch. 59, pp. 144–5. Cf. Rosalynn Voaden, 'Beholding Men's Members: The Sexualizing of Transgression in *The Book of Margery Kempe*', in *Medieval Theology*

lief, God withdraws all good thoughts and contemplation. Margery learns only later that the Devil had deluded her and caused her almost to fall into despair. She is in the hell of disbelief until a good angel comes to tell her that God has chastised her for her disbelief. Her response is simple, but it conveys her internal progress: she submits herself, saying: 'Lord, now wyl I lyn stille & be buxom to þi wille' (ch. 59, p. 146, line 32).

This experience of doubt and delusion is similar to Julian's experience of a devil tempting her to doubt her revelations. In chapter 69, Julian recounts the return of the Devil, but she is delivered by thinking of Christ's Passion.[37] The Devil embodies 'the psychological forces which run counter to the dynamic of love – impatience and despair' and ultimately a sense of the devil undermines the skilful balance that is indispensable for discretion.[38] Temptation by the Devil paradoxically enables both Margery and Julian to banish the Devil from their souls, and we learn that the experience of temptation, however painful, is necessary because it is a prerequisite to embracing what Julian describes as the working of the Holy Spirit:[39]

> He is not abil for the time to perceivyn the soft comfort of the Holy Gost till he have vnderstonding of this drede of peyne, of bodily deth and of gostly enemyes. And this drede stirrith us to seken comfort and mercy of God; and thus this drede helpith us to sekyn comfort and mercy of God and abileth us to have contrition be the blisfull touching of the Holy Gost. (LT, ch. 74, pp. 118–19)

The following chapters show that the ordeals Margery suffered are actually steps by which she develops spiritually. She increases in contrition, in holy dread of God, and in the knowledge of her own frailty – all of which are gifts of the Holy Spirit.[40] Significantly, Margery recounts in chapter 72 that her mind and thoughts are attuned to God's inward presence by the process of time and that these ordeals transformed her vision of human life: she now sees Christ in and through every human situation she encounters:

> So be processe of tyme hir mende & hir thowt was so ioynyd to God þat sche neuyr forgate hym but contynualy had mende of hym & behelde hym in alle creaturys. & euyr þe mor þat sche encresyd in lofe & in deuocyon, þe mor sche encresyd in sorwe & in contrycyon. (ch. 72, p. 172, lines 11–15)

Her compassion culminates in her imitation of St Francis when she kisses the lepers. Her spiritual power is now being used to help her fellow humans. In this

and the Natural Body, ed. Peter Biller and A. J. Minnis, York Studies in Medieval Theology I (Woodbridge, 1997), pp. 175–90 at pp. 175–6.

37 LT, ch. 69, pp. 111–12. Cf. Marion Glasscoe, *English Medieval Mystics: Games of Faith* (London, 1993), p. 302.

38 Glasscoe, *English Medieval Mystics*, p. 259.

39 Hilton also argues that 'God allows those whom he chooses to be wearied and tempted, and afterward he comforts them and makes them secure in grace'. See Walter Hilton, *The Scale of Perfection*, trans. John P. H. Clark and Rosemary Dorward (New York, 1991), I, ch. 39, p. 109.

40 See BMK, ch. 72, p. 172.

period Margery helps the woman with post-partum insanity, just as Jesus had rescued her.[41] But the summit of her loving charity is attained in her reunion with her senile husband. Her spiritual growth enables her to see Christ in her husband, although her clumsy obsession with sexual sin within marriage still overshadows the way she recounts the event. But she helps her sick husband, saying 'for þi mercy grawnt me grace to obeyn þi wil & fulfille þi wil & late neuyr my gostly enmys han no powyr to lett me fro fulfillyng of þi wil' (ch. 76, p. 180, lines 34–6). Margery now serves him as if she were serving Christ.[42]

This transformed state of mind finally ushers in the long discourse of Christ in chapter 77, in which natural order in the creation of God is discussed in the context of the traditional attributes of the persons of the Trinity: Godhead as might and creating force, the Second Person as wisdom, and the Holy Spirit as love. Christ expounds the natural order in which the planets and other natural phenomena are obedient to his will:

> Dowtyr, þu seist how þe planetys ar buxom to my wil, þat sum-tyme þer cum gret thundirkrakkys & makyn þe pepil ful sor a-feerd. And sumtyme, dowtyr, þu seest how I sende gret leuenys þat brennyn chirchys & howsys . . . I fare wyth þe myth of my Godheed; it may not be seyn wyth mannys eye, & ȝyt it may wel be felt in a sympil sowle wher <me> likyth to werkyn grace, as I do in þi sowle. &, as sodeynly as þe leuyn comith fro Heuyn, so sodeynly come I in-to thy sowle, & illumyn it wyth þe lyght of grace & of vndir-standyng, & sett it al on fyr wyth lofe, & make þe fyr of lofe to brenn þerin & purgyn it ful clene fro alle erdly filth.
>
> (ch. 77, p. 182, lines 11–15 and 19–27)

Christ's discourse on the Trinity is illuminated by traditional Augustinian theology, which appropriates the characteristics of the Uncreated Trinity of Father, Son, and the Holy Spirit to Power, Wisdom and Goodness respectively:[43] Christ tells Margery that he would manifest the might of his Godhead, causing an earthquake that arouses fear in her. But suddenly he comes into her soul and illumines it with the light of grace and understanding. This is the perfect charity that God gives to her. The wisdom of the second person is known to Margery by virtue of her renewed understanding, which is enabled by the love of the Holy Spirit. The Holy Spirit also makes the fire of love burn inside her soul and purges

[41] Margery recounts that the woman beholds many fair angels round her. This might suggest that Margery has increased confidence in divine protection. See BMK, ch. 75, pp. 177–9.

[42] See BMK, ch. 76, p. 181, lines 9–15.

[43] See Clark, 'Trinitarian Theology', p. 125. The Long Text constantly alludes to two triads: that of the human memory, reason and will on the one hand and, on the other, that of the traditional attributes of the persons of the Trinity – might, wisdom and love. See Nicholas Watson, 'The Trinitarian Hermeneutic in Julian of Norwich's *Revelation of Love*', in *MMT* V, pp. 79–100 at pp. 97–8. Bridget's revelations about the Trinity elucidate Christ's discourse on that subject, although they are grounded on more subtle and sophisticated implications. See *The Liber Celestis of St Bridget of Sweden: The Middle English Version in British Library MS Claudius Bi, Together with a Life of the Saint from the Same Manuscript*, vol. I, ed. Roger Ellis, EETS OS CCXCI (Oxford, 1987), Bk I, ch. 50, p. 91, lines 7–8 and Bk III, ch. 26, p. 234, lines 21–8.

it clean from all earthly filth, thus preparing it to receive divine illumination. Despite her lack of intellectual vocabulary, Margery absorbed the theology of the Trinity and deepened her understanding of the love of the Trinity.

Furthermore, in her unbidden tears and cries, Margery feels the force of a power operative in the universe – the working of God, to which she must submit her whole being in obedience. As she is further illumined, God reveals to her five tokens that are known only to chosen souls and assures her that he resides in her soul. She responds to God with obedience which leads her closer to contemplative experience: 'I wolde, Lord, for þi lofe be leyd nakyd on an hyrdil, alle men to wonderyn on me for þi loue . . . ȝyf þu wer plesyd þerby & no mannys sowle hyndryd, þi wil mote be fulfillyd & not myn' (ch. 77, p. 184, lines 19–25). She is spiritually mature enough now to receive the gift of the Holy Spirit in her total surrender to the will of God. It is at this stage that Margery describes herself as a mature recipient of the grace of God. Chapter 83 relates both outward and inward evidence for *discretio*. Two priests take her to a church in the fields to find whether she is an attention-seeking hypocrite, only to learn that she cries as loudly when away from people as when among them. The experience of having her behaviour tested increases her trust in God, leading her to feel that her crying greatly profits the merit of those who trust her. Ultimately, faith in divine love, the crucial internal criterion of *discretio*, is firmly established in her transformed mind. She is certain that Christ, not the devil, visited her, for 'sche lakkyd no grace but whan sche dowtyd er mistrostyd þe goodnes of God, supposyng er dredyng þat it was þe wyle of hir gostly enmy to enformyn hir er techyn hir oþerwyse þan wer to hir gostly hele' (ch. 83, p. 201, lines 14–17).

In the Long Text Julian explores how 'the essential moral dynamism of the christian life is vested in faith, which flows from our substance into our sensuality'[44] and argues that, through the work of the Holy Spirit, faith is the source of all the soul's virtues:

> And our feith is a vertue that comith of our kynd substance into our sensual soule be the Holy Gost, in which al our vertuys comith to us – for without that no man may receive vertue – for it is not ell but a rythe vnderstondyng with trew beleve and sekir troste of our beyng that we arn in God, and God in us, which we se not . . . Crists mercifull werking is in us, and we graciosly accordand to him throw the gefts and the vertues of the Holy Gost. (LT, ch. 54, p. 87)[45]

Noticeably, Margery begins increasingly to express the counsel of God with the vocabulary of contemplative experience:

> Whan sche beleuyd þat it was God & no euyl spiryt þat ȝaf hir so mech | grace of deuocyon, contricyon, & holy contemplacyon, þan had sche so many holy thowtys, holy spechys, and dalyawns in hir sowle techyng hir how sche xulde louyn God, how sche xulde worschepyn hym & seruyn hym . . . it weryn so hy abouyn hir bodily wittys þat sche myth neuyr expressyn hem wyth hir bodily tunge liche as sche felt hem. (ch. 83, p. 201, lines 28–33 and 36–8)

44 Tugwell, *Ways of Imperfection*, p. 199.
45 See also LT, ch. 57, p. 92.

Arguably, part of her spiritual transformation is seen in this abstract description of her inner state of mind. She recounts that her understanding becomes more enlightened as the boisterous vocal crying diminishes without her ceasing to receive the gift of tears.[46] She is coming closer to contemplative *unitas*.

Her total trust in the work of the Holy Spirit culminates in her image of each person of the Trinity sitting on a cushion in her soul.[47] This image signifies that the human soul is God's true dwelling place. Significantly, Margery sees this image at the stage at which she feels that she now has a true faith and that God acknowledges her for her obedience to the working of his will in her: 'I sitte in þin hert & knowe euery thowt þat is þerin, boþe good & ylle, & þat I parceyue þe lest thynkyng and twynkelyng of thyn eye' (ch. 77, p. 184, lines 12–14). The same image is vividly illustrated in Julian's sixteenth revelation, in which she sees the glorious city of the soul. She understands that the soul finds rest in none but God, whose seat is in the soul, and who rules all things:

> And than our lord opened my gostly eye and shewid me my soule in midds of my herte . . . He sitteth in the soule even ryte in peace and rest. And the Godhede ruleth and gemeth hevyn and erth and all that is; sovereyn myte, sovereyn wisedom, and sovereyn goodnes. The place that Iesus takith in our soule, he shal never removen it without end as to my syte; for in us is his homliest home and his endles wonyng.
> (LT, ch. 67, pp. 109–10)

Furthermore, Julian links this vision with a sense of confidence and security of mind attained by her conviction that it was God who had shown her all she had seen previously:

> And this was a singlar ioy and bliss to me that I saw him sitten; for the sekirnes of sitting shewith endles dwelling. And he gave me knowing sothfastly that it was he that shewid me al aforn . . . [he said]: 'Wete it now wele that it was no raveing that thou saw today . . . troste thou therto, and thou shalt not be overcome' . . . And ryte as in the first worde that our good lord shewid, menyng his blissfull passion – 'Herwith is the devill overcome' – ryte so he seid in the last word with full trew sekirness, menand us all: 'Thou shalt not ben overcommen'.
> (LT, ch. 68, pp. 110–11)[48]

Margery echoes the sense of confidence that Julian feels. Margery's description of her spiritual manner at the end of Book One shows that she is learning *discretio* as she is transfigured in the course of spiritual pursuit:

> It [dalyawnce] wil be had but in gret qwyet of sowle thorw long excersyse. Of þis maner speche and dalyawnce sche was mad mythy & strong in þe lofe of owr Lord & gretly stabelyd in hir feith & encresyd in mekenes & charite wyth oþer good vertuys. & sche stabely & stedfastly beleuyd þat it was God þat spak in hir sowle & non euyl spiryt, for in hys speche sche had most strength & most comfort & most encresyng of vertu. (ch. 87, p. 214–15, lines 34–6/1–6)

46 See BMK, ch. 85, p. 209.

47 See BMK, ch. 86, pp. 210–11.

48 Julian argues that God's presence in our soul produces wonderful certainty when there is true faith, and gives us hope and an awe that is sweet and delightful. See LT, ch. 65, pp. 106–7.

Julian was an expert in *discretio spirituum*, the sense of which was sharpened by her intellectual and spiritual growth. Through Julian's illuminating counsel Margery gains a new kind of knowledge of God and learns *discretio spirituum*, as she is psychologically repaired in an interior realisation of the love of God and transformed into a new awareness of the meaning of redemption. Margery discerns the working of the Trinity in her and increases her faith in 'a redemption of this life, not a redemption *from* it'.[49]

49 Tugwell, *Ways of Imperfection*, p. 201.

* I am grateful to Dr Denise N. Baker for reading and commenting on an earlier draft of this paper.

‘THISELF A CROS TO THISELF’: CHRIST AS *SIGNUM IMPRESSUM* IN THE *CLOUD*-TEXTS AGAINST THE BACKGROUND OF EXPRESSIONISTIC CHRISTOLOGY IN LATE MEDIEVAL DEVOTIONAL THEOLOGY

KARL HEINZ STEINMETZ

Introduction

IT IS ALMOST SUPERFLUOUS to mention the fact that according to Christian self-understanding the person of Christ plays a key-role in any form of Christian spirituality and mysticism. Hence recent research on the Christology of the anonymous Middle English *Cloud*-texts,[1] which we presume were written in the last decades of the fourteenth century by a Carthusian author,[2] had no problems demonstrating Christ’s presence in the *Cloud*-corpus.[3] Nonetheless, such an initial reflection raises as many questions as it answers – and these questions deserve a detailed investigation. After all, between the extremes of Arianism, the exaggeration of the human aspect of Christ, and of Monophysitism, a certain form of neglecting the human dimension of Christ, there is a broad spectrum of possible orthodox Christologies. Furthermore, the life of Christ itself contains a richness of different episodes such as the Incarnation, the preaching and ministry in Palestine, the Passion and Crucifixion in Jerusalem, the Resurrection and Ascension. Finally, the Middle Ages witnessed many ways of imitating Christ such as pastoral work, meditation, contemplation, almsgiving, ascetic life, flagellation and so on. It seems desirable then to go beyond previous studies, to determine more precisely the character and the function of the mystical Christology of the *Cloud*-author and to highlight its emphases against the background of various Christologies in the fourteenth century. This essay considers the Christology of the *Cloud*-corpus from the perspective of the History of Theology. Such a perspective tries to take seriously the theological claims made by the *Cloud*-author himself, with the conviction that such claims can only be interpreted when deciphered in their historical context.

1 The edition used in this essay is *The Cloud of Unknowing and Related Treatises on Contemplative Prayer*, ed. P. Hodgson, Analecta Cartusiana III (Salzburg, 1982). All references are by abbreviated title, page and line number in this edition.

2 For a discussion of the identity of the author see *The Cloud of Unknowing*, pp. ix–xii, with further literature.

3 See P. F. O’Connell, ‘The Person and Work of Christ in “The Cloud of Unknowing” ’, *Contemplative Review* xiv/2 (1981), pp. 1–9; xiv/3 (1981), pp. 15–21 and W. Johnston, *The Mysticsm of ‘The Cloud of Unknowing’: A Modern Interpretation*, Religious Experience VIII (St Meinrad, Ind., 1975), pp. 67–79.

Theology of Meditation: A rather chaste beholding of Christ

The proper starting-point for a theology of prayer is anthropology. According to Genesis 1:26 every human being is a wonderful image of God. Augustine draws rather complex conclusions from this simple sentence: since God is a Trinitarian God every human being is an image of this Trinity. Hence, analogous to the procession of the divine Son and the Holy Spirit from the divine Father is a procession from the depth and midst of the human person (*mens*), the theoretical mind (*intellectus*) and the practical mind (*affectus*). This Augustinian psychology is the common ground on which different vernacular authors build their Middle English terminology, such as the well-known tripartite expression *mynde-witte(reson)-wille*.[4] Furthermore, most Middle English authors are influenced by Richard of St Victor's *Beniamin minor* when they speak of the sub-organ of *imaginacioun*.[5] Due to the Christological focus of this investigation there can be no detailed discussion of Middle English terminology here. So a brief summary will suffice. *Mynde* is the centre of human personality, the depth of the mind, where the theoretical and practical mind have their root. *Witte*/*reson* is the organ of the theoretical mind, an inner eye so to speak, which can grasp the form and structure of an object of knowledge and imprint it as a mental concept on the mind. Under normal conditions knowledge can only be achieved within a structure of images and pictures; therefore the *witte* uses the sub-organ of *imaginacioun* for this imaginative dimension. *Wille* or *affeccioun* is the organ of the practical mind, the power of the soul, which can produce an act of will to strive for a worthy object and to acknowledge and enjoy its goodness.[6]

If a human being tries to approach God, s/he has to turn both the theoretical mind, the *witte* with *knowyng*, *seeyng*, *imaginacioun*, *beholdyng* and *thynkyng*, and the practical mind, the *wille* with *affeccioun*, *entent*, *felyng*, *lovyng*, *listyng*, *steryng* and *tastyng*,[7] to God and to the mirror of Holy Scripture, in which God is present.[8] The mystics-to-be must work with their theoretical and practical mind

4 On the Augustinian background see M. Schmaus, *Die psychologische Trinitaetslehre des heiligen Augustinus*, Muensterische Beitraege zur Theologie XI (Muenster, 1976), pp. 235–81 with a detailed discussion of the Augustinian sources. On *mynde-witte-wille* in the *Cloud*-corpus see for instance Pr. 104/12; Cl. 9/14, 9/33–4, 25/38–9, 44/8, 64/7–8, 64/17 and B. M. 129/4.

5 For a discussion of the imagination in the *Cloud*-corpus and for more literature on this topic see D. Renevey, ' "See by Ensaumple". Images and Imagination in the Writings of the Author of The Cloud of Unknowing', *Micrologus* vi (1998), pp. 225–43.

6 For a detailed account see the doctoral thesis (in print) of K. H. Steinmetz, 'Affectus non affectuosus. Mystische Erfahrung und mystisches Wissen in den mittelenglischen Cloud-Texten', Doctoral Thesis of Ludwig-Maximilians-University (Munich, 2002), pp. 27–39.

7 See Steinmetz, 'Affectus non affectuosus', pp. 36–9.

8 See Cl. 39/37–40/13 as a creative adoption of a passage from Gregory's *Moralia in Iob* 2.1.1, ed. M. Adriaen, Corpus Christianorum Latinorum CXLIIIA (Turnhout, 1979), p. 59.

intensively on the Holy Scripture through *lectio-meditatio-oratio-contemplatio*: the praying person has first to read the text aloud (*redyng*), second to digest the text with both organs in order to be nourished by it (*thynking*) and third to respond to the claims of the Holy Scripture by saying prayers (*preying*).[9] Only after such preparatory exercises can the praying person turn the mind directly to God in order to touch Him and even to reach mystical union.

More support for such a view into the mirror of Holy Scripture and such a beholding of Christ can be gained from the middle part of *Privy Counsel*, where the anonymous author explains John 10:9–10 in a way that recalls parallel passages in Bonaventure's *Itinerarium mentis* or the Pseudo-Augustinian *Liber de spiritu et anima*: God has revealed himself in an unsurpassable manner in Jesus Christ. If a person focuses on Christ as presented in Holy Scripture, he or she will find the visible Christ as the entrance and door through which one can approach God. Such a turn to the visible Christ, though, cannot be regarded as the highest form of communication with God. Since God revealed himself as God in Jesus Christ, the humanity of Christ is only the door to God. In order to really attain God one must walk through the door, cross the threshold and then proceed to the Godhead, by which Christ is sitting, so to speak, behind the door as porter.[10] Such a Christological reflection, demonstrating Christ's revelatory function and Christ's humanity as the medium of his Divinity, is not uncommon in Middle English texts and can also be found in Walter Hilton's *Scale of Perfection*.[11]

Admittedly such an abstract formula is not really fitting for meditation; it has to be transformed into more accessible instruction as to how the approach to God can be performed. The ascent to God through Christ can be characterised as a passion-meditation with three different steps. The first apprehension of passion-meditation is the wretchedness of the human being and its function as a motivating principle of the divine love. The second perspective is the pain which Christ had to endure in his human nature during his cruel crucifixion. The third aspect is the salvific grace and atoning love of the divine nature of Christ.[12] Such a three-step meditation of the Passion is a standard component of medieval spiritual life and a central topic in the theology of prayer in the *Book of Margery Kempe*, to mention but one example.[13]

9 See P. C. 39/22–36 as a reinterpretation of Guigo's *Scala claustralium* 2, ed. E. Colledge and J. Walsh, Sources Chretiennes CLXIII (Paris, 1970), pp. 82–4.

10 This exegesis appears in P. C. 90/41–92/2. The standard theological background occurs in Bonaventure's *Itinerarium*, prologue 3, Opera Omnia V (Quaracchi, 1891), p. 295 and in *Itinerarium* 4.2, p. 306. Another possible source is the Pseudo-Augustine *De spiritu et anima* 9, PL XL, col. 785.

11 On the revealing function see *Scale of Perfection* 1.91, ed. T. Bestul (Kalamazoo, Mich., 2000), lines 2583–609.

12 This three-step meditation is summarised in P. C. 91/13–21.

13 On the role of the humanity and Deity see *Book of Margery Kempe* 35, ed. L. Staley (Kalamazoo, Mich., 1996), pp. 91–4. On the three steps see *Book of Margery Kempe* 85, pp. 195–7.

In the subsequent sentences in this chapter the *Cloud*-author illustrates the exclusiveness of Christ as the way to God and mentions the danger of pseudo-meditation by explaining the phrase 'qui vero non intrat per ostium sed assendit aliunde, ipse fur est et latro'. The *beholdyng of the passion of Criste* is the door through which a meditating person can attain God. But aside from true believers there are also robbers and thieves, prowling in the dark past the door in order to break in from elsewhere. The *Cloud*-author unfolds a creative interpretation of the two Latin terms *fur* and *latro*, that far exceeds in originality the comparable passage of Walter Hilton in his *Scale*.[14] The terms 'robber' and 'thief' stand for misled persons who produce pseudo-meditations through uncontrolled and scattered thinking ('wilde wantoun wittes'), perform quibbling investigations ('sotil seching') and practise over-picturesque imaginations ('fantastic worching'). Such a pseudo-meditating person is on the one hand a day-robber (equivalent to the Latin *latro*) since he or she imitates the highest steps of mysticism in order to impress other people, while not really entering the way of Christ. On the other hand he or she is a night-thief (equivalent to the Latin *fur*) because of the darkness of arrogance and the unwillingness to shape oneself according to the example of humble Christ.[15]

Another positive description of how to meditate on Christ can be found in the *Cloud*: in order to prepare oneself for contemplation one must first build a solid foundation of *goostly meditacioun*, *besy beholding* and *ymaginaciouns* of the centre of revelation.[16] The *Cloud*-author again introduces a three-step pattern of Christ-centred meditation and even adds the emotional attitude in which the meditating person should try to unlock the depth of the *mysteria Christi*: first comes the meditation of one's own *wrechidnes* with the attitude of *sorow* and *contricion*; second the *Passion of Criste* with the attitude of *pite* and *compassion*; third the *chiftes and joyes of heven*, *of oure Lady* and *of seintes and aungelles* with the attitude of *thankyng* and *preysing*.[17]

After this brief examination of the author's instructions for meditation a short evaluation is needed. Even if the *Cloud*-corpus has much in common with other vernacular works of religious instruction – for example the emphasis on *compassio* as the aim of meditation – a certain tendency stands out through which the *Cloud*-author holds a privileged position within the fourteenth-century theory of meditating on Christ. The *Cloud*-author consistently limits the focus of meditation to the inner saving and liberating effect of the Passion of Christ, to the atoning and salvific love of Christ, not allowing any colourful image, any detailed illustration or

14 See the topic of the 'gate and entré to contemplacioun' in *Scale of Perfection* 2.27, lines 1617–774.

15 On this creative exegesis see P. C. 91/25–92/2.

16 For the terms *meditacion*, *ymaginacion* and *beholding* see also Cl. 17/26; Cl. 29/35; P. C. 90/13; P. C. 90/31 and P. C. 91/13.

17 Relevant passages for this three-step pattern appear in Cl. 16/15–16; 17/26–30; 21/27–8; 29/35–7; P. C. 90/13–15 and 91/13–24.

picturesque allegory of the passion-scene or the life of Christ. The specific position of the *Cloud*-author becomes very clear when we read the texts against the background of the mainstream Christology between the twelfth and fourteenth centuries. Medieval Christology very often presents the life of Christ and his human nature in user-friendly images and pictures ready for meditation.[18] Bernard of Clairvaux, for example, concluded from the fact of the Incarnation that meditation had to start at the level of the *humanitas Christi* in order to grow from a sensible love to the spiritual love of *amor castus*, and he offers examples of how to meditate on the humanity of Christ.[19] Aelred of Rievaulx insisted, far more than Bernard, on the importance of constantly meditating on the humanity of Christ; he embedded this meditation of the humanity into anchoritic spirituality and thus fertilised English devotional theology.[20] In his *Summa theologiae*, Thomas Aquinas went through each stage of the life of Christ, the *mysteria vitae Christi*, in order to demonstrate in an exemplary mode the relevance of the *humanitas Christi*. In his work *Lignum vitae* Bonaventure offered carefully worked-out examples of how to meditate on the life of Christ.[21] The Pseudo-Bonaventure *Meditationes vitae Christi* gained popularity and were translated into Middle English at the beginning of the fifteenth century by Nicholas Love under the title *Mirror of the Blessed Life*.[22] *Stimulus amoris*, another Pseudo-Bonaventure work written by James of Milan, was translated into the vernacular (probably) by Walter Hilton and stimulated English devotional theology.[23]

[18] See É. Ledeur, 'Imitation du Christ II. Tradition spirituelle', *Dict. spir.* VII/2 (1971), pp. 1562–87 and J. Hourlier, 'Humanité du Christ II. Chez les spirituels médiévaux', *Dict. spir.* VII/1 (1969), pp. 1053–63.

[19] On the Christology and Passiology of Bernard see W. Baier, *Untersuchungen zu den Passionsbetrachtungen in der 'Vita Christi' des Ludolf von Sachsens. Eine Quellenkritischer Beitrag zu Leben und Werk Ludolfs und zur Geschichte der Passionstheologie*, vol. II, Analecta Cartusiana XLIV/2 (Salzburg, 1977), pp. 238–45. On the relevance of Bernard for devotional theology in England see C. Atkinson, *Mystic and Pilgrim: The Book and the World of Margery Kempe* (London, 1983), pp. 137–8; G. Constable, 'The Popularity of Twelfth-Century Spiritual Writers in the Late Middle Ages', *Renaissance Studies in Honour of Hans Baron*, ed. A. Molho and J. A. Tedeschi (Florenz, 1971), pp. 3–28 and A. Louth, 'Bernard and Affective Mysticsm', *The Influence of St Bernard*, ed. B. Ward (Oxford, 1976), pp. 2–10.

[20] On Aelred see Atkinson, *Mystic and Pilgrim*, pp. 134–7; Baier, *Untersuchungen*, pp. 218–20; G. Mursell, *English Spirituality: From Earliest Times to 1700* (Louisville, 2001), p. 193.

[21] Aquinas, *Summa Theologiae* III qq. 35–59, Ed. Paulinae (Milan, 1988), pp. 2033–160. Bonaventure, *Lignum Vitae*, Opera Omnia VIII (Quaracchi, 1902), pp. 68–87.

[22] For further information on the *Meditationes* see Baier, *Untersuchungen*, pp. 325–9. The vernacular text of Nicholas Love is published as *The Mirrour of the Blessed Lyf of Jesu Christ*, ed. J. Hogg and L. F. Powell, 3 vols, Analecta Cartusiana XCI/1–3 (Salzburg, 1989–95). For some further hints see E. Salter, *Nicholas Love's 'Myrrour of the Blessed Lyf of Jesu Christ'*, Analecta Cartusiana X (Salzburg 1974), pp. 55–118.

[23] The text of James of Milan is published as *Stimulus amoris*, Bibliotheca Franciscana Ascetica IV (Quaracchi, 1949); the vernacular version as *The Prickynge of Love*, ed. H. J. Kane, Elizabethan and Renaissance Studies XCII:10 (Salzburg, 1983). For further information see Baier, *Untersuchungen*, pp. 374–5.

The most famous source for meditation, literature and the arts in the later Middle Ages, though, was certainly Ludolf of Saxony's *De vita Christi*.[24]

Devotional theology in fourteenth- and fifteenth-century England adopts such stimulating patterns to a large extent: the focus on the humanity of Christ is present in sermons, spiritual instructions, mystery plays, lyrics, book-illustration, altarpieces, stained glass and frescos, which deal with the visible aspects of Incarnation, Resurrection, Ascension and above all the Passion of Christ.[25] The stimulating patterns of classical Latin Christology stand behind the passion-portraits in the vernacular texts of Richard Rolle, Edmund of Abingdon, Walter Hilton, Julian of Norwich and Margery Kempe.[26] They occur in William Langland's lively description of Christ as a noble and brave knight[27] or in Henry of Lancaster's invitation to adore the child Jesus.[28]

Little of this can be found in the *Cloud* group; there are no detailed portraits of the humanity of Christ. The *Cloud*-author neither shows the Nativity nor mentions the stations of the cross. There is no scene of the Crucified One with Mary and John standing beneath.[29] Furthermore, the anonymous author seems to quickly pass over a spirituality of emotional compassion. In his *Cloud* the author anticipates the possible question of the reader about the value of deploring the Passion of Christ, of *weeping ful hertly*.[30] Such a deploring of the Passion is an important aspect of the spirituality of Margery Kempe; moreover, it can be called the central element of her piety, the practice she embraced most willingly, even when she incurred

24 The standard work for detailed information remains Baier, *Untersuchungen*.

25 On some aspects of this devotional theology see V. Gillespie, 'Strange Images of Death: The Passion in later medieval English devotional and mystical writing', *Zeit, Tod und Ewigkeit in der Renaissance-Literatur*, vol. I, ed. J. Hogg, Analecta Cartusiana CXVII:1 (Salzburg, 1987), pp. 111–59; Mursell, *English Spirituality*, pp. 188–91; J. W. Robinson, 'The Late Medieval Cult of Jesus and the Mystery Plays', *Proceedings of the Modern Language Association* lxxx (1968), pp. 508–14.

26 For Richard Rolle see '*Super Canticum Canticorum* from Ms. Trinity College Dublin 153', ed. E. M. Murray, unpublished diss. Fordham University (New York, 1958), p. 45, lines 5–24. For Edmund of Abingdon see *Speculum religiosorum and Speculum ecclesiae* 23, ed. H. P. Forshaw, Auctores Britannici medii aevi III (London, 1973), p. 91. For Walter Hilton see *Scale of Perfection* 1.35, lines 898–934. For Julian of Norwich see *The Shewings of Julian of Norwich. Long Text*, ed. G. R. Crampton (Kalamazoo, Mich., 1994), 4, lines 114–18; 7/241–55; 10/346–81; 12/473–80 and 16/589–614. For Margery see *Book of Margery Kempe*, 28–9, ed. Staley, pp. 74–80 and 73–82, pp. 167–89. On the cross in the writings of Richard Rolle and in *Piers Plowman* see A. V. C. Schmidt, *The Treatment of Crucifixion in Piers Plowman and in Rolle's Meditations on the Passion*, Analecta Cartusiana XXXII:2 (Salzburg, 1983).

27 For more information see J. A. Alford, ed., *A Companion to Piers Plowman* (Berkeley, 1988), pp. 53–5.

28 This adoration of Henry of Lancaster occurs in *Le Livre de seyntz medicines*, ed. E. J. Arnould, Anglo-Norman Texts Society II (Oxford, 1967), pp. 34–5.

29 A standard account of the *imitatio Christi anglicana* is offered by R. Lovat, 'The Imitation of Christ in Late Medieval England', *Transactions of the Royal Historical Society* xviii (1968), pp. 97–121.

30 See Cl. 16/15–16.

suspicion and offence because of her uncontrollable outbursts of *weeping* and *sobbing*.[31] The *Cloud*-author neither discusses nor criticises this practice of *compassio affectiva* in detail, but tries to pass over quickly without touching it too much. The point he wants to impress upon the reader is almost the opposite of *compassio affectiva*: He is anxious about the non-imaginative, non-sensualistic and 'objective' character as the decisive factor of a valuable passion-meditation. He warns against a piety and devotion infected with *curiositas*. He opts for a 'chaste' and discrete meditation of Christ, for beholding Christ with *amor castus* and *discretio*, and without any *fantastic worchyng*.

This very tendency can also be found in the *Cloud*-author's reservation against the devotion of the Name of Jesus. Inspired by influential texts of Bernard of Clairvaux and Henry Suso authors like Richard Rolle propagated a devotion of the Name of Jesus.[32] In *devotio popularis* obviously even grosser forms of constant repetition of the Name of Christ came into practice. Hence, Walter Hilton is willing to defend a Devotion of the Name of Jesus as such, but at the same time he pronounces a severe warning against the over-enthusiastic use of the Name-of-Jesus-Prayer, leading to psychological projections, illusions and sensational dysfunctions.[33] Even more careful is the teaching of the *Cloud*-author: He does not forbid the devotion of the name of Christ, but he does not ascribe to this practice any deeper value regarding the higher steps of spiritual life, either.[34]

This 'chaste' Christology that we have encountered is not an invention of the *Cloud*-author but a distant echo of christological models developed centuries earlier: the three famous abbots of Cluny (Odo, Odilo and Hugo) as well as some theologians of the Gregorian reform argued for a chaste Christology, focusing on the *paupertas* and *nuditas* of Christ.[35] In contrast to the rich visualisation of Aelred of Rievaulx in some of his writings[36] the Carthusian Guigo I, for instance, opted for a remarkable soberness and temperance during the meditation of Christ's life.

31 See *Book of Margery Kempe* 57, ed. Staley, pp. 137–40 and 78–9, pp. 176–82. On the theological and sociological background see H. Weissman, 'Margery Kempe in Jerusalem. Hysteria compassio in the late Middle Ages', *Acts of Interpretation: The text and its context 700–1600. Essays in Honor of E. Talbot Donaldson*, ed. M. J. Carruthers and E. D. Kirk (Norman, Oklahoma, 1982), pp. 201–17.

32 See *Form of Living* 3–25, ed. S. J. Ogilvie-Thomson, EETS CCXCIII (London, 1988), p. 18, lines 610–25. For a brief summary see Mursell, *English Spirituality*, p. 191.

33 See *Scale of Perfection* 1.44, lines 1188–276. For further information see J. Catto, 'Religious change under Henry V', *Henry V: The practice of kingship*, ed. D. L. Harris (Oxford, 1985), pp. 97–115 at p. 109; H. E. Allen, *Writings Ascribed to Richard Rolle Hermit of Hampole and Materials for his Biography*, The Modern Language Association of America, Monograph Series III (New York, 1927), p. 72.

34 See Cl. 50/9–17.

35 See J. Leclercq, 'La christologie clunisienne au siècle de Saint Hugues', *Actes du Colloque scientifique international. Cluny Septembre 1988* (Cluny, 1990), pp. 523–35.

36 See M. L. Dutton, 'The Face and Feet of God: The Humanity of Christ in Bernard of Clairvaux and Aelred of Rievaulx', *Bernardus Magister: Papers presented at the Nonacentenary Celebration of the Birth of Saint Bernard*, ed. J. R. Sommerfeldt, Cistercian Studies CXXXV (Spencer, 1992), pp. 203–23.

According to Guigo the relevant point of meditation is the imitation of Christ's moral attitude and internal way of acting, which implies *caritas*, *patientia* and *amor castus*. Additional external pictures and 'experiences', let alone 'emotions', are more or less irrelevant.[37] The advice of the Carthusian Adam of Dryburgh is similar: the dwelling on the humanity of Christ is only a preparatory stage of contemplation to be abandoned at the higher ranks of spiritual life.[38] Such similarities or analogies do not enable us to specify the sources of the *Cloud*-author at this stage of analysis. Nevertheless, it is safe to say that the teaching of the *Cloud*-corpus on the meditation of Christ is reminiscent of the 'chaste' Christology developed by theologians of Cluny, of the Gregorian reform and of the anchoritic and monastic movement of the twelfth century. Because of its 'chaste pattern' the Christology of the *Cloud*-author differs significantly from the mainstream devotional theology of the fourteenth century.

There is one possible objection against our suggestion of an echo of 'chaste' Christology in the *Cloud*-texts: the absence of the visible Christ in meditation could just be the natural consequence of the obvious reception of the apophatic theology of Dionysius the Pseudo-Areopagite in the *Cloud*-corpus. The apophatic shift of the *Cloud*-author's theology is beyond question,[39] but is it really enough to explain the specific form of the Christology of the *Cloud*-texts? By a deeper investigation of the role of Christ in contemplation we will try to show that the 'presence of the visibly absent Christ' both in meditation and contemplation cannot be explained by apophatic theology alone but has to be understood as the result of a creative reinterpretation of 'chaste' Christology.

Theology of Contemplation: *Signum impressum* versus *signum expressivum*

Contemplation of the Godhead

There can be no detailed historical or systematic discussion of the term *contemplatio* here.[40] For our purpose it is sufficient to say that contemplation is the direct and immediate turn of the theoretical and practical mind, of *thinkyng* and *felyng*, to God in Jesus Christ, without using specific media – as opposed to meditation, which uses scriptural passages, pictures and imaginations a great deal. Most authors of devotional theology, however, do not draw a sharp distinction between meditation and contemplation. A good example of this tendency can be found in the *Book of*

[37] For a detailed discussion and a more complete account see B. Rieder, *Deus locum dabit. Studien zur Theologie des Kartaeuserpriors Guigo I (1083–1136)*, Veroeffentlichungen des Grabmann-Instituts, Neue Folge XLII (Paderborn, 1997), pp. 101–2.

[38] See *De Quadrapartito Exercitio Cellae,* PL CLIII, col. 831.

[39] For a detailed account see R. A. Lees, *The Negative Language of the Dionysian School of Mystical Theology. An Approach to the 'Cloud of Unknowing'*, Analecta Cartusiana CVII:1–2 (Salzburg, 1983).

[40] On contemplation in the *Cloud*-corpus and the theological background (Cassian, Augustine, Jerome, Bernard, the Victorines, Bonaventure and Hugh of Balma) see Steinmetz, 'Affectus non affectuosus', pp. 139–50.

Margery Kempe: meditation is the beholding of Christ's humanity, and so is contemplation, which is just a prolongation of meditation and a deeper and clearer beholding of Christ. Not only in meditation but also in contemplation Margery focuses on the humanity of Christ and in her contemplative visions she can see the whole *conversatio Christi in mundo*, from the nativity through the Passion to the Resurrection.[41] It is almost impossible to subdivide Margery's spiritual turn to God into distinct steps: reading Scripture, meditating, having a vision, talking with God and contemplating are only different grades of intensity within one life-long communication with God.

The *Cloud*-author, in contrast, does draw a very clear distinction between meditation and contemplation. Meditation is linked with the humanity of Christ whereas contemplation is completely decoupled from it. Real contemplation forgets the humanity and focuses on the Deity, as can be discerned from the story of Mary and Martha. Mary was not concerned about the needs of Christ, not attentive to the holy body of the Saviour and to the sweet voice and words of Jesus, but she was completely submerged in the abounding wisdom of Christ's Deity, hidden behind the dark words of his humanity.[42] When Mary fixed her awareness and her contemplative love on the *Deitas Christi*, she could penetrate the Cloud of Unknowing with her *affeccioun*. The lesson of contemplation according to the instruction of the *Cloud*-author is simple: the *fote of love* has to climb upwards, straight into the Cloud of Unknowing of the Deity of Christ. The *Cloud*-author's teaching of the *fote of love* is in marked contrast to a text like 'Doctrine of the Hert'. In this work of religious instruction the contemplative is taught to immerse his contemplative awareness completely in the Passion of Christ, that is to say, to plunge the mind into the blood and water flowing down from the Crucified and to make red the foot of love with Christ's precious blood.[43] The *Cloud*-author wants the foot of love rather penetrating the incomprehensibility of the Deity than being blood-red.[44]

Mystical Imitation of Christus nudus, crucifixus et ascensus

The middle part of the *Book of Privy Counsel* demonstrates the Christological dimension of contemplation in detail. The author mentions three decisive steps of Christ's life and works out their relevance for contemplation: first of *Christus nudus*,

41 See *Book of Margery Kempe* 28–29, ed. Staley, pp. 74–80 and 73–82, pp. 167–89.

42 See Cl. 26/8–27. For the theological background see also a parallel passage in Richard of St Victor's *Beniamin maior* 1.1, PL CXCVI, col. 65.

43 Oxford, Bodleian Library, MS Laud misc. 330, fol. 25v: 'drenche thin affecions and thi thouchtes in Christis passion consideryng both the shedyng of his blode and watir . . . wolde God that the fote of thin affecion were made rede in the licore of his precious blod'. For more background information see D. Renevey, 'L'imagerie des travaux ménagers dans The Doctrine of the Hert. Spiritualité affective et subjectivité', *Micrologus* xi (2003), pp. 519–54.

44 On the ascent with the foot of love and penetration of the incomprehensibility of God see Cl. 8/13; 8/16; 62/31–32. On the theological background see also V. Gillespie, 'Mystic's Foot: Rolle and Affectivity', *MMT* II, pp. 199–230.

the naked Christ; secondly of *Christus cucifixus*, the crucified Christ; and thirdly of *Christus ascensus*, the ascended Christ.

One decisive incident of Christ's life happened at the end of the *via crucis* and prior to the Crucifixion when Christ was deprived of his clothes. The historical fact has an inner spiritual meaning, which can be unlocked by exegesis. Being stripped is the outward expression of Christ's *kenosis* (i.e. Christ's self-giving and self-emptying love), his patience, his obedience to the divine Father and his mission. Patristic theology was deeply fascinated by *Christus nudus* and impressed upon all believers the demand of becoming naked in order to imitate the naked Christ. Jerome puts this theological thought into the well-known formula 'nudus Christum nudum sequi', calling everyone to the imitation of the naked Christ by becoming naked.[45] Throughout history this motto was interpreted in several ways: as the underlying principle of the anchoritic or monastic lifestyle during the Gregorian reform and in Cluny, as the ideal of the Cistercian way of life, of Franciscan poverty or of the lay-movement.[46] From early on such a theology of nudity, demonstrating the *kenosis* of Christ and the imitation of this *kenosis* in spiritual life, included key sentences from the letters of St Paul. Important traces of this theology of nudity can be found in the *Cloud*-texts, but they appear in a creative reinterpretation, emphasising the mystical stripping of contemplation.[47]

Every created being is not its own being but has its being as a gift from the divine Being. A created being as such is 'nothing', since it has its entire 'being' only through the mode of receiving itself from the divine Being.[48] Even if this metaphysical lesson seems to be rather difficult and complex the underlying simple ontological fact can be used as a bridge for the mystical union with God: if a praying person wants to find his or her own centre of personality, he or she just has to focus on the pure and naked being, the 'existing', the 'that-it-is' or 'being-here'.[49] Since this being is emanating from the divine Source by *creatio continua*, the contemplating person can 'follow' this 'flowing down' or 'receiving itself' back to the divine Source. Then, by focusing on the pure and naked divine

[45] This formula occurs in Jerome's *Homilia in Lucam Evangelistam* 16, ed. M. Morin, Corpus Christianorum Latinorum LXXVIII (Turnhout, 1958), p. 514. The same point is made in *Epistola* 125 *ad Rusticum* 20, ed. K. Hilberg, Corpus Scriptorum Ecclesiasticorum Latinorum LVI (Leipzig, 1918), p. 142. On the topic see also the passage in Hilton's *Scale of Perfection* 2.31, lines 2127–40.

[46] For a more complete treatment of this point see M. Bernards, 'Nudus nudum Christum sequi', *Wissenschaft und Weisheit* xiv (1951), pp. 148–51. The basic work on this topic remains J. Châtillon, 'Nudum Christum nudus sequere. Note sur les origines et la signification du thème de la nudité spirituelle dans les écrits de Saint Bonaventure', *S. Bonaventura 1274–1974. Vol. IV: Theologica* (Grottaferrata, 1974), pp. 719–71.

[47] The relevant passage is P. C. 88/39 – 90/7. For further insightful information see J. P. H. Clark, *The Cloud of Unknowing: An Introduction, Volume 3: Notes on 'The Book of Privy Counselling': Bibliography, References*, Analecta Cartusiana CXIX:6 (Salzburg, 1995), pp. 2–3 (annotations on 135/20–1).

[48] See P. C. 75/31–76/6.

[49] On the contemplation of one's own being see P. C. 77/36–7; 78/14–16; 78/38; 79/4; 79/26–7; 79/32–4; 80/30–2; 80/43–81/1; 81/20–1; 86/25–31 and 88/36–8.

Being a contemplating person can find mystical union, which is an ecstatic forgetting of one's own being, the abandoning of the 'separate' mind in order to reach the unified mind – thus being one with God.[50]

This way to mystical union can be illustrated by a theology of nudity. The first step of contemplation is the awareness of one's own *nakid beyng*. Within the awareness of one's own being God's being is present only as the hidden ground; it is wrapped, so to speak, into the beholding of one's own being. At the end of the way of the cross Christ was deprived of his clothing and stripped to nakedness. If a contemplating person really wants to follow Christ and reach the higher level of contemplation, he or she has to unwrap or unclothe the naked divine being from the wrapping of the awareness of one's own being. By this mystical stripping, the contemplating person can reach the naked awareness of the naked divine being, the abandoning of the separate mind in order to reach the unified mind in mystical union with God. By this mystical nudity the contemplating person can hope to be dressed with Christ himself, who is the 'ample garment of love and eternity'; that is to say, he or she can hope to be dressed with the mystical experience of unification with God.[51]

The way of the cross did not stop with the nudity of Christ but led to the Crucifixion. Hence, the teaching of the mystical stripping cannot be considered as the very centre of contemplation; it must be deepened to the mystical crucifixion. Here again the *Cloud*-author relies heavily on the theological tradition. In his *Itinerarium mentis* Bonaventure worked out in exemplary mode the Cross as the centre of contemplation: The way to mystical experience and to mystical union depends on the ardent love for the crucified, and only through the imitation of Christ is the passing-over from the world to the Father possible.[52] The contemplation of the cross, though, requires more than just looking upon or even staring at the cross as *signum expressivum*, as the visible sign expressing the *kenosis* of Christ; it demands the willingness of the praying person to take the cross personally as *signum impressum*, as an imprinted sign – as can be clearly seen in the stigmata of St Francis.[53]

Within the English writings of religious instruction the *signum crucis*, the sign of the cross, is omnipresent. Walter Hilton, for instance, demonstrates the opening of

[50] For a detailed discussion of contemplation in ontological perspective and its theological background (the creative reception of passages from Bernard of Clairvaux's *De consideratione* for instance) see Steinmetz, 'Affectus non affectuosus', pp. 151–60.

[51] See P. C. 89/8–22. For helpful background information see Clark, *Notes on 'The Book of Privy Counselling'*, pp. 46–7 (annotations on 156/13–15 to 156/24–5) and W. Riehle, *Studien zur englischen Mystik des Mittelalters unter besonderer Beruecksichtigung ihrer Metaphorik*, Anglistische Forschungen CXX (Heidelberg, 1977), pp. 93–6.

[52] The relevant passages are *Itinerarium* prologue 2, p. 295 and *Itinerarium* 7.6, p. 313.

[53] For the expression *expressiva et impressa* see *Hexaemeron* 22.23, Opera Omnia V (Quaracchi, 1891), p. 441. More insightful information appears in H. U. von Balthasar, *Herrlichkeit. Eine Theologische Aesthetik. Volume 3/1: Im Raum der Metaphysik, Teil 2: Neuzeit*, 2nd edn (Einsiedeln, 1965), pp. 277–9.

the spiritual eye to the cross, and the insight into its function as *signum expressivum* of Christ's *kenosis*, as the essential part of contemplation.[54] The visions of Julian of Norwich, just to mention another example, mainly refer to the *signum expressivum* of the cross. In her visions Julian can see the outward expression of Christ's *kenosis*, comprising the crown of thorns, the dripping blood, the wounds, the discoloured body, the horrible thirst of Christ and his dried-out flesh and skin.[55] And she understands the inner meaning of the exterior expression; she realises the underlying principle of the inner-trinitarian love, bridging all possible gaps in the world, even the gap of sin, in order to make all thing well. In the *Book of Margery Kempe* the vision of the cross and crucifixion appears as the midst of spirituality: *mulier pia* Margery can see all the details of the Passion and the Crucifixion as if it were through the eyes of the mother of God.[56]

In the writings of Walter Hilton, Julian of Norwich and Margery Kempe the *signum crucis impressum* is not excluded from the contemplation of the *signum expressivum* but included as its immanent aim: the beholding of the cross must lead to *compassio*, which then impresses the sign of the cross into the human person as *signum impressum*.[57] The mainstream instruction of contemplation, however, always unfolds the *signum crucis expressivum* into illustrative and imaginative passion-pictures.

Very little of this can be found in the *Cloud* group. The *Cloud*-author explains the traditional sentence of Matthew 16:24 'si quis vult venire post me, abneget semetipsum; tollat crucem suam et sequatur me' in order to work out the taking of the cross as the centre of contemplation,[58] a sentence that is a commonplace in Christian spirituality and appears, for example, in Walter Hilton's *Scale*.[59] The decisive and distinctive point of the *Cloud*-author's creative theological reflection, though, is his strong emphasis on the cross as *signum impressum*. Instead of offering the illustrative description of the Crucifixion that is present in almost every late medieval work of religious instruction, he offers a specific lesson of mystical self-crucifixion: in order to reach mystical union, the contemplating person has to learn first to forget the awareness of all created things and to focus on one's own naked being. But now, at a higher step of contemplation, the contemplative must learn to forget or to abandon even any form of self-awareness (*wetyng and felyng of thi being*).[60] But when the praying person really tries to abandon the self-awareness and the separate mind in order to reach the unified mind and the mystical awareness of God, the contemplative will realise the impossibility of overcoming

[54] See for instance *Scale of Perfection* 1.35, lines 898–934.

[55] On the passiology of Julian see *Shewings*, 4, ed. Crampton, lines 114–18; 7/241–55 and 12/473–80. For the discoloured body see 10/346–81. On the thirst and drying out see 16/589–614 and 17/615–65.

[56] See *Book of Margery Kempe* 78–80, ed. Staley, pp. 176–85.

[57] A fine example are the three prayers of Julian of Norwich in *Shewings*, 2, lines 48–71.

[58] See the carefully composed passage in P. C. 88/6–90/7.

[59] See *Scale of Perfection* 1.42, lines 1132–9.

[60] See P. C. 88/39–43.

self-awareness by one's own strength. The self-awareness stands against the contemplative, it lies between the mind and God, it is like a heavy and painful burden on the shoulders. The *Cloud*-author speaks of a total transformation of the whole person into a cross, of becoming *thiself a cros to thiself*.[61] This typos of self-crucifixion plays a key-role in Carthusian and early Cistercian Christology, in works of Guigo I and Nicholas of Clairvaux for example, which seems to be an interesting analogy, even if there is no proof of a direct relation of these sources to the *Cloud*-texts.[62]

With this lesson of self-crucifixion the *Cloud*-author holds a privileged position within English devotional theology and religious instruction: according to the teaching of the *Cloud*-author, contemplation is not so much a *contemplatio ut visio* of the *signum crucis expressivum*, such as plays an important role in the writings of Julian of Norwich, Margery Kempe and in the almost uncountable minor works of religious instruction, but mainly a *contemplatio ut passio* of the *signum crucis impressum*, a painful burden, so to speak, imposed on the shoulders of a contemplating person, when he or she tries to overcome the separate self-awareness in order to reach the unified awareness of mystical union. Since no human being can overcome self-awareness through one's own strength, the contemplative falls into a dramatic situation: the ascent to mount Sinai is transformed into the way of the cross to Golgotha, the contemplative prayer becomes a mystical crucifixion. The contemplative dwells in the Cloud of Unknowing, participating in the darkness of the Cross.

Christ died on the cross, rose from the dead and ascended into heaven. From the perspective of ascension it becomes obvious that the external beholding of the *humanitas Christi* cannot be considered as the highest form of communication with Christ. The real communication with God in Jesus Christ has to be the 'blind view of faith', focusing on the invisible. This is the lesson Augustine was concerned about, when he interpreted the biblical story of the Ascension of Christ. In his *Sermo 143* and in his *Commentary on the Gospel of St John*, Augustine demonstrated the spiritual meaning of *ascensio Domini*: in his Ascension Christ withdrew his bodily presence from men in order to teach them the ascent from the lower form of communication through *visio corporalis* to the higher form of communication through *fides*.[63] Based upon this exegesis, Bernard of Clairvaux built his *20th Sermon on the Song of Songs*: Christ ascended into heaven in order to signify the ascent from *amor carnalis* to *amor spiritualis*.[64] These theological patterns also fertilised devotional theology in England. In his *Scale* Walter Hilton explains the

61 See P. C. 89/23–90/7.

62 For Guigo I see *Epistula* 7.2, ed. G. Greshake, Fontes Christiani X (Freiburg, 1992), p. 149: 'Crucifixum crucifixus et ipse crucifigendis misistis'. For Nikolaus of Clairvaux see *Sermo in exaltatione crucis*, PL CXLIV, col. 762: 'Venis ad hominem crucifixum? Crucifixus venias aut crucifigendus.'

63 See *Sermo* 143.4, PL XXXVIII, col. 786. The same point is made in *In Epistolam Johannis ad Parthos Tractatus* 94.4–5, PL XXXV, col. 1869.

64 See *Sermones super Cantica Canticorum* 20.4–5, ed. J. Leclercq and H. M. Rochais, S. Bernardi Opera I–II (Rome 1957), pp. 117–21.

story of the Ascension exactly in Bernard's way, in the sense of an ascent from *amor carnalis* to *amor spiritualis*.[65] In *Privy Counsel* the *Cloud*-author takes the pattern both from Augustine and Bernard and draws conclusions for a theology of contemplation: the awareness of Christ's humanity with the help of imagination and the inner senses (*goostly wittes*) is only the minor level of prayer called meditation. By withdrawing his corporal presence in the Ascension Christ made clear what the perfection of contemplation implies: not a beholding of his humanity but a loving contemplative awareness of his Deity (*felyng and love of the Godheed*).[66] In the *Cloud* the anonymous author warns against misunderstanding *imitatio ascensionis* in a similar way: the imitation of Christ in contemplation does not require any visualisation. Imitation of the ascended Christ does not mean a *contemplatio ut visio*, a process of imagining the Ascension through the *goostly wittes* or a turning upwards of the psychological organs of *witte* and *wille*. This wrong contemplation would only lead to a dangerous 'contortion' of the contemplative mind.[67] The motto of real contemplation is simple: forget the external beholding of the humanity of Christ in order to strengthen the internal 'blind' awareness of the invisible Deity, the *felyng and love of the Godheed.*

Conclusion

The *Cloud*-texts offer a coherent theology of contemplation, even if the anonymous author does not develop a theological 'system' (which would be rather inappropriate for religious instruction). As demonstrated elsewhere, this theology of contemplation can be subdivided into different but nonetheless coherent and compatible perspectives, structuring the theological reflection: the ontological, psychological, christological, eschatological and spousal perspective.[68] The ontological and psychological perspectives rely heavily on the reception of the pseudo-Dionysian theology. This reception, however, is not sufficient to explain the Christology of the *Cloud*-corpus, since Christology is the weak point in pseudo-Dionysian theology. The Christology of the anonymous author can be summarised thus: as a baptised Christian a contemplative has to imitate the normative structure of the life of Christ. This structure of Christ's life is *kenotic*, finding its visible expression in the figures of *Christus nudus* and *Christus crucifixus*. This structure of *kenosis* is also normative for the approach to God: real contemplation means more than just visualising the life of Christ (*contemplatio ut visio*); it is the existential imitation of Christ's kenotic love

65 See *Scale of Perfection* 1.35–6, lines 898–957. A similar point can be found in 2.30, 2042–93.

66 See P. C. 98/8–24.

67 On the danger of the 'contortion' of the contemplative mind see Cl. 59/8–63/35.

68 See Steinmetz, 'Affectus non affectuosus', pp. 150 and 222–8 for a summary; pp. 151–60 on the ontological dimension; pp. 161–76 on the psychological perspective; pp. 177–83 on the christological aspect; pp. 184–90 on the eschatological perspective and pp. 191–4 on the spousal dimension.

(*contemplatio ut passio*). The proper object of such an ascending and kenotic contemplation, hence, can only be the presence of the visibly absent *Christus ascensus*.

This Christology seems to be the fruit of a creative reinterpretation of christological patterns developed within the Greek and Latin tradition: Greek church fathers like Irenaeus of Lyon, Clement of Alexandria and Origen propagated Christ in his function as teacher, *Christos didaskalos*, a concept that was introduced into Latin monasticism by Evagrius Ponticus, John Cassian and the father of Lérins, by the *Regula Magistri* and the *Regula Benedicti*. Latin authors such as Augustine, Gregory the Great and Jerome created the expression of Christ as master and example, *Christus ut magister et exemplum*. From the ninth century onwards various theological schools developed different styles of *Christos-Didaskalos*-Theology: The common ground for all of them is the rediscovery of the humanity of Christ. The Christology of Cluny, present in the works of Odo, Odilo and Hugo, is characterised by its focus on the poverty and the nudity of Christ. Cistercian Christology starts at the same point, but then tries to demonstrate how meditation on the humanity can incite an 'experiential' love in the heart of the praying person.[69] This experiential Christology can be found in the works of St Bernard, William of Saint-Thierry and especially in the writings of Aelred of Rievaulx; it is present in Bonaventure's works and in Franciscan piety; it is the source and starting-point for the mainstream devotional theology of the fourteenth and fifteenth centuries. But beside this experiential Christology there is also a small but nonetheless vivid tradition of chaste Christology, going back to Cassian, Jerome and Benedict, growing in Cluny and flourishing in the Christology of the Carthusian Guigo I. This tradition is distantly echoed in the *Cloud*-corpus in the form of a chaste Christology, that stands out by its interpretation of the humanity of Christ as pure transparency and perspicuity (as opposed to an 'object' of meditation and contemplation).

This result is certainly not strong enough to provide proof for the heavily discussed Carthusian provenance of the *Cloud*, since chaste Christology is not exclusively Carthusian. But this result is, first, cogent with this suggestion and secondly coherent with the *Cloud*-author's psychology, which contains a critique of the career-theology of fourteenth-century scholasticism as the outcome of the misled theoretical mind (*witte*/*reson*), of an over-picturesque *devotio popularis* as the result of an unruled imaginative mind (*imaginacioun*), and of an over-experiential mysticism as the offspring of an uncontrolled practical mind (*affeccioun*). And it can, thirdly, well explain why the *Cloud*-corpus did not fulfil the expectations of the late medieval audience: Richard Rolle's 'expressionistic spirituality' with inner sweetness and music was far more attractive for the mystics-to-be, whereas the teaching of the *Cloud*-author with the *signum impressum* of the cross and the motto *thiself a cros to thiself* faced some difficulties in finding a broader audience – as can be seen from the number of extant manuscripts.

69 'Experiential' here refers to *cognitio experimentalis*, which is the common technical term for 'religious experience' in medieval mysticism.

'THE PROPHETYCAL LYF OF AN HEREMYTE': ELIJAH AS THE MODEL OF THE CONTEMPLATIVE LIFE IN *THE BOOK OF THE FIRST MONKS*

VALERIE EDDEN

'You are at our shoulder, . . .
. . . cautioning us
to prepare not for the breathless journeys
into confusion, but for the stepping
aside through the invisible
veil that is about us into a state
not place of innocence and delight.'
(R. S. Thomas)[1]

> The ende of þe wyche lyf [þe relygyous lyf of an heremyte] is doble: on þe wych we getyn be the grace of God, helpynge be our labour and vertuows exercyse, and that is to offeryn to God an hooly herte and a clene fro actual fylthe of synne, wych ende we atteyne & neyhyn when we arn perfyth & in Caryth . . . Anothyr ende of thys lyf ys of þe clene ȝyfte of God ȝeven vnto vs, þat is for to seyne not alonly aftyr deth but now in thys dedly lyf sumwhat to tastyn in herte and prouyn in sowle þe vertu of þe presens of God and þe swetnesse of euerelastynge blysse. (II ii, fol. 50v)[2]

IN THIS WAY *The Book of the Institution of the First Monks*[3] describes the aims of the Carmelite life, proposing Elijah as the model of the spiritual life. The Carmelite life is presented as one of solitude, contemplative prayer, a life led to allow the best opportunity for experiencing fully the presence of God in this life.

> Wyth how much sekyrnes of mende, we, folwyng forme of thys conuersacyoun, mak redy a weye to owre Lord vnto owr hertys, not be novelteys takyn ne by veyn fabelys, but be þe fyrst exaumplys of al þe lyf of a monk apprevyd & þat we mak

1 R. S. Thomas , 'Wrong?', *No Truce with the Furies* (Newcastle-upon-Tyne, 1995), p. 26.

2 Quotations in Middle English are taken from Thomas Scrope's translation in London, Lambeth Palace Library MS 192. I am preparing an edition of this text for Middle English Texts. Quotations in Latin are taken from Paul Chandler, 'The Book of the First Monks', unpublished Ph. D. thesis, University of Toronto, 1991. Chandler is preparing an edition for publication.

3 'Institution' is an inadequate translation, as everyone who has worked on the text has pointed out. The Latin *Institutio* includes in its meaning not only 'foundation' but also 'discipline' and 'formation.'

> ryhtful patthys to owr God of comyng vnto vs, þat whan he comyth and callyth anon we may openyn vnto hym, þe quych seyth: 'Behold! I stand at þe dore & knokke'.
> (Fol. 49v, quoting Revelation 3:20)

In its almost exclusive use of the Elian model, the *Institution* differs from most medieval mystical writings, whose models of encountering God are more usually Moses, to whom God appeared in the burning bush and, later, hidden in a dense cloud on Sinai, Jacob with his dream of a ladder reaching up to heaven and the love of the bridegroom for the Shulamite woman in the Song of Songs. This focus on Elijah (first found in Carmelite writing in 1281)[4] is a way of reminding the order of its eremitic origins and of the prophetic role assigned in the scriptures to those voices crying in the wilderness and of showing how the Carmelites differed from the other orders. In so doing, it also goes some way towards defining a Carmelite spirituality.[5]

The *Institution*, a work linked to the name of Felip Ribot (d. 1391),[6] was translated into English in the second half of the fifteenth century by the Carmelite Thomas Scrope, who himself lived for a number of years in an anchor-cell near the entrance to Norwich friary.[7] Ribot claimed that the work was a compilation of ancient texts and ascribes Books I–VII to John forty-fourth Bishop of Jerusalem, claiming it was written in Greek in 412 and translated into Latin by Aimeric, patriarch of Antioch (1142–1196). Such a claim is clearly false,[8] though its recent editor, Paul Chandler, thinks that Book I may have been an earlier, independent work which Ribot incorporated.[9] Nonetheless it is hardly a pre-medieval text. The authenticity of the *Institution* is not relevant for our purpose, which is to consider it as a text in circulation and probably written in the later Middle Ages, one known and read in fifteenth-century East Anglia and seminal in the thought of both Teresa of Avila and John of the Cross. The main purpose of the *Institution* is polemic: to put the case for a continuous succession of monks on Carmel from Elijah until the Saracen incursions in the twelfth century and therefore to prove that the Carmelites were the most ancient of the fraternal orders and also that they had a unique relationship with their patron, Mary. It appears to be a response to the debate on the topic between John Hornby and Peter Stokes,[10] which took

4 In the 'Rubrica prima', *Medieval Carmelite Heritage: Early Reflections on the Nature of the Order*, ed. Adrianus Staring, Institutum Carmelitanum (Rome, 1989), p. 40.

5 For a discussion of Carmelite spirituality, see Valerie Edden, 'The Mantle of Elijah: Carmelite Spirituality in England in the Fourteenth Century', *MMT* VI, pp. 67–83.

6 See the article on Ribot by Paul Chandler in *Dict. spir.* XIII (1988), pp. 537–9.

7 For information on Scrope see Rotha Mary Clay, *The Hermits and Anchorites of England* (London, 1914), pp. 163–4. Scrope's translation is preserved in a single copy in Lambeth Palace Library MS 192 (see above, n. 2).

8 The authenticity of the text was first queried by Clemens Kopp, *Elias und Christentum auf dem Karmel* (Paderborn, 1929); see also Norman G. Werling, 'The Date of the *Institution*', *The Sword* xiii (1949), p. 283.

9 Chandler, 'Book of the First Monks', p. lx.

10 J. P. H. Clark, 'A Defence of the Carmelite order by John Hornby, O. Carm.', *Carmelus* xxxii (1985), pp. 73–106, reprinted in *Carmel in Britain: Essays on the Medieval*

place in Cambridge in 1374. The Chancellor found in favour of the Carmelites.[11] I have argued elsewhere that Ribot is perhaps even more concerned to prove the existence of authentic Carmelite documents which predate the founding of the other orders.[12]

Book VIII of the *Institution* quotes the earliest text of the Carmelite rule in its entirety, the so-called 'primitive text' drawn up by Albert, Patriarch of Jerusalem, some time between 1206 and 1214.[13] It provides a compromise between a monastic rule and a life of total seclusion. Each brother is to stay in his cell at prayer (primarily reciting the psalms), except when other duties occupy him. The cells are separate; that of the prior is to be placed at the entrance, so that the prior may be the first to see anyone attempting to visit any brother. It is a life of prayer, solitude, silence, penance, poverty and manual work (the brothers provide their own food), focussed clearly on obedient service to Christ and designed to help each brother to become a warrior, waging battle against Satan. 'Each one of you is to stay in his own cell or nearby, pondering the Lord's law day and night and keeping watch at his prayers unless attending to some other duty.'[14] Silence was required from Vespers until Tierce the next day.

The Albertine Rule is much influenced by Cassian. What it achieves is to bind these hermits very loosely into a community, with the appointment of a prior to whom obedience must be given, the provision of a chapel where Mass is celebrated daily for the whole community and some elements of common discipline. The mitigation under Innocent IV moved the order further towards communal life, with the provision of a communal refectory, the communal recitation of the canonical hours and a reduction in the length of the 'long silence'. Nonetheless, the order remained distinctive in its emphasis on the place of silence, solitude and contemplative prayer and was, as Ribot claims, using Isidore's categories,[15] an order of eremitic monks, though of course by the fourteenth century the order had become an order of friars and had an active apostolate.

The *Institution* also is much indebted to Cassian and other earlier writers for whom Elijah is not so central and it is instructive to see how it develops their ideas. Its view of the Christian life owes much to Neoplatonism: the world of the spirit and the material world are held to be in permanent conflict and the indi-

English Carmelite Province, ed. Patrick Fitzgerald-Lombard, vol. II (Rome, 1992), pp. 1–34.

11 Cambridge, Cambridge University Library MS Ff vi.11, fol. 23v.

12 Valerie Edden, 'Felip Ribot's *Institution of the First Monks*: Telling Stories about the Carmelites', *Journal of the Early Book Society* (forthcoming).

13 Ribot's text is used by Bede Edwards in his edition and translation of the rule in *The Rule of Saint Albert* (Aylesford and Kensington, 1973); on the authenticity of this early version of the rule see pp. 75–6. The discussion of the Rule which follows in the next paragraph is indebted to Edwards' introduction. For Scrope's translation of the Rule, see Lambeth Palace Library MS 192, fols 125r–26v.

14 *The Rule of St Albert*, p. 83.

15 Isidore, *De Officiis* 16.2, PL LXXXIII, col. 794C.

vidual soul to be distracted from its true destiny of union with God by bodily temptations and the attacks of the devil. The eremitic life is presented as the best way to overcome the temptations of the flesh and to achieve a purity of heart which paves the way for the soul to be united with Christ. Gregory comments that in the presence of God, Elijah covers his face with his mantle out of consideration for his own infirmity, and the cave in whose entrance he stands may be taken to represent his corruptible dwelling place, i.e. his body. Similarly God's presence is hidden from Moses by a cloud.[16]

Cassian writes:

> As God loves us with a love that is true and pure, a love that never breaks, we too will be joined to Him in a never-ending unshakable love, and it will be such a union that our breathing and our thinking and our talking will be 'God'. And we will come at last to that objective which I have mentioned, the goal which the Lord prayed to be fulfilled in us: 'That they may all be one as we are one, as I am in them and you in me so that they are utterly one' (John 17: 22–23). . . . This, then, is the goal of the monk. All his striving must be for this so that he may deserve to possess in this life an image of future happiness and may have the beginnings of a foretaste in this body of that life and glory of heaven. This, I say, is the objective of all perfection, to have the soul so removed from dalliance with the body that it rises each day to the things of the spirit until all its living and all its wishing become an unending prayer.[17]

Ribot writes in a similar way about the aim of the monastic life. Where he differs from Cassian is by putting the words in the mouth of Jesus himself, turning an objective statement into a personal message from Jesus to his beloved. Scrope translates:

> Al thys I counseyl the, to thys ende that of thyn clene herte procede a feruent and a gret loue, makyng pesable al thyn herte, be the wych þou may altogedere be ioynyd and knyt to me, withowtyn geyn, besynesse or wythstandyng, that thyn herte fele vttyrly ryth nowt wythtaryyng to my loue, but that it reste altogedere pesable in my loue. (I viii, fol. 55v)

The first two books of *The Institution* offer a sustained meditation on the life of Elijah as presented in 3 Kings 17–19. I shall consider Book I separately because of the possibility that it is a discrete text. The biblical account of Elijah's experience on the holy mountain Horeb (Sinai) is designed to evoke comparison with those of Moses, to whom God spoke after an angel appeared in the burning bush (Exodus 3) and to whom God appears in a thick cloud after the mountain resounded with peals of thunder and flashes of lightning and a loud trumpet blast. Later he hides in the crevice of a rock and God covers him with his hand lest he see his face. It is to Moses' encounter with God that we may trace the origins of the tradition of speaking of mystical experience using metaphors of darkness, of clouds and of covering. When God reveals himself on Carmel to the

16 *Moralia* V.xxxvi.32, CCSL CXXXXIII (Turnhout, 1979) p. 265.

17 John Cassian, *Conferences*, transl. Colm Luibheid (New York, 1985), Conference 10.7, pp. 129–30.

assembled gathering including the priests of Baal, his presence is accompanied with equal drama. On Horeb in contrast God is not present in the earthquake, wind and fire but in the 'sound of a slight breeze'.[18] Prior to either of these theophanies God calls upon Elijah to prepare himself by withdrawing into the wilderness, where he drinks from the stream and is fed by ravens. It is this incident which furnishes the *Institution* with its model of the 'perfect end' of the life of contemplation. Elijah's experience of God on Horeb in the 'sound of a slight breeze' is given surprisingly little prominence and figures only, much later in the text (III ii), to illustrate how God defends his followers from their persecutors.

By reading the biblical text 'not alonly hystoryaly but rather goostly', the two-fold aim of the eremitic monk is exemplified: his withdrawal into the wilderness shows Elijah offering a holy heart to God and prompts his experience of God's power and glory on Horeb. Literally the text is interpreted to mean that those who desire to lead a contemplative life should flee the common dwelling of men, hide in the wilderness and live as monks in the desert (I ii). They may say with the Psalmist: 'O God, my God, I watch for you from the morning light. My soul thirsts for you and my flesh also. In a desert land, impenetrably wild and without water, I have come into your holy place so that I might see your power and your glory' (Ps. 62:1–2).[19]

There is a sustained spiritual reading of God's message to Elijah: 'Go hence, go against the East; hide in the brook of Carith, which is against Jordan and there you shall drink from the stream and I have commanded ravens to feed thee there.' The first four clauses provide the four steps of preparation necessary to living the life of the eremitic monk.

(1) Go hence: forsake all worldly possessions (Book I iii).

(2) Go against the East: first, crucify all fleshly concupiscence; secondly, abandon your own desires and follow only the will of God (I iv).

(3) Hide in the brook of Carith: flee the company of men and especially of women (I v). Carith, which is against Jordan, is interpreted through the pun on Carith/*caritas*, as loving God above all and living in charity with one's neighbour (I vi).

(4) The final clause gives God's promise: 'I have commanded ravens to feed thee there.' The ravens are the prophets who will provide spiritual food to sustain the eremitic monk until he is offered the fullness of life everlasting (I vii and viii).

[18] The phrase has passed into English as a 'still, small voice', the reading of the King James Bible. The phrase provides something of a problem in the Hebrew text: see Robert Davidson, *The Courage to Doubt: Exploring an Old Testament Theme* (London, 1983), p. 98. The Vulgate has *sibilus aurae tenuis*, 'the sound of a slight breeze', suggesting possibly an intense silence out of which God spoke.

[19] Modern English translations of biblical passages are mine. Generally Ribot is following the Vulgate, though at times he is either adapting it slightly or using a variant text. Since his argument is based on a close reading of these passages, I have provided a literal translation of the text quoted in the Latin version of the *Institution*, one chosen to reflect Ribot's understanding of the passage.

In this way, it is made clear that one can only hope to attain a sense of the presence of God in the soul by a life of rigorous self-discipline. The first three clauses in the message commend a monastic discipline of poverty, chastity and obedience and withdrawal into solitude.

> Seek þou with besy stody tho thyngys the wych callyn the to feruowr of my loue, as arn the preceptys of my lawe and tho thyngys þe wych therfore I counseyled the first, as pouerte and crucifyyng of flesschly concupiscence, obedyence and forsakyng of thy awne wyl, contynence and the contynuaunce of wyldernesse.
> (I vii, fol. 55r)

Each step is explained in detail, firstly, 'Go hence!' The eremitic life is a withdrawal from this world, from home and family and earthly possessions, for worldly things prove a distraction from godly things; they are like the tares that grow up and strangle the good seed. This is a first step towards the perfect end of life and offers monks a foretaste of heavenly bliss in this life and the promise of life everlasting.

'Go east, against Jordan'. The life of prayer requires a proper moral disposition and is grounded in purity of heart. The metaphor of 'crucifying' the flesh leads to a meditation on crucifixion, which is spoken partly by Christ himself. The eremitic life is presented as a form of crucifixion. Many late medieval meditations on the cross dwell on the physical torment, an emphasis which tends to lead to a commendation of mortification of the flesh in imitation of Christ. Even whilst speaking of the crucifixion of fleshly concupiscence, Ribot's emphasis is different; the cross is the ultimate example of obedience, of total submission to the will of God. Jesus reminds his followers, 'I came down from heaven, not to do my own will but the will of my father who sent me' (John 6:38, quoted in I iv). Ribot eschews the commonplace images of the anchor-cell as either a tomb or a prison and yet conveys a clear sense of the eremitic life as one of total loss of individual freedom. The crucified one cannot move and is constrained utterly by the will of others and so the hermit is constrained utterly by the will of God. He is dead to the world, not concerned about the past or for the morrow, save in that it will bring his passing from this life. He is not moved by pride or contention or strife, revenge or envy. In this spiritual state, the monk prepares to hide his life with Christ in God, and in so doing his life is transformed until at the last he appears with him in glory, as promised in Col. 3:3–4.

'Be hid in the bek of Carith', is to live in continence, avoiding the company of men and especially of women. The exposition of this clause makes it clear that 'continence' goes far beyond 'sexual continence'. A life of proper self-restraint is almost impossible amongst the busy throngs of men in the life of cities. What is commended is not so much chastity *per se* as total solitude. We are reminded of the derivation of the word 'monk', *monachus*, which according to Gratian's *Decretals* derives from Greek *monos* ('alone') and *akos* ('melancholy').[20] However this withdrawal from the company of others is not a life of self-concern,

20 *Decretum magistri Gratiani*, ed. Aemilius Friedberg (Liepzig, 1879), p. 763.

for paradoxically it is only by withdrawal into solitude that the monk is free to embrace the penitential life, lamenting not only his own sins but those of all humanity. Following Gregory, he compares the man who has chosen a solitary life in the wilderness to the wild ass in Job 39:5–6, which is given its freedom and has its haunts in the wilderness,[21] for he is freed from the thraldom of sin. Total submission to the will of God is in fact the perfect way to freedom, for it allows God to loosen the bonds of sin.

The final requirement of the eremitic monk is that he lives 'in Carith, which is against Jordan'. Here again, the exposition depends on etymology to explain the role of love in the penitential life. Drawing on Jerome's *On Hebrew Names*,[22] 'Jordan' is interpreted as 'their descent' and 'Carith' as 'division', as well as 'charity, love'. So love is the only remedy against man's fall from grace, dividing man from sin. 'Love causes every sin to be forgotten' (Prov. 10:12). Once again, Jesus himself addresses the monk, demanding from him a total commitment of love, leaving mother and father and all else for his sake. He asks him to commit himself 'wyth swych zeel', a word which takes us back to Elijah with his 'I have burnt with zeal for the love of the Lord of Hosts' (3 Kings 19:10). The text continues with a discussion of the nature of love which is broadly Augustinian, in which God is to be loved for himself alone and our neighbour for God's sake and not his own and in which love's remedy against sin can be embodied in Paul's observation 'Love is the fulfilment of the law' (Rom. 13:10), for a perfect love leads the soul to love God so fervently that it no longer desires for anything which is contrary to God's will. When fervent love proceeds from a pure heart, then Jesus promises that the soul will be truly joined to him. 'Al thys I counseyl the, to thys ende that of thyn clene herte procede a feruent and a gret loue, makyng pesable al thyn herte, be þe wych þou may altogedere be ioynyd and knyt to me' (I vii, fol. 55v). The 'joining' here is *coniungens*, a word so commonly used for marriage, friendships and other close relationships that it hardly strikes the reader as a metaphor; once more the emphasis is on the intimacy of the monk's relationship with Jesus.

And so, the soul tastes of the stream of Carith, as the Psalmist promises: 'You give them to drink from the stream of your delights' (Ps. 35:9). What it is to drink from the stream is explained through a spiritual reading of Job 22, in which Job's false friend Eliphaz tells of the rewards to be given by God to the godly. Ribot allegorises: 'He will give you a flintstone for earth' and addresses the reader directly: he will offer a strong and fervent love in exchange for your abandoning of earthly affections; 'He will give streams of gold in exchange for the flintstone' – he will offer sweet spiritual delights beyond words for strong and fervent love, and will then defend you from your enemies. And so at last 'your silver will be piled up', that is you will come to the end of the contemplative life. You will enjoy converse with God ('diuino colloquio') and hidden things and future things

21 Gregory, *Moralia* XXX.xv.50, CCSL CXLIII B (Turnhout, 1985), pp. 1525–6.

22 Jerome, *Liber de interpretatione hebraeorum nominum*, CCSL LXXII, pp. 67, 100.

will be revealed to you, for the follower of Elijah is called to be a prophet too and finally 'Than schal þou be plentevows with delytys, vnabyl to be gyssyd vpon and þou schal lyftyn vp to beheldyn frely the face of thy sowle to God' (I vii, fol. 56r).

In the final chapter of Book I, Ribot expounds God's promise to Elijah that ravens will feed him in Carith. This allows him to restate the need to prepare the heart through penitence, for the ravens are the prophets, who point to the infirmity of the human condition and who support the contemplative in his life of prayer, particularly at times when he does not feel the sweetness of God's presence. There is an extended meditation on Job 38:41: 'Who provides food for the raven, when its chickens cry, wandering about because they have no food', prompted by God's promise to Elijah, that the ravens will feed him in Carith. Firstly he relates the folk-lore, borrowed from Gregory,[23] that the raven will not feed her chicks until their black feathers begin to show and she can be sure that they are really hers. And so the Christian soul is not permitted to taste the sweet refreshment of the joy of the divine presence until, prompted by the warnings of the prophets, he acknowledges and laments his own sinfulness, and so grows black, his blackness indicating his withdrawal from the lustre of the world.

It is important to understand that the sweet sense of the presence of God comes as a fleeting moment, which cannot be sustained. As the disciples experienced a dark cloud which cast a shadow over the transfigured Christ, so the frailty of the flesh prevents the perfect sweetness lasting more than a moment. In the *Institution*, whilst purity of heart is a necessary condition for union with Christ, the joyous moment is pure gift, not an inevitable reward for those who strive for it, 'noȝt of thyn owyn deservys but of my grace' (I viii, fol. 57v). Nor can one mark progress towards it. It is instructive to notice the metaphors avoided by Ribot; there is no pilgrimage of the soul, no journey, no ladder of perfection to climb. It is a moment outside time, as Thomas puts it, the rare 'stepping aside through the invisible veil' that surrounds us.

Whilst, as we have said, it is likely that Book I is an earlier text, incorporated later in the *Institution* (though of course possibly an earlier work by Ribot himself), later books expand on material in this first one. Book II differs from Book I in approach. Whereas Book I gave a spiritual reading of 3 Kings 17, Book II reads the events of Elijah's life historically and subsequent books follow it in having a chronological framework, charting the history of the order, though historical events are often discussed in terms of the lifestyle and aims of contemporary monks. There is a shift in emphasis from Carith to Carmel, since Carith had no water and was therefore uninhabitable and so the first followers of Elijah settled on Carmel. Their story is told with an emphasis on solitude and silence, on the importance of individual cells, on devotion to Mary and on the role of prophecy within the life of the eremitic monk, so that, in dealing with Carmelite

23 Gregory, *Moralia* XXX.ix.33–5, CCSL CXLIII B (Turnhout, 1985), pp. 1513–15.

history and practice, the emphasis is always on the inner life rather than on externals.

So, for example, the Carmelite habit, with its modifications over the years, is given symbolic significance in Book VII. The earliest hermits on Carmel were clad in leaves and goatskins, but, according to Ribot, when this style of dress led to derision it was replaced by rough, dark-coloured tunics ('kootes' in Middle English). The harshness of this clothing signifies contrition and the colour signifies the judgement which sin deserves. The monk is girt round the loins to signify chastity. The scapular signifies the yoke of obedience to God's will and, with its hood and open arms, a continual readiness to labour for God. The changing colour of the mantle, which had been the cause of controversy between the Carmelites and other orders,[24] is also symbolic. The original white mantle, about which legend recounts that it was foretold in a dream by Elijah's father, Sabach,[25] signifies purity of soul as well as of body. When they were forbidden to wear white by the Saracens because it was their royal colour, they adopted the famous striped ('barred') mantle. This garment signifies the purity of observance of the Gospel, for it recalls the four-cornered linen cloth with its unclean beasts, of which Peter dreamt (as recorded in Acts 11), to teach him that it is God who purifies. The four stripes signify the four evangelists and their one gospel, the three stripes the three stages of penance: contrition, confession and satisfaction. There was a return to the white mantle after the migration to the west. Finally the Carmelite carries a staff, to remind him of the staff carried by Elisha and used in the raising of the son of the Shunammite woman (4 Kings 4:29–37) and to signify the need to be armed against vices at all times.

We are also given further insight into the mystical encounter with God. In the second book, Ribot ventures a fuller account of Elijah's experience in Carith.

> The herte of the wych Helye, whyl it waxyd hoot in desert wythinne hymself of feruent charyte and the feer of godly loue, gan to brennyn in hys meditacyon, he tastyd oftyn tyme the glorye of God, vnabyl to be spokyn, and he sat, that is to sey he restyd, in the bek of a godly lust where God ȝevyth drynk to men, louying hem. Seyng the prophet: 'Thow schal ȝevyn drynk to hem of the bek of thy lust.' But thoȝw Hely that tyme forsyd to restyn besyly in contemplacyon as wel of ineffabyl rychessys as delytys, nederdelesse he, oppressyd be a corruptyble body, myth not ryth longe contynuyn in hem. (II i, fol. 70v)

Here new language for the mystical encounter with God is provided by the Psalms, always a pervasive influence in the text. Like the Psalmist, Elijah's heart burnt within him and, as he meditated, 'there kindled a flame' (Ps. 38:4), – Ribot adds 'a flame of God', and so he tasted the ineffable glory of God, and (drawing again on the Psalms) he drank from the stream of delights (Ps. 35: 9). With 'the stream of pleasure', Ribot adds *voluptas* to *suavitas* and *dulcedo* (sweetness) to describe the indescribable experience of the presence of God, a word wholly

24 Clark, 'A Defence', p. 87.

25 He cites Peter Comestor in support of this legend, *Historia Scholastica* 4 Kings 2, PL CXCVIII, col. 1387.

appropriate, for throughout the Vulgate it is the word used for the Garden of Eden, where Adam enjoyed a perfect relationship with God.[26] The stream of delights may be understood also as 'the fount of wisdom' (Pr. 18: 4), which is Christ himself.[27] As in other mystical texts, the mystical encounter is described using verbs of taste (*fruor, gusto*). Ribot makes the eucharistic connotation explicit, for sin is said to separate man from the 'pryuy partytakyng of God' ('ab illa arcana participatione Dei'). *Participatio* is a rare word in scripture, but this phrase seems to derive from Paul's account of the Eucharist as 'a sharing in the body of Christ' ('participatio corporis Domini sui') (1 Cor. 10:16). The individual who experiences the presence of God within the soul experiences at a personal level the indwelling of God which is enacted ritually in the sacrament of the Mass. As Marion Glasscoe has commented, 'If the Mass enacted the social reality of the body of Christ, it also enacted the recognised pattern of personal contemplative experience. . . . The contemplative who had a cell adjoining the church would have a window through which the altar could be seen. Thus at the canon of the Mass he or she would be able to identify the realities of personal experience and the sacred participation in *communitas* with the presence of Christ.'[28] One of the ways in which the Carmelite Rule is distinctive is that it enjoins a daily celebration of the Mass.

The experience of the early hermits living in solitude in their cells on Mount Carmel is discussed, drawing on Paul's second letter to the Corinthians (III viii). Paul contrasts the revelation under the Old and New Law (2 Corinthians 3:12–18). He reflects on the veil that covered Moses' face on his descent from Sinai with the two stone tablets, suggesting that maybe the glow on his face is already fading. Ribot boldly claims for these followers of Elijah the lifting of the veil claimed by Paul as the new dispensation.

> They, dystroyyng the opyn conflyctys and stryvys of develys, reysyd vp with swych a myth here mendys in the contemplacion of God to the exawmple of Helye, prynce of hem, that they were supposyd to be translant among hevynly companyys and to seen the ioye of God wyth hys face schewyd and to vsyn speche and talkyng wyth God, to whom they clevyd with clene mendes. (III viii, fol. 87r)

'Talking with God' introduces a new metaphor into the text, indicating the intimate relationship with God which grows from a life of prayer. Here he quotes Isidore, who describes anchorites in this way: 'So þe most secret and vttyrly remevyd fro the syith of alle men, vsyd godly speche and talkyng, to whom they clevyd with clene mendys and for whos loue they forsoke not alonly the world but the felachepe of men' (III viii, fol. 87v).[29]

26 'Paradisum voluptatis' (Genesis 2:8, 2:15, 3:23, 3:24); 'locus voluptatis' (Genesis: 2:10) and see also Ezekiel 31:9, 31:16, 31:18, 36:35.

27 *Glossa Ordinaria*, PL CXIII, col. 896.

28 Marion Glasscoe, *English Medieval Mystics: Games of Faith* (London, 1993), p. 23.

29 Isidore, *De Officiis* 16.2, PL LXXXIII, col. 794C. Scrope's translation, 'vsyd godly speche and talkyng', is infelicitous if not actually erroneous, since Isidore's Latin text makes it clear that anchorites speak *with* God: 'diuino tantum colloquio perfruuntur, cui puris mentibus inheserunt, et propter cuius amorem . . .'.

Solitude and silence are advocated as a means of cultivating this relationship with God. A clear distinction is made between being 'alone', separated from God, and being 'solitary', 'a recluse', who abandons his own freedom in and for God. *Cella* is derived from *celando*, 'hiding', for Elijah was ordered to hide in the beck of Carith. There is a long quotation from William of St Thierry's 'Golden Letter to the Carthusians' on the nature of the cell.[30] The cell provides the best opportunity to develop a loving relationship with Christ. It resembles heaven because it is a holy place, the place where the child of grace, the fruit of its womb, may be nurtured and brought to perfection, and prepared for 'talking with God'. As Moses was commanded to take off his shoes on holy ground, so the solitary must cast off all that is detrimental to the soul. The cell is thus neither a prison nor a grave but a house of peace, in which intimate relationships may be fostered:

> A cell ought not to be seyd a closyng of necessyte but a lityl hows of pees, a dore schet not to the deen, but secret and preuy. Cellys and the habytacyon of heuene are cosenys. For as heuene and a *cella* arn seyd to han togedere sum kynrede of name, lychwyse of mekenesse. Heuene and a celle arn seyn to takyn here dyryuacyon and name of thys word *celando*, that ys as moche to sey as to hylyn or kewryn, for that that ys kewryd in heuenys ys kewryd in cellys and that that is doon in heuenys ys doon in cellys. What is that to mene? To ȝeuyn entent to God, to hauntyn and vsyn God. In a celle oftyntyme the Lord and hys seruaunt spekyn togedere as a man to hys frend, in the wych I beleue a trew soule ys ioynyd to the word of God, a spowse ys felachepeyd to here husbonde, and heuenely thyngys arn iyonyd to erdely and godly thyngys to manly. (III vi, fol. 85r)

Using Elijah as both the founder and paradigm of the Carmelite life inevitably raises the prophetic role of his followers, for it is as a prophet primarily that Elijah is presented in the scriptures. His role was to call the people of Israel back to the true God after Ahab and his queen Jezebel led them into the worship of Baal, and his first public act was to foretell the drought in Samaria. The phrase 'the prophetycal lyf of an heremyte' (or 'a monk') is used throughout the *Institution*. Reflecting not only on Elijah but on the sons of the prophets in the time of David (1 Chronicles 25), Ribot observes that a prophet is not to be defined by the ability to foretell the future (though some prophets did) but 'in so myche that they sang devoutly to God wyth instrumentys of musyk' (II ii fol. 73v), maintaining the worship of the true God. He writes of a monastic community on Carmel, established by the followers of Elijah. They fulfilled both aspects of the prophetical life, worshipping God with psalms and music and warning the people of Israel of the consequences of their actions. Thus Micaiah prophesies the death of Ahab (3 Kings 22); Elisha advises in the war between Israel and the Aramaeans (4 Kings 6); Jonah (son of the widow of Zarephath, according to Jerome)[31]

[30] *The Golden Epistle of Abbot William of St. Thierry*, transl. Walter Shewring (London, 1930), Chapter 4. In the fourteenth century Carmelites believed that this epistle had been addressed to a Carmelite audience.

[31] Jerome, *Commentaria in Jonam prophetam*, PL XXV, col. 1118.

preached to the people of Ninevah (Jonah 3). In Book VI, which deals with the order's special relationship with Mary, it is claimed that they changed their name from 'the sons of the prophets' to 'brothers of the Blessed Virgin Mary', in part because they ceased playing musical instruments in their worship (VI v).

Following earlier fourteenth-century Carmelite writers like Baconthorpe, it is claimed that Elijah prophesied the Virgin birth in the little cloud of rain which rises from the sea (3 Kings 18:44).[32] Ribot extends this by a symbolic reading of the whole incident, in which Elijah instructs his boy to tell Ahab to mount his chariot and depart lest the rain prevent him, and 'the heavens grew dark, overcast with clouds, and the wind blew and there was a great downpour of rain' (3 Kings 18:44). Here the chariot signifies the son of God, because a chariot (*sc.* a chariot's wheel) is circular and able to carry a burden, and Christ is eternal, his burden (it is implied rather than stated) is the burden of human nature. The heavens signify his power, the wind is the Holy Spirit and the cloud signifies the Virgin, in whom Christ became incarnate, and the rain is the fountain of grace which his incarnation initiates. Mary is thus linked to Elijah both because she follows him in her pure virginity and because through her showers of grace fell from heaven.

There has been a tendency to assume that the development of the order from its eremitic origins to its establishment as one of the four mendicant orders led to its losing sight of the original Carmelite calling. Some have seen the *Institution* as echoing Nicholas of Narbonne (*Ignea Sagitta* 1270–1)[33] in recalling the brothers to their eremitic, contemplative origins.[34] However, it seems clear that the influence of the *Ignea Sagitta* has been exaggerated.[35] It is certainly true that late medieval friars lived in towns and amongst people rather than as solitaries in the wilderness but whether Ribot or his contemporaries saw this as a betrayal of their past is open to question. One may argue that the *Institution*, with its account of Elijah's roles as proto-monk, hermit and prophet led to a different emphasis from that of Nicholas. Whilst Ribot undoubtedly put contemplative prayer at the centre of the Carmelite life, he also commended a commitment to follow Elijah in 'the prophetycal lyf of an heremyte'.

We may reflect that this accounts for the way in which so many late medieval Carmelite friars, in England at any rate, combined elements of the contemplative life with a public role. I cite some obvious examples: John Swaffham (d. 1398)

32 John Baconthorpe (d. 1348), Carmelite theologian, English provincial 1326–1333, taught at Oxford, Cambridge and Paris. For his works, see Staring, *Medieval Carmelite Heritage*, pp. 184–253. For this passage, see 'Laus religionis Carmelitanum', cap. IX, ed. Staring, p. 226.

33 Nicholas of Narbonne, *The Flaming Arrow*, transl. Michael Edwards (Dartington, 1985). This translates A. Staring, 'Nicolai Prioris Generalis Ordinis Carmelitarum Ignea Sagitti', *Carmelus* ix (1962), pp. 237–307.

34 Andrew Jotischky, *The Carmelites and Antiquity: Mendicants and their Pasts in the Middle Ages* (Oxford, 2002), p. 143.

35 See Richard Copsey, 'The *Ignea Sagitta* and its readership: a re-evaluation', *Carmelus* xlvi (1999), pp. 164–73.

was Bishop of Cloyne and later of Bangor; Robert Mascall (d. 1416) was Bishop of Meath and then of Hereford; Thomas Peverell (d. 1419) was successively Bishop of Ossory, then Llandaff and finally Worcester; Stephen Patrington (d. 1417) was Bishop of St David's and John Stanberry (d. 1374) Bishop of Bangor and then Hereford. The House of Lancaster had a succession of Carmelite confessors and Walter Diss, prior of the Norwich house from 1376, played an active part in the career of John of Gaunt as well as being his confessor. There are many examples of friars during their lives embracing both contemplative and active lifestyles, though not generally simultaneously. A striking one is Thomas Scrope (Bradley), whose translation of the *Institution* we have been using. His life included a period of several years in the 1440s when he lived as a hermit in a cell near the entrance to Norwich friary but, later in his life, he held a number of livings in East Anglian parishes, was appointed Bishop of Dromore in 1449 (a see ruled by absentee bishops from 1420 until the 1450s), suffragan bishop of Norwich (1450–1477) and of Canterbury (1469) and acted as papal legate in 1462. Those who led such a life, allowing themselves both space for contemplation and some opportunity for active ministry, could undoubtedly look to Elijah as their model, for he too had a public role in his dealings with Ahab and Jezebel and the priests of Baal.

The *Institution* can be seen to reflect a spirituality which has much in common with other medieval contemplative writings, especially Carthusian. Nonetheless in focussing on Elijah as the model of the spiritual life, it promotes a distinctive approach to contemplative life. It advocates an ascetic way of life, a preparation of the heart in purity to experience the presence of God. It advocates a knowledge of God which is experiential rather than intellectual (there is, for example, no mention of reading), the height of which is the mystical encounter with God through love, an intimate relationship with Christ developed in the solitude of the cell through a life of prayer. Such encounters are necessarily transient, limited by the infirmities of the human condition. Ribot also calls on the Carmelite brothers to consider prophecy as part of their vocation, including amongst the promises to those who follow Elijah's example that 'hyd thyngys and thyngys for to comyn schal be schewyd sumtyme among fro God vnto the' (II vii, fol. 56r). Elijah, who encountered God on Carmel and on Horeb and was sustained by him when in solitude in the wilderness, was indeed the model for 'the prophetycal lyf of an heremyte'.

'MAKEDES OF ME/WRECCHE ÞI LEOFMON & SPUSE': MYSTICAL DESIRE AND VISIONARY CONSUMMATION

SUSANNAH MARY CHEWNING

'The dreamer is an inadequate vessel for the experience of his dream'
(A. C. Spearing, *Medieval Dream-Poetry*)

I

IN SHAKESPEARE'S *A Midsummer Night's Dream*, Bottom, upon awakening from his disturbing experience among the fairies, says, 'I have had a dream, past the wit of man to say what dream it was. . . . The eye of man hath not heard, the ear of man hath not seen, man's hand is not able to taste, his tongue to conceive, nor his heart to report, what my dream was' (IV.i.209–10, 214–17). Bottom's lack of awareness about almost anything is comically apparent here, where he misidentifies the senses which, should they be applied to understanding his dream, would fail to comprehend it. In spite of its comic and confusing nature, this quotation works well to define, to some extent, what makes dreams and visions so very difficult to categorize and to recognize based on traditional methods. Dreams are complicated because they represent extensions of the unconscious, desires which make us uncomfortable when we are conscious and participating in our regular lives. Still, the wishes we fulfill in our dreams, however uncomfortable they may make us feel when we dream them, are genuine to some extent, in spite of, as Freud writes, their 'strangeness and obscurity'.[1]

In medieval literature, the genre of the dream vision is wrapped up closely with that of mysticism because both deal with experiences which occur outside of human consciousness.[2] Most scholars who address these two genres see them

1 Sigmund Freud, *Interpretation of Dreams*, trans. A. A. Brill (London, 1942), p. 1.

2 In spite of its lack of recognition as an actual genre, I will discuss mysticism as such in the context of this study. Because mysticism is not typically understood as a genre, it is usually included within other genres – poetry, devotional treatise, instruction manual, autobiography. Its nature is difficult to define, but mysticism should, I believe, be included as a separate genre of medieval literature because it serves, as I will demonstrate, a separate, distinguishable purpose with respect to other genres. Indeed, recent critics have begun to describe mysticism with more authority, such as Nicholas Watson, who describes what he terms 'the canon of "Middle English mystics"'. Rather than seeing mysticism as a motif within other forms of medieval literature and rhetoric, I find there to be a mystical impulse within medieval writers who choose it as the means

separately. Mysticism, for example, is seen by most who study it as a physical (or at least sensual) phenomenon, based on a specific experience of transcendence, and experienced differently based on a mystic's gender and social role. Traditional definitions of mysticism generally view it as a process that is achieved through successful completion of either the *via negativa*[3] or what has become known as the *via mystica*,[4] a three-tiered process combining prayer, contemplation, and meditation. Mysticism, because of its experiential nature, has not until very recently been taken seriously as a genre – in fact, for some, it still remains a marginal form of expression, at best, made up of what some might characterize

with which to express themselves. They are not poets (or prose writers, or theologians – writers of other *known* genres) who use mysticism to get their ideas across; rather, the very point of mysticism is to transcend what is known, and thus we must view them separately, and their work, however it is constituted, must also hold a unique position within our modern sense of medieval literature. For a fuller discussion of the genre of mysticism, see Nicholas Watson, 'The Middle English Mystics' in *The Cambridge History of Medieval English Literature*, ed. David Wallace (Cambridge, 1999), pp. 539–65.

3 The *via negativa*, connected to Eastern Christian mysticism through Pseudo-Dionysius, is characterized by an absence of human knowing – God cannot be known, in this definition, through humans' understanding or language, so all senses of human understanding must be surrendered in order to gain access to the Divine. John P. H. Clark has characterized the *via negativa* through its connection to Pseudo-Dionysius. He writes, 'Pseudo-Dionysius bids his reader leave behind both the senses and the operations of the intellect and follow Moses in his ascent of the mountain and entry into the "truly mystical darkness of unknowing", where he is united . . . with God at a supraintellectual level.' The *via positiva* is another means by which the mystic may pursue union with God. It is opposed to the *via negativa* in that it is an approach to the Divine that relies upon human knowledge and wisdom. The *via negativa* is the surrendering of understanding in order to reach the Divine; the *via positiva* pursues the Divine by making use of the understanding that the *via negativa* eradicates. See John P. H. Clark, '*The Cloud of Unknowing*', in *An Introduction to the Medieval Mystics of Europe*, ed. Paul Szarmach (Albany, 1984); quotation from p. 277.

4 In Christian mysticism, as it was established in the early Middle Ages, there are three steps to union with the Divine Other through access to the 'way of mysticism', or the *via mystica*. These three steps are the *via purgativa*, the *via illuminativa* and the *via contemplativa*. In the *via purgativa* the mystic separates herself from the thoughts and activities of daily life through prayer, eliminating from her mind the concerns and needs of worldly life. 'Passions' are to be eradicated at this stage, as well. Many mystics reach this stage through fasting, isolation, or other sensual deprivation. In the *via illuminativa* the mystic has reached a point of separation from the sensual, human world and loses her connection with human discourse. At this point the mystic begins to feel a sense of enlightenment and illumination from the source of her concentration, the divine Other. From this point on, communication between the mystic and the Divine takes place within the realm of the soul, separated from the body and from human language. In the *via contemplativa*, the mystic reaches her moment of communication with the presence of the Divine. This communication can take many forms; the mystic may hear a voice, see a vision, feel a strange atmospheric sensation. De Marquette calls it 'the supreme achievement of human destiny, the return of the differentiated creature to the resplendent infinitude of the Creator'. See Jacques de Marquette, *Introduction to Comparative Mysticism* (New York, 1949), p. 26.

as the near-psychotic rantings of unbalanced, disturbed religious fanatics. A brief examination of how Margery Kempe has been perceived over the last century will support this claim. Dream visions, however, hold a privileged position within the discourse of scholars of medieval literature.

E. V. Gordon writes that for medieval audiences dream visions 'allowed marvels to be placed within the real world, linking them with a person, a place, a time, while providing them with an explanation in the phantasies of sleep, and a defence against critics in the notorious deception of dreams'.[5] Dream visions, for Gordon, and for most scholars of the genre, fall into the category of allegory, a narrative describing 'in other terms some event or process'.[6] Thus dream visions, in spite of Freud's insistence that dreams are strange and obscure, represent some sense of reality, some real event described in the language of allegory. Perhaps this is the problem faced when one tries to connect dream visions and mysticism. If a dream vision is the allegorized re-telling of an event occurring in reality, then a mystical work may be seen as a factualized re-telling of a symbolic or allegorical experience – the difference being that dreamers always return to reality, whereas mystics – when they are mystics – can only exist in the liminal state of experience beyond words.

In this paper, and within the larger framework with which I am examining this subject, I would like to argue that most critics who separate mysticism and dream visions miss a crucial connection that brings them together within the same context. Gordon himself says it in his definition: that a dream vision allows marvels to be placed within the real world. What else is mysticism than a re-claiming of an experience that *transcends* this world by the mystic, who dwells *in* this world? A mystic transcends her self and her reality.[7] She moves beyond what is known into a realm of consciousness that cannot be fully comprehended through human language. A dreamer does much the same thing – he moves from a state of 'reality' into the realm of the unconscious, seeing the world as he wants it to be rather than the way it is. Rather than finding it difficult to see dreams and mystical visions as the same, one might ask why they were ever viewed as different.

For the purposes of this study, I will use specific texts as a means of defining and exploring the relationship between mysticism and dream visions. The mystical texts with which I am working are known as the *Wohunge Group*. They were written by a male author in the latter half of the twelfth century. This author, although he is mostly unknown to us, is possibly the same author who wrote *Ancrene Wisse*. Even if the authors are different, the relationship between the *Wohunge Group* and *Ancrene Wisse* cannot be ignored. These works grow out of a need felt during the twelfth century by religious women for spiritual and social

5 *Pearl*, ed. E. V. Gordon (Oxford 1986), pp. xiv–xv.

6 Ibid., p. xiv.

7 For reasons that will become clear as I make my argument, in this study I will distinguish between the persona of the dream vision as masculine and that of the mystical vision as feminine.

direction, and from a need on the part of the author to give these women metaphors through which to describe and articulate their own mystical experiences of the Divine. The dream vision I wish to analyze within this context is the fourteenth-century Middle English allegory, *Pearl*, written by a similarly unknown author for an unknown purpose, and because it is found in the same manuscript with *Sir Gawain and the Green Knight*, *Patience*, and *Cleanness*, assumed to be authored by the same poet. The author of these works is known, depending on the context of his description, as either the *Pearl*-poet or the *Gawain*-poet, although obviously, for my purposes, I would prefer to associate him with *Pearl*. In part, I have chosen these texts because they define their respective genres well. They also serve, however, to define each other and to provide a broader context within which to see the two genres as part of one larger motif.

II

Although I have argued that mysticism and dream visions do need to be regarded together, the argument may as yet be unconvincing. As such, I would like to explain, briefly, why the two genres belong together and, perhaps, why they have thus far always been separated by scholars. When discussing dream visions, two scholarly names immediately come to mind, at least to mine. One is A. C. Spearing, whose *Medieval Dream-Poetry* is a must-read for any medievalist.[8] Spearing discusses mysticism in his introduction when he defines the genre of the dream vision. He refers to mystical works as 'scriptural and Christian visions' (p. 11), citing scriptural and late classical examples, as well as what he calls 'the use of the other-world vision for theological and political polemic' (p. 14) in such allegorical works as the *Divine Comedy* and *Pearl*. Spearing sees the dream and the vision as existing within the same larger genre of dream poetry, rarely examining mysticism specifically except with respect to similarities of metaphor and language. His work seeks to define and examine the dream poem and its place, particularly within the vernacular poetry of Ricardian England. The second, more recent volume devoted to dream visions is Steve Kruger's *Dreaming in the Middle Ages*, published in 1992.[9] Kruger does not pick up where Spearing leaves off, as one might imagine. Instead, he re-theorizes medieval dream literature, categorizing it by century and within various sub-categories. He focuses on the binary opposition of divine and mundane dreams and a middle ground between them, what he calls the 'middle vision'.[10] Kruger's treatment of dreams includes

8 A. C. Spearing. *Medieval Dream-Poetry* (Cambridge, 1976).

9 Steven Kruger, *Dreaming in the Middle Ages* (Cambridge, 1992).

10 Kruger writes: 'In certain dream visions, however, mundane and celestial qualities are more evenly matched. Such "middle visions" powerfully exploit the double nature of the dream, locating themselves midway between the two poles of the literary genre' (p. 129). He characterizes the dreams of Chaucer, Boccaccio, and Langland as 'all middle visions, evoking the possibility of revelation as they nervously question their own reliability' (p. 130).

some mystical writers, such as Hildegard and Julian of Norwich. However, when he discusses them, he, like Spearing before him, uses the term *vision*, which covers both genres but does not clearly indicate where the dream ends and the mystical truth begins. I make this point because of a fundamental issue which I think has prevented scholars from looking at dreams and mysticism together until now. Dreams are not *real*. Living in a post- Freudian world, we can almost not see dreams as anything beyond wish fulfillment, unconscious desire, and fantasy. Even in the Middle Ages, dreams were seen as arbitrary and vague, sometimes divinely inspired but just as often the work of devils or pagan sorcerers. Dreams are created in the mind; they do not have existence in reality except when we describe them. A good example of this is Chaucer's dream visions, which always begin with some introductory matter about how he fell asleep – and that sleep is the premise of the dream. In *The Book of the Duchess* he has been reading about Ceyx and Alcyone and the power of Morpheus, the pagan god of sleep. He himself has been suffering from a lack of sleep and offers to bribe Morpheus if he will allow him one good night's rest.

> I hadde unneth that worde ysayede,
> Ryght thus [as] I have tolde hyt yow,
> That sodeynly, I nyste how,
> Suche a luste anoon me tooke
> To slepe, that right upon my booke
> Y fil aslepe, and therewith evene
> Me mette so ynly swete a swevene,
> So wonderful, that never yitte
> Y trow no man had the wytte
> To konne wel my sweven rede (*Book of the Duchess* 270–9)[11]

He is thinking about poetry – about ancient myth, fiction, and love; he is tired, he falls asleep, and he dreams about a courtly lover and his lady. Whatever his dream will entail, however, he makes it clear that it *is* a dream, and he has fallen asleep. In *The Legend of Good Women*, Chaucer has been walking on a beautiful summer's day and has been struck by the beauty and sensuality of the flowers around him, particularly the daisies. At sundown he bids his men make a bed for him in his arbor and, in honor of the new summer, 'I bad hem strowe flouris on my bed./ Whan I was layd and hadde myn eyen hid,/ I fel aslepe withinne an our or two' (*Legend of Good Women* 101–3). Again, inspired, this time by nature itself, Chaucer falls asleep and dreams, in this case about the god of Love. Chaucer and other dream vision poets make it clear that what follows in the poem did not happen in reality, but in the unconscious, where one is suggestible and often misled by what he dreams.[12] Dreams can, because their source is always in question, be false, and therefore they must be seen as not real. Mysticism,

[11] Geoffrey Chaucer, *The Riverside Chaucer*, ed. Larry D. Benson (Boston, 1987).

[12] Of course, although we know Chaucer is asleep in this work, we do not necessarily see him wake up – he almost seems to begin writing the poem during his dream (*Legend of Good Women*, 578–9).

however, is, for those who experience it, extremely real. It occurs when they are conscious, although sometimes in extremity due to physical injury or illness.

A mystical experience provides one with access to the 'transcendent realm for which we yearn',[13] but it differs from a dream because it *does occur.* As Evelyn Underhill describes it, mysticism is 'experience in its most intense form'.[14] For example, Julian of Norwich's vision, which she describes in her *Book of Showings*, began when she fell seriously ill at the age of thirty and a half. Those around her believed she was dying, and a priest was sent for who gave her a crucifix to look upon as she died.

> I agreed to fix my eyes on the face of the crucifix if I could, and so I did. . . . After this my sight began to fail. It grew as dark about me in the room as if it had been night, except that there was an ordinary light trained upon the image of the cross, I did not know how . . . And suddenly at that moment all my pain was taken from me, and I was as sound . . . as ever I was before. . . . Then suddenly it came into my mind that I ought to wish for the second wound as a gift and a grace from our Lord, that my body might be filled full of recollection and feeling of his blessed Passion.
> (*Showings*, p. 180)[15]

Although Julian states that her body seems to fall away from her at this moment of transcendence, and that physically she feels like she is dying, she never says that she loses consciousness or leaves the physical reality that surrounds her. She could be perceived as going into a trance, but she is conscious, sentient, and aware of all that is going on around her. This is no dream, but the vision is dream-like. She says, for example, that she sees things which most people would say cannot be seen in the realm of reality. She writes: 'I saw the red blood running down from under the crown, hot and flowing freely and copiously, a living stream, just as it was in the time when the crown of thorns was pressed on his blessed head . . . I saw [our Lady Saint Mary] spiritually in her bodily likeness' (pp. 181–2). Julian does not say she *thinks* she saw the blood of Christ dripping over her bed or the face of Mary; she never says she fell asleep. She says she really saw them – they were there, in front of her, in her conscious reality.

While a dream vision author can say almost anything, because it was a dream and is therefore not subject to human logic or truth, a mystic often makes equally unbelievable claims without the security of the vision having been a dream. Mystics are questioned, ridiculed, and rejected by the Church because of what they see and how they describe that vision. If they were simply to describe their visions as dreams, then perhaps society, both medieval and modern, would be less likely to reject them. The problem of mysticism for many scholars, however, is the mystic's insistence that her vision was real, that the Divine sought her out when she was sick or otherwise out of sorts, and that it was not a dream. Still,

13 Kruger, *Dreaming,* p. 130

14 *Mysticism* (New York, 1955), p. 82.

15 All citations taken from the *Showings* of Julian of Norwich, Long Text, trans. Edmund Colledge and James Walsh (New York, 1978). Parenthetical citations refer to page numbers in this edition.

although it is not a dream, no mystic's vision is easily understood, even by the mystic herself. Julian's visions are, of course, difficult for her to understand, and she says that her understanding of the visions did not occur until fifteen years after the experience, at which time she is told, in yet another vision, 'What, do you wish to know your Lord's meaning in this thing? Know it well, love was his meaning. Who reveals it to you? Love. What did he reveal to you? Love. Why does he reveal it to you? For love' (p. 342). Love, then, embodied as Christ and Mary, has visited Julian and made her aware of its power and authority. Love, of course, is *real*, and has real cultural and spiritual power. If Love exists as an entity, however, not merely as a human emotion, then it must be perceived in a physical context which is, at least for Julian, the premise of the mystical experience itself.

This notion of mysticism as real and dream as not real has separated the genres on two levels. First, there are those who see dreams, however false or arbitrary they may seem to be, as natural manifestations of the human mind, strange, sometimes, but always attributable to something, whether it is a suggestion planted in the unconscious during the day, an as yet unarticulated wish or desire, or a late-night meal. We all have dreams – even animals appear to dream. Dreams are normal. Mystical visions, although the mystic always insists that they are true, are not natural. They do not occur to all of us, and many of those to whom they have occurred, such as Joan of Arc, Margery Kempe, or Marguerite Porete, appear to be insane, and have suffered for what they saw, usually at the hands of those to whom they reported it. Mystics are *not* normal. The second separation of the genre is based on the first. Medieval and Renaissance writers who use dreams as metaphors in their writing (or who describe dreams that they claim to have actually experienced) are the mainstream, traditional poets of European literature, such as Dante, Chaucer, Langland, Boccaccio, Gower, and Shakespeare. We trust these writers; they have a real identity within our modern perception of the Middle Ages. They are all, I might add, men. Dreams are natural; traditional, patriarchally sanctioned poets write about them. Mystical writers are known to us, for the most part, only because of their visions. They do not exist outside of the genre of mysticism, except as a footnote, sometimes, to a larger event. They are unstable, often physically weakened, isolated by their religious lives. Many mystics are women, too many are completely anonymous, and as such always already Other in medieval society. Mysticism is unnatural, and with a few exceptions, unnatural or at least extremely unusual people participate in it.

In spite of these differences, or, perhaps, because of them, my goal has been to reunite the mystic and the dreamer as participating in one tradition. Both styles of writing include the same basic ingredients: a speaker (dreamer or mystic) who has a supernatural vision in which a message of wisdom or compassion is bestowed by a spiritual figure of authority. In a typical dream vision the dreamer falls asleep (sometimes under unusual circumstances) and dreams about a problem or concern with which he has been struggling in his waking life. In the dream, he is addressed by a figure, often a woman, which I will call the Dream Lady, who gives him advice or comfort in order to solve his problem, recover, and return to his life enhanced in some way as a result of the dream. In a mystical vision, the mystic contemplates an image or idea associated with God, usually during an experience of poor health or mental anguish. She does not pursue the vision – it pursues her, and she finds herself in the presence of a divine figure, Christ, Mary, or a physical embodiment of divine love who offers the mystic some hidden spiritual truth about love, divine justice, or spiritual authority. What makes these two forms of writing so alike is the focus of the vision: the Dream Lady of the dream vision and the voice of the Divine in the mystical vision. In both cases this spiritual Other provides comfort, wisdom, and peace to the dreamer/mystic who is forever changed by the encounter. Ultimately, I would like to argue that the dream vision and the mystical vision operate under the same assumption: that through the authority of a heavenly voice earthly problems and griefs can be dispelled and a higher level of human awareness can be achieved. Both the dream vision and the mystical vision operate under this same metaphor, deriving, perhaps, from biblical exchanges of a similar nature, but developing separately for, in turn, secular and spiritual medieval audiences.

III

For the purposes of this work I would like to focus on the twelfth-century mystical treatise, *Þe Wohunge of Ure Lauerd* and the fourteenth-century alliterative poem, *Pearl*. I find, however, that the parallels that I seek to draw between these forms of expression go far beyond these two works. In Dante's *Comedia*, for example, we find a dreamer who has all but surrendered to despair who is given a vision, provided through Beatrice by God, which saves his soul and cures his depression. In Chaucer's *The Book of the Duchess*, the presence of the dead Blanche provides salvation, of a sort, to both the dreamer and his subject, the Black Knight. In Chaucer's *Legend of Good Women*, the god of love and his queen, 'who in appearance is like a transfigured daisy',[16] offer the dreamer wisdom and a spiritual and professional challenge. In *Piers Plowman*, Holychurch commands Piers to follow her doctrine, informing him of her wisdom and the power of divine love. All of these figures have in common their supernatural state, and in the cases of the work of Dante, Chaucer, and a number of other dream visions, that state is provided through death. This, of course, is the case in *Pearl*, in which the dead daughter of the dreamer appears in order to offer her father wisdom and relief from the grief he has suffered since her death. The dead Lady of the dream vision – such as Beatrice, Blanche, and the *Pearl*-maiden – takes on a similar position in comparison with the divine figures who speak in the vision of the mystic. Christ and Mary, although their roles in the afterlife are clearly representative not of death but of new life, are, at least in their physical, historical contexts, dead. They are figures who have transcended death and

16 Spearing, *Medieval Dream-Poetry*, p. 101.

appear to the mystic in order to bring her some form of divine truth (and I think it is no accident that the vision often comes to the mystic when she herself is facing physical illness and death). The common form of these works might make better sense when seen as a diagram:

Dream Vision	**Mystical Vision**
1. The dreamer is depressed, isolated, experiencing insomnia, or some other state/form of emotional restlessness.	1. The mystic is sick, close to death, starvation, or some other physical ailment.
2. The dreamer falls asleep.	2. The mystic transcends her body.
3. The Dream Lady appears and provides spiritual and emotional consolation.	3. The Divine figure appears and offers wisdom, comfort, and love.

The similarities exist in the articulation of emotion for both the dreamer and the mystic, as well. In *Þe Wohunge of Ure Lauerd*, the speaker meditates on the crucifixion, re-enacts it, and attempts to participate in Christ's death as her own. Her vision is extremely sensual; she sees Christ's blood and sweat and feels as if she, too, has been crucified, and she feels great joy in her own suffering:

> A . iesu swa swet hit is wið þe
> to henge . forhwen þat iseo o þe
> þat henges me biside . þe mu-
> chele swetnesse of þe . rea-
> ues me fele of pine (*Wohunge*, 598–602)[17]
>
> [Ah Jesus, so sweet it is to hang with you. For when I look on you who hang beside me, your great sweetness snatches me strongly from pain.][18]

The *Pearl* narrator, surrounded by great natural beauty as his vision begins, is faced with potential physical harm, as well, but the possibility of joy that he feels will come from his vision gives him the courage to face what lies ahead:

> Bote woþe mo iwysse þer ware,
> Þe fyrre I stalked by þe stronde.
> And euer me þoȝt I schulde not wonde
> For wo þer weleȝ so synne wore
> Þenne new note me com on honed
> Þat meued my mynde ay more and more. (*Pearl*, 151–6)

The sensuality of the dream vision and the mystical encounter is only one of several similarities that unite the two genres. In a sense, dream vision and mysticism serve as two versions of the same medieval impulse: to find the meeting point of the human and the Divine and to articulate it for the enrichment and

[17] *Þe Wohunge of Ure Lauerd*, ed. W. Meredith Thompson, EETS OS 241 (London, 1958), p. 36. Citations throughout refer to line numbers in this edition.

[18] Anne Savage and Nicholas Watson, *Anchoritic Spirituality: 'Ancrene Wisse' and Associated Works* (New York, 1991), p. 256. Subsequent references to Savage and Watson's translation will be given in the text.

salvation of mankind. Dream vision poets see themselves as changed, improved upon somehow by their dreams; Dante, for example, in recollecting his dream, argues that Beatrice, by arranging for his vision and guiding him to Paradise in his dream, has provided him with a means of salvation through the power of divine love: 'Here force failed my high fantasy; but my/ desire and will were moved already – like/ a wheel revolving uniformly – by/ the Love that moves the sun and the other stars'.[19] Mystics recover from life-threatening illness and live to tell their stories about the power of divine love. As Julian of Norwich writes, explaining her vision and her new understanding of the world, 'all is one love' (p. 363). Mystic and dreamer alike are motivated by making sense of and putting into words that which does not make logical sense and cannot, ultimately, be expressed in human language. Again, it is Dante who, when finally visualizing the center of Paradise, reminds us: 'How incomplete is speech, how weak, when set/ against my thought! And this, to what I saw/ is such – to call it little is too much' (*Paradiso*, XXXIII.121–3).

My two examples above represent both the two genres of dream vision and mystical vision, as well as authors of both genders, and this choice is deliberate. It is, I think, central to this discussion that most (if not all) medieval dream visions are authored by men whereas the majority of later medieval mystical works are female authored. This being the case it seems important to examine the motivations and focus of the dream vision as, perhaps, a male author's context for mystical expression, one in which he can re-create woman in his own way; while moving away from the textual and liturgical categories applied to visions and mystical transcendence by the Church, the author of the dream vision can still participate in the extra-linguistic experience of the mystic. One must keep in mind that for modern audiences mystics seem unorthodox and strange, but for many medieval writers they were represented as spiritually superior to other Christians. Most mystics whose work remains extant participated in the religious life as nuns or anchoresses if not before then certainly after their visions. Secular writers like Dante and Chaucer lived very much in the political and social arenas of their times and could not have given up those lives for religious contemplation. Thus it seems reasonable to argue that the authorship of dream visions gives secular writers access to the spiritual life, offering them the spiritual sanction of the mystic without the theological commitment. It is not surprising, again, that the two genres are separated by literary convention and style as well as gender, for it is clear that gender determines many aspects of human personality, not the least of which being artistic and spiritual composition. Men and women write differently, and they write about different subjects in very different ways.

I have discussed elsewhere[20] that mysticism can be perceived as culturally

[19] Dante Alighieri, *The Divine Comedy of Dante Alighieri: Paradiso*, trans. Allen Mandelbaum (New York, 1984), canto XXXIII, lines 144–5.

[20] Susannah Chewning, 'Mysticism and the Anchoritic Community: "a time . . . of veiled infinity" ', in *Medieval Women in their Communities*, ed. Diane Watt (Cardiff, 1997), pp. 116–37.

feminine based on the notion of *l'écriture feminine* and the means by which gender determines authorship. If this is the case, then one might wish to argue that the dream vision is, traditionally, a masculine form of writing. This has, indeed been argued elsewhere, particularly due to the idea of the gaze and its gendered determination. Sarah Stanbury interprets the dreamer in *Pearl* (a grieving father whose dream focuses upon his deceased daughter) as 'the true scopophilic, enraptured with sight . . . the experience of looking in, from without, even doubly removed . . . is ecstatic, a kind of visual *jouissance* that culminates in his attempt to cross the stream and fracture the divide between his body and the object of his gaze'.[21] *Scopophilia*, the joy of looking, voyeurism, is the process by which a male subject gazes at a female object and derives (often erotic) pleasure from what he sees. It is often applied to film and the camera, for which 'woman is always on display before the male gaze'.[22] The voyeur's pleasure, in fact, comes from looking, not participating in what he witnesses. The male dreamer, then, might well be seen as a voyeur (and has been seen as such by several critics, most notably A. C. Spearing in his book, *The Medieval Poet as Voyeur: Looking and Listening in Medieval Love-Narratives*).[23] Since voyeurism and the gaze are almost exclusively described by literary critics and psychoanalysts alike as masculine, there is a clearly masculine impulse behind the authorship of the dream vision.

The mystic, whether male or female, can be seen, particularly through her abjection and denial of subjectivity, as feminine. This can be seen in any number of mystical works, in both male- and female-authored mysticism in the act of self-denial. Marguerite Porete, for example, writes that the perfected soul must be without a will of its own, completely in denial of all personal will and self-involvement: '[free souls] no longer possess any will, and if they would desire anything, they would separate themselves from Love . . . Such souls do not know how to consider themselves good or evil, no longer possessing understanding of themselves, nor knowing how to judge if they are converted or perverted.'[24] Mystics by the very nature of the process of transcendence become submissive to the subjectivity of the Divine, spiritually feminized, in a sense. Thus, if the mystic is feminine and the dreamer is masculine, these genres can, ultimately, be seen as masculine and feminine expressions of the same process, the persona of one constructed as a gazer and of the other as a participant, dreamer and dream.

In the two works that I have examined thus far, *Pearl* and *Þe Wohunge of Ure Lauerd*, the gender of the author is ultimately unknowable, and thus the reader is

21 Sarah Stanbury, 'Feminist Masterplots: The gaze on the Body of *Pearl's* Dead Girl' in *Feminist Approaches to the Body in Medieval Literature*, ed. Linda Lomperis and Sarah Stanbury (Philadelphia, 1993), pp. 96–115. See also Sarah Stanbury, *Seeing the 'Gawain'-Poet: Description and the Act of Perception* (Philadelphia, 1991).

22 Kaja Silverman in Stanbury, 'Feminist Masterplots', p. 105.

23 Cambridge, 1993.

24 Marguerite Porete, *The Mirror of Simple Souls*, trans. Ellen L. Babinsky (New York, 1993), pp. 86–7.

free to imagine the author through the composition of the speaker, or persona, of these works. In the case of *Pearl*, whose author's gender has never seriously been questioned, the narrator is clearly male – in fact, he refers to himself as a man early on in the text: 'No gladder gome heþen into Grece/ þen I' (230–1). The narrator of *Þe Wohunge* is feminine, identifying herself as Christ's lover (and him as her darling, her honey drop) but, more specifically, as a woman: 'þu . . . makedes me lauedi/ ouer all þin schaftes þat tu schop/ on eorðe' (82–6).[25] *Þe Wohunge* is a powerfully feminine text, whether its author is male or female,[26] filled with images of erotic love and abjection. Thus, although both authors are unknown to us, and, indeed, are most probably both male, their work is gendered in its style and construction and thus represents a gendered perception of transcendence in medieval poetry.

It seems clear that medieval dream vision authors and medieval mystics articulate similar expressions of spirituality and creativity. Within the specific works, as well, there are similar tropes of transcendence, desire, and sensuality. As I noted above, in fact, the sensuality of mysticism and dream vision poems may be the first similarity one notices. This may stem from their common sources, and I do not have space in this context to explain those sources in detail. However, it seems obvious that biblical sources and late classical and early medieval notions of spirituality serve as similar sources for both types of works.[27] Whether it is St Bernard and the *Song of Songs* or Macrobius and the *Somnium Scipionis*, or indeed a text which I believe influences both genres quite directly, Boethius' *De Consolatione Philosophiae*, all of these texts share a perspective on sensuality and spiritual intimacy which both dreams and mystical visions share. The physical nature of desire and consummation seem to run through both types of works, as well. For example, in *Þe Wohunge of Ure Lauerd* the speaker contemplates the body of Christ in his beauty, his suffering and, ultimately, his death.

> Hwa ne mei
> luue þi luueli leor? Hwat her
> te is swa hard þat ne mei to mel
> te iþe munegunge of þe? Ah
> hwa ne mej luue þe luueli-
> che iesu? (5–10)

[25] Savage and Watson translate this passage as follows: 'you . . . made me lady over all the created things you shaped on earth' (p. 249).

[26] Most critics agree that the author is probably male. See Bella Millett, 'Women in No Man's Land: English Recluses and the Development of Vernacular Literature in the 12th and 13th Centuries' in *Women and Literature in Britain, 1150–1500*, ed. Carole Meale (Cambridge, 1993), pp. 86–103 and Savage and Watson, *Anchoritic Spirituality*, pp. 245–7.

[27] Critics have traditionally argued for biblical sources for the mystical works I have discussed here, particularly the Song of Songs; see Denis Renevey, 'Enclosed Desires: A Study of the Wooing Group' in *Mysticism and Spirituality in Medieval England*, ed. W. F. Pollard and R. Boenig (Cambridge, 1997), pp. 39–62. For a traditional reading of the sources and inspiration for fourteenth-century dream vision poetry, see Spearing, *Medieval Dream-Poetry*, pp. 1–24.

> ['Who cannot love your lovely face? What heart is so hard that it cannot melt in the memory of you? Ah, who cannot love you, lovely Jesus?' (p. 248)]

The narrator continues to express her desire to enjoy physical intimacy with Christ, and her desire to participate with him in his passion. 'A þat/ luuelike bodi þat henges swa rewli/ swa blodi & swa kalde' (532–5) ['Ah! That lovely body, that hangs to pitifully, so bloody, and so cold' (p. 255)]. The narrator contrasts images of Christ's beauty with his bloodied, violated body, seeing him as beautiful in the brutality and his death and seeing herself as redeemed through participation in his death and her own.

In *Pearl*, the narrator also makes a number of references to the *Pearl*-maiden's unique beauty, not as she dies (which is not part of the narrative) but after her death. In fact, the maiden is described using the traditional characteristics of the courtly mistress, including a 'fayre face,' (169); a high brow and ivory skin ('her fayre frount,/ Hyr visage whyt as playn yuore' (177–8)); and 'yȝen graye' (254).[28] The relationship between the dreamer and the Dream Lady in this poem is complicated, of course, because the poet seems to load his descriptions of their relationship and his desire for her with erotic language and imagery. This has led some critics to argue for the desire between the father (dreamer) and his daughter (the maiden) as incestuous.[29] Although I do not wish to make this claim, I do feel that desire as it is expressed in this poem, and in most other dream visions, is problematized in much the same way that it is in mysticism. Wooer and wooed are confused in these works, and the desire of the narrator, although physically chaste, can often be expressed only in terms of erotic desire. This is clear in *Þe Wohunge* when the narrator asks of Christ, 'makedes of me/ wrecche þi leofmon & spuse' (571–2).[30] She articulates her desire for Christ as erotic, not because of genuinely erotic desire, but because the literary conventions of her time, especially courtly literature and dream vision poetry, assume that desire, even that between a father and child, can only be understood as such.

[28] For further discussions of the courtly qualities of the maiden's appearance and of the poem itself, please see María Bullón-Fernández, ' "Byȝonde þe water": Courtly and Religious Desire in *Pearl*', *Studies in Philology* xci (1994), pp. 35–49; David Aers, 'The Self Mourning: Reflections on *Pearl*', *Speculum* lxviii (1993), pp. 54–73, and Charlotte Gross, 'Courtly Language in *Pearl*' in *Text and Matter: New Critical Perspectives of the 'Pearl'-Poet*, ed. Robert J. Blanch, Miriam Youngerman Miller, and Julian N. Wasserman (Troy, NY, 1991), pp. 79–92.

[29] See Jane Beal, '*The Pearl*-Maiden's Two Lovers', *Studies in Philology* c (2003), pp. 1–21.

[30] According to the editors of MED, *leofmon* and its various forms is used in several secular texts, as well as in secular ways in some spiritual works (they include the *Wohunge*). Its first recorded use as 'a spiritually beloved one . . . a believer in Christ . . . the Virgin Mary . . . [or] Christ' is in *Hali Meiðhad* (part of the Katherine Group) in 1225. See *Hali Meiðhad* in *Medieval Prose for Women from the Katherine Group and 'Ancrene Wisse'*, ed. Bella Millett and Jocelyn Wogan-Browne (Oxford, 1990), pp. 2–43.

IV

Space does not allow me to examine all the similarities in either *Pearl* and *þe Wohunge* specifically or dream visions and mysticism generally. However, my intention has been to examine and re-assess the relationship between these two styles of writing in order to argue that the relationship between them is not that of a smaller group of works (mysticism) within a larger genre (dream vision) or even of two separate genres (necessarily) among the larger world of medieval literature. Because of their association with the unconscious mind and of both desire and transcendence, these two types of literature must, I believe, be seen together. In a sense, what this argument seeks to do is to deconstruct current (and traditional) notions of the dream vision, clearly the privileged half of this binary, and in so doing define each not by its difference from the Other but by the Other itself in an effort to understand them both more fully. As Spearing points out in *Medieval Dream-Poetry*, 'the dreamer is an inadequate vessel for the experience of his dream' (p. 126). Just as Dante states that language fails when it seeks to explain profound spiritual truths, it seems the dreamer fails to understand his own experience. This is often true, as well, of the mystic, who seeks mostly to explain what happened to her, not necessarily what it means. Both dream visions and mysticism share this connection to the failure of human beings to make sense of the divine. Perhaps both genres exist as a means to bridge that gap in understanding, one originating in humans who seek to make sense of themselves with respect to the Divine (and the unknown), and one originating with a divine presence which seeks to form a more tangible connection with the experiences of human beings. Ultimately the source of the impulse seems less interesting than the persistence of the impulse itself: to know and to be known in a transcendent, extraordinary manner.

LORDSHIP, SERVICE AND WORSHIP IN JULIAN OF NORWICH

ALEXANDRA BARRATT

'AND WHOSOEVER WILL BE first among you, shall be the servant of all.' That verse from the Gospels (Mark 10:44) would have echoed in medieval ears with greater contemporary resonance and relevance than it does today. As we have been rightly reminded, 'Service has some claim to be considered the dominant ethic of the middle ages'[1] and Julian of Norwich was a woman of her time. Such an ethic, closely associated with concepts of 'lordship' and 'worship', thoroughly imbues her *Revelation of Love*. We do Julian a profound disservice if, with the laudable desire of making her accessible to our own time, we occlude the way in which she is firmly embedded in a specific historical era.

I have already argued that Julian's characterisation of the Holy Spirit as 'our good lord' can only be understood properly within the framework of so-called bastard feudalism.[2] What Julian's contemporaries thought constituted a 'good lord', a 'lord who looked after his servants' interests',[3] is implicit in numerous late-medieval texts. A 'good lord' was one's patron, with whom his man had a profound personal bond: the lord would reward his 'service' not by the grant of land as in the earlier Middle Ages but by fees or other material rewards, by his favour and patronage and, above all, by support in his 'lawful causes' (and on occasion in those not so lawful) in a court of law. The later-medieval 'good lord' was, therefore, in the most literal sense of the word a 'paraclete' – an advocate to stand at one's side in court – and therefore a suitable metaphor for the Holy Spirit.[4] Although it is easy enough to descry these features of good lordship in the society of the time, it is virtually impossible to find any contemporary definition that delineates it so baldly: 'Significantly . . . this concept never needed to be defined, but was simply invoked.'[5]

1 Rosemary Horrox, ed., *Fifteenth-century Attitudes: Perceptions of Society in Late Medieval England* (Cambridge, 1994), p. 61.

2 ' "Bastard feudalism" . . . is in fact a misnomer which has no justification except a vague prejudice against the later Middle Ages', G. A. Holmes, *The Estates of the Higher Nobility in Fourteenth-Century England* (Cambridge, 1957), p. 83. On the history of this disputed term, see J. M. W. Bean, *From Lord to Patron: Lordship in Late Medieval England* (Manchester, 1989), p. 3.

3 Horrox, *Fifteenth-century Attitudes*, p. 66.

4 Alexandra Barratt, 'Julian of Norwich and the Holy Spirit, "Our Good Lord" ', *Mystics Quarterly* xxviii (2002), pp. 78–84.

5 Horrox, *Fifteenth-century Attitudes*, p. 66. Cf: 'In asking for lordship, contemporaries

But 'lordship' and 'good lord' are merely part of a nexus of words and concepts drawn from bastard feudalism that we find in Julian's writings. We need also to pay attention to 'service' and 'servant'; to 'office', and to 'worship' and its derivatives in all its senses. By revisiting some key passages in *A Revelation of Love* where these words occur, we can attempt to deepen and re-focus our understanding of Julian through a heightened awareness of her historical context.

Both lord and servant, as Rosemary Horrox puts it, lived in 'a society where standing was intimately bound up with "face" – what contemporaries called *worship*'.[6] This concept is particularly emphasised by the first passage to be studied. In the late fourteenth century, the most common meaning of 'worship' as a noun was one that is now obsolete: 'the condition . . . of deserving, or being held in, esteem . . . honour, distinction, renown; good name, credit'.[7] This single sense actually subsumes a pair of meanings that mirror each other: the intrinsic honour, credit or reputation possessed by a great lord, to which the servant may contribute; and the rewards, both abstract and concrete, that the lord may choose to bestow on his servant and which will enhance his status. In the first sense, 'worship' was in part the reputation that a lord gained from his proven status as 'good lord':

> By demonstrating his mastery through the successful defence of his clients' interests – by being a 'good lord' – a magnate made it known that he was a man worth following and thus attracted yet more support.[8]

It was thus essentially identical with 'political power' or

> the quality a landowner expected to have if he used his resources properly. [Worship] defies modern definition, but can best be described as the worth or credit that was earned by living up to one's status as a landowner in all publically-visible aspects of life, from housing and food through litigation to dealing with the king or his officers.[9]

From as early as chapter 2 of *A Revelation of Love*, the theme of worship bubbles along, surfacing dramatically in chapter 7 in the 'opyn example' of 'a solemne king or a grete lord'.[10] When Julian relates her original desire for a near-death experience so that she might 'after lyven more to the worshippe of God because of that sekenesse' (p. 3), worship is something that already belongs to God but that she can augment by her service in this life. When granted her desire, she resigns herself to an early death with the words, 'Good lord, may my

rarely felt it necessary to define what they wanted', Rosemary Horrox, *Richard III: A Study in Service* (Cambridge, 1989), p. 2.

6 Horrox, *Fifteenth-century Attitudes*, p. 62.

7 Oxford English Dictionary, *s.v. worship* I. 1. a.

8 Christine Carpenter, 'The Beauchamp Affinity: a study of bastard feudalism at work', *English Historical Review* xcv (1980), pp. 514–32 at p. 528.

9 Christine Carpenter, *Locality and Polity: A Study of Warwickshire Landed Society 1401–1499* (Cambridge, 1992), pp. 198, 245.

10 Marion Glasscoe, ed., *Julian of Norwich: A Revelation of Love* (Exeter, 1976, rev. edn 1993), p. 11. All subsequent references (given within the text) are to this edition.

living no longer be to thy worshippe!' (p. 4). This kind of worship seems to be closely associated in Julian's mind with life on earth. In chapter 42, on prayer, she writes that we should pray 'that [God] reule us and gyde us to his worshippe in thys lif and bryng us to his bliss'; if we do not perceive this, 'it makyth us hevy and doubtful; and that is not to his worshippe' (p. 59). And in chapter 81 she reflects that it is 'the most worshippe to him of onything that we may don, that we leven gladly and meryly, for his love, in our penance' (p. 130). Presumably we can contribute to God's 'worship' only while on earth, as at least in part it has do to with how He is perceived by human beings.

Her preoccupation with 'worship' continues in chapter 5. After the famous hazel-nut vision she prays, 'God, of thy goodnesse, give me thyselfe; for thou art enow to me and I may nothing aske that is less that may be full worshippe to thee' (pp. 7–8). In the next chapter she expands this thought: God's honour demands that we should ask him only for himself and for nothing else, invoking his goodness alone:

> it is more worshippe to God, and more very delite, that we faithfully pray to himselfe of his goodness . . . than if we made all the menys that herte can thinke; for if we make all these menys, it is to litil and not full worshippe to God. (p. 8)

This sense of 'worship' as something possessed by God is associated with certain other divine attributes. In chapters 22 and 23, where Julian meditates on Christ's words, 'It is a ioy, a blis, an endles lekyng to me that ever suffrid I passion for the' (pp. 31–2), she links 'worship' and 'blis' or glory. As she envisages the Father acting towards his Son in a typically feudal fashion, bestowing on him a reward in return for his 'dedes', she sees how, 'by the curtes geft of his Fader we be his blis, we be his mede, we be his worshippe, we be his corone' (p. 32). (A very similar passage occurs at the end of the parable of the lord and the servant: see below p. 185.) Her train of thought continues into the next chapter: 'for the ioy I vnderstode the plesance of the Fader; and for the blis, the worshippe of the Son. . . . The Fader is plesid, the Son is worshippid' (p. 33).

Elsewhere, 'worship' is linked with the divine will: in chapter 57 Julian declares that, with respect to our 'substance', God 'made us nobil and so rich that evermore we werkyn his will and his worship' (p. 91). In chapter 65 at the end of the fifteenth revelation, she hears Christ say: 'What shuld it than agrevyn the to suffre a while, sith it is my will and my worshippe?' (p. 107). If 'worship' is at times close in meaning to 'power' or 'might', it is not surprising that it collocates with 'will'.

This 'worship' that is intrinsic to God but to which we can contribute while on earth is also associated with eschatological advantages to ourselves, linked with our 'profit' or salvation. When God himself, appropriately, teaches a soul how to conduct itself in contemplation, 'that is most worshipp to him and profitt to thyselfe . . . for a soule that only festinith him on to God with very troste . . . it is the most worshipp that he [*sc.* the soul] may don to him, as to my sight' (chapter 10, pp. 16–17). A few pages later, Julian reflects that 'in God may be no wreth, as to my syte, for our gode lord endlesly hath regarde to his own worshippe and to the profite of al that shall be savid' (chapter 13, p. 20). 'Worship' is also associated with our heavenly 'ioy'. In chapter 47 she reflects on the intermittent nature of our perception of God in this life: 'this manner syte of Him may not be continuant in this lif, and that for his owen worship and for encreas of our endless ioy' (p. 67). In chapter 62 she points out that even when we are apparently falling into sin, 'he kepyth us in this tyme as tenderly and as swetely to his worship and as sekirly to our salvation and therto he . . . turnyth it [*sc.* sin] al to his worship and to our ioye, withoute end' (p. 101).

This sense of 'worship' as a divine attribute is a minor theme in the lead-up to chapter 7: the chapter itself foregrounds 'worship' as the honour or glory that God can bestow on us. This chapter is the final movement of Julian's great first revelation. It consists of three apparently discrete sections: a 'ghostly sight' of the Blessed Virgin Mary; a continuing 'bodyly sight' of Christ's bleeding head with the distinctive similes of water falling from the eaves and of herring scales; and finally Julian's thoughts on God's courtesy and 'homlyhede'.

The shewing of the Virgin Mary may at first seem to have no bearing on our theme. On closer inspection, however, it can be seen to relate to the theme of service, rewarded by 'worship'. The opening of chapter 7 is largely a recasting of the final section of chapter 4, which reads:

> In this he browght *our blissid lady to my understonding*. I saw hir ghostly in bodily likeness, a simple mayde and a meke, young of age and little waxen above a child, in the stature that she was wan she conceived with child. Also God *shewid* in party *the wisedam and the trueth* of hir soule, wherein I understood the *reverend beholding* that she beheld hir God and *maker*, mervelyng with greate reverence that he would be borne of hir that was a simple creature of his makeyng. And *this wisdam and trueth*, knowyng the *gretenes* of [her] maker and the *littlehede* of hirselfe that is made, caused hir sey full *mekely* to Gabriel: 'Lo me, Gods handmayd.' In this sight I undestode sothly that *she is mare than all that God made beneath hir in worthyness and grace*. (p. 6)

In comparison, chapter 7 reads:

> And to lerne us this, as *to myne understondyng*, our lord God *shewed our lady* Saint Mary in the same tyme; that is to mene [*the*] *hey wisedome and trewth* she had in *beholding of hir maker* so grete, so hey, so mightie and so gode. This *gretenes* and this noblyth of the *beholdyng* of God fulfilled her of *reverend* drede, and with this she saw hirselfe so *litil* and so low, so simple and so pore, in reward of hir lord God, that this reverend drede fulfilled hir of *mekenes*. And thus, by this grounde, she was fulfillid of *grace* and of al manner of vertues and *overpassyth all creatures*. (p. 10)

The italicised words and phrases indicate the considerable overlap in thought and expression between the two passages. What the passage from chapter 7 omits, however, – but which it must imply – are the references to the Virgin as 'a simple mayde and a meke, young of age and little waxen above a child, in the stature that she was wan she conceived with child', and her response to Gabriel's message: 'Lo me, Gods handmayd.' These are not mere affective details: rather, both draw attention to the idea of service. The Middle English word 'handmayd' translates, of course, the Vulgate *ancilla*, of which it has recently been said that 'we have no single meaning . . . but rather a multiplicity of meanings that may shade into one another'.[11] Youth, however, seems to have been one important element in the definition,[12] and here the Virgin's youth is particularly stressed: she is 'young of age and little waxen above a child'. So chapter 4 explicitly, and chapter 7 implicitly, present the Virgin as God's handmaid or servant. Indeed the very adjectives – 'pore' and 'simple' – used to describe the 'servant' of the exemplum are also those applied to the Virgin.

The exemplum itself[13] is designed to illustrate the courteous intimacy of God's revelation of Christ's sufferings. It reads as follows:

> it is the most worshippe that a solemne king or grete lord may doe a pore servant if he will be homely with him. . . . Than thinkyth this pore creature thus: 'A! What might this nobil lord doe more worshipp and ioy to me than to shew me, that am so simple, this mervelous homlyhede? Sothly it is more ioy and likeing to me than he gave me grete gifts and were himselfe strange in maner.' (p. 11)

This exemplary story demands to be placed within its late-medieval social and political context. First, we must appreciate that 'service' was not regarded as demeaning:

> the term is used variously in respect of the relationship of individuals to God, of children to their parents, of employees to their employers, and of lovers to their beloved. What these relationships have in common is a sense of mutual obligation, which may well be contractual and based on consent. . . . For medievals 'servant' does not generally appear to have been a pejorative or demeaning term. It implied as much a relationship – between servant and master, mistress, or Divinity – as a status.[14]

Not only was service not demeaning: on the contrary, 'service to the right master generated reflected glory rather than degradation',[15] and 'conferred on the retainer some of the respect due to his lord. It enhanced his prestige and authority.'[16] Furthermore, service 'was defined not by the nature of the tasks being performed, but by the relationship involved: that of master and man'.[17] This was a symbiotic relationship: consequently, service is something that God

11 P. J. P. Goldberg, 'What Was a Servant?', in *Concepts and Patterns of Service in the Later Middle Ages*, ed. Anne Curry and Elizabeth Matthew (Woodbridge, 2000), p. 2.

12 'From at least 1260 living-in servants were equated with children; probably they already owed the unquestioning obedience and suffered the absolute paternal authority of their master assumed in early modern England', Michael Hicks, *Bastard Feudalism* (London, 1995), p. 84.

13 Joan M. Nuth, *Wisdom's Daughter: The Theology of Julian of Norwich* (New York, 1991), p. 31, rightly regards this exemplum, and also the passages from chapter 14 discussed below, as 'intimations' of the parable of the lord and servant in chapter 51. She does not however comment on their shared secular imagery but rather on the parable's 'scriptural ties' (p. 32). Marion Glasscoe also points to the links between these passages in *English Medieval Mystics: Games of Faith* (London, 1993), p. 251.

14 Goldberg, 'What Was a Servant?', p. 2.

15 Carpenter, *Locality and Polity*, p. 227.

16 Hicks, *Bastard Feudalism*, p. 149.

17 Horrox, *Fifteenth-century Attitudes*, p. 63.

himself may offer us. As early as chapter 6, Julian declares that he 'hath no disdeyne to serve us at the simplest office that [t]o our body longyth in kinde' (p. 9). This service is 'nerest in kind and ridiest in grace' (ibid.), phrases that foreshadow the terms 'nerest, redyest and sekirest' which in chapter 60 Julian is to apply to 'the mother's service', the service assumed by God when he took flesh, 'himselfe to don the service and the office of moderhede in allthyng' (p. 97). In the following chapter, Julian again uses 'office' as a synonym for 'service': 'the swete gracious hands of our moder be redy and diligently aboute us; for he in al this werkyng usith the office of a kinde nurse. . . . It is his office to saven us, it is his worship to don [it]' (p. 101). Indeed, this metaphor of the mother's service illustrates how in human society, too, the superior may serve – and gladly serve – the inferior, and that the most menial forms of service do not disparage the one who serves. The distinction between honourable and menial service was based on the status of the servant, not the nature of the service performed: 'even quasi-menial service could become honourable when performed by someone of sufficiently superior status'.[18]

Just to be in the service of a great lord would generate 'worship': as Mark Ormrod has said, 'To be within the affinity of a great nobleman – or the king – was therefore to be a person of rank and importance: as contemporaries would have put it, to enjoy both "good lordship" and "worship".'[19] In Julian's story, 'worship' is not bestowed by anything as tangible as 'grete gifts', the giving of which, 'usually in the form of food, sometimes of cloth or jewels . . . was an important social function' of the lord in later medieval society.[20] Rather, Julian's lord rewards his servant with genuine intimacy ('homlyhede') and respect, which are specifically seen as preferable. This form of 'worship' – essentially the validation of the servant by the lord – is linked with 'ioy', just as elsewhere Julian links it with 'solace' and 'bliss' (chapter 48, p. 68), 'goodness' (chapter 59, p. 95), and 'pretioushede (chapter 62, p. 101).[21]

Ideas of service are foregrounded even more precisely by my second passage. Chapter 14, which constitutes the sixth revelation, opens with the Lord thanking Julian for her service: 'I thanke thee of thy travel and namely of thy youthe' (p. 21). She then sees him 'as a lord in his own house', having invited to a feast 'al his derworthy servants and freinds' (pp. 21–2). (The medieval noble household comprised 'a collection of servants, friends and other retainers, around a noble and possibly his immediate family'.[22]) He reveals to her the three degrees

[18] Ibid., p. 64.

[19] W. M. Ormrod, *Political Life in Medieval England, 1300–1450* (Houndsmill, 1995), p. 52.

[20] Kate Mertes, *The English Noble Household, 1250–1600: Good Governance and Politic Rule* (Oxford, 1988), p. 93.

[21] Conversely, 'worship' is opposed, implicitly or explicitly, to 'peynys' (chapter 21, p. 31), 'wounds' (chapter 39, p. 54), and 'our tribulations and al our wo' (chapter 49, p. 70).

[22] Mertes, *The English Noble Household*, p. 5.

of glory to be enjoyed by 'every soule . . . that wilfully hath servid God in any degre in erthe' (p. 22). The stress is on voluntary, not forced or constrained, service: in the secular analogy, 'the dependency of the servant to the employer . . . because voluntarily entered into, may be characterised by good will on both parts'.[23] The rewards for this voluntary service are once again intangible. They consist, first, of God's thanks – 'worshipful thanke', we may note – and, secondly, of the publication of this 'worshipfull thankyng' to the inhabitants of heaven. This is illustrated by another 'example' of a king: 'a king, if he thanke his servants it is a gret worship to hem, and if he makyth it knowen to all the reme, than is his worshippe mekil incresid' (ibid.). Presumably 'his worshippe' here means the honour accorded the servant, though it could mean the king's honour. One of the features of 'worship' is that it is reciprocal: the servant's service may bestow 'worship' on his lord, while the lord may in turn reward that servant with 'worship'.

In addition, Julian perceives:

> the age of every man shal be knowen in hevyn, and shal be rewardid for his wilful service and for his time; and namely the age of hem that wilfully and frely offir her yongith to God passingly is rewardid and wonderly is thankyd. (ibid.)

She was herself only thirty and a half years old at the time of the shewings and when she thought she was dying was much preoccupied with her youth: 'And in youngith yet, I thought great sweeme to dye' (chapter 3, p. 4). She explains that there was nothing on earth that she wished to live for, but she wished 'that I might have loved God better and longer tyme' (ibid.). By this exemplary story, therefore, God reassures her that to die young can be an additional source of honour. For she further grasps that 'the more that the lovand soule seeth this curtesy of God, the lever he is to serve him al the dayes of his life' (p. 22). Service, then, could be said to be a self-reinforcing activity: as Rosemary Horrox puts it, 'Service was its own reward, and most people wanted to serve at least as much as lords wanted service.'[24]

Finally, service and lordship, as we have already seen, must be reciprocal: no servant without a lord, no lord without a servant. It would be impossible to write about service and lordship in Julian and ignore chapter 51, the 'wonderful example of a lord that hath a servant', that falls between the fourteenth and fifteenth revelations. This parable endlessly eludes completely satisfactory exegesis and I have no intention of offering yet another interpretation.[25] By drawing attention, however, to its political and social framework, we may at least appreciate its inner logic a little more.

23 Goldberg, 'What Was a Servant?', p. 10.

24 Horrox, *Fifteenth-century Attitudes*, p. 56.

25 See for instance the references given by Christopher Abbott, who comments: 'The example of the lord and servant has attracted significant critical attention (though less than might have been expected given its obvious weight within the text)', *Julian of Norwich: Autobiography and Theology* (Cambridge, 1999), p. 90 n. 21.

In chapter 51 Julian sees the servant setting out 'to don his lords will' (p. 72): she must think this important as she uses these words three times in five lines. (In the secular world the servant's own honour required 'a readiness to carry out the lord's specific commands'.)[26] In the process, however, perhaps because he acts 'suddenly' and 'in grete haste', he falls into a 'slade' and lies there wallowing helplessly, unable to look up and see his lord. His 'curtes' lord looks on him with compassion and says:

> Lo, lo, my lovid servant. What harme and disese he hath takeyn in my service for my love, ya, and for his good will! Is it not skyl that I award hym his afray . . . ? . . . fallith it not to me to gevyn a geft that be better to hym and more worshipfull than his own hole shuld have ben? And ell me thynkyth I dede hym no grace. (p. 73)

Here he speaks as would any responsible 'good lord'. The servant was voluntarily serving his lord; while attempting to carry out the lord's will he has suffered through no fault of his own. In return, even though he has failed, the lord owes him an honourable gift. If the lord failed to give him this, he would be denying his servant his 'grace' or favour and detracting from his own honour, for 'A lord's honour . . . demanded that he uphold the interests of his servant.'[27] All this should be familiar by now; the one new element is that the bond between lord and servant is a bond of love. This is much more than the 'mutual obligation',[28] 'good will'[29] or 'tie that was honourable and binding'[30] which modern historians describe as characterising the servant–lord relationship. (It is perhaps significant that in all the material I have gathered on 'bastard feudalism', the word 'love' does not occur once.) Granted a supernatural insight into the lord's thoughts, Julian particularly notes the role of love and comments:

> I saw that it behovith neds to ben, stondyng his grete and his own worship, that his dereworthy servant which he lovid so mech shuld ben verily and blisfully rewarded . . .; ya and so ferforth that his fallyng and his wo . . . shall be turnyd into hey and overpassing worship and endless bliss. (p. 73)

Here the nexus of obligation, honour, service, love and reward is inescapable. For the sake of the lord's own credit or reputation, it is essential that the servant, whom he loves dearly, should receive a reward. Not only will the servant be rewarded, but his very failure and suffering will be transformed into a source of honour and glory.

At this point the shewing vanishes and in the subsequent passage, in which Julian relates her initial reaction to, and pondering of, the exemplum, references to 'worship' and 'lordship' slip into the background. They come forward once more, however, when nearly twenty years later she is instructed to reconsider certain details that she had earlier ignored. In the original vision she had noted,

26 Horrox, *Fifteenth-century Attitudes*, p. 70.
27 Ibid., p. 68.
28 Goldberg, 'What Was a Servant?', p. 2.
29 Ibid., p. 10.
30 Carpenter, 'The Beauchamp Affinity', p. 531.

'The lord sittith solemnly in rest and in peace' (p. 72), and one tends to assume he must be seated on a throne. But now she perceives that the 'place that our lord sat on was symple, on the erth barren and desert' (p. 75). This, she realises, is significant: he sits on the ground because he has no more fitting place to sit: 'he made mans soule to ben his owen cyte and his dwellyng place' but as yet he may not sit there, as man 'was not al semly to servyn of that noble office' (p. 76).

Not only does this passage juxtapose 'serve' and 'office': in addition, Julian for some reason associates this idea of man's soul as the 'cyte', where the lord desires to sit and where he will eventually take his seat or 'see', with various words derived from 'worship'. In chapter 56 she is to write of the 'worshipfull cyte that our lord Iesus sittith in' (p. 90), while in chapter 67, as she contemplates the soul, she understands that 'it is a worshipful syte. In the midds of that syte sitts our lord Iesus . . . heyest bishopp, solemnest kinge, worshipfulliest Lord: and I saw him clad solemnly and worshiply' (p. 109). Then almost at the end, in chapter 81, she recurs to this theme, recalling that 'our good lord' had revealed himself as reigning 'principally' in the human soul: 'He hath taken there his resting place and his worshipfull cyte; oute of which worshipfull see he shall never risen nor removen without end' (p. 130).

What exactly does Julian mean by 'worshipful'? One is tempted to suspect just a vague term of approval when, for instance, she writes of 'many privy points longing to our faith which be worshipfull to knowen' (chapter 7, p. 12). Here the word probably means 'notable' or 'outstanding', but elsewhere (and possibly it is significant that all these examples come after chapter 51) she uses it to mean 'showing or bringing with it worship or honour', surely fully aware that it derives from 'worship'. When in chapter 80 she writes that God, who is 'nerest and mekest' (words that recall 'the moders service'), does not only what is necessary but also 'all that is worshipfull, to our ioy in hevyn' (p. 129), we remember that she has earlier linked 'ioy' and 'bliss' with 'worship' (see above, p. 179). In addition, she uses 'worshipful' to modify 'asseth' and 'nobleth' in chapter 52 (p. 84), and 'onyng' in the phrase 'the worshipfull onyng . . . betwix the soule and body' in chapter 55 (p. 89).

More important, perhaps, is the use of the word to refer to what brings 'worship' to God. In chapter 45, which looks forward to chapter 51, 'worshipful' is associated with the first promptings that result in Julian's ventures into theodicy:

> Than was this my desire: that I myte sen in God in what manner that the dome of holy church herin techyth is trew in his syte, and how it longyth to me sothly to knoyn it; wherby thei myte both [*sc.* the judgement of God and of the Church] be savid, so as it wer worshipfull to God and ryte way to me. And to al this I had non other answere but a mervelous example of a lord and of a servant. . . . (pp. 63–4)

For Julian, to reconcile the teachings of the Church on the subject and her own revelation of God's judgement[31] becomes something to which she aspires because it

31 There is a useful tabulation of the apparent contradictions between orthodox doctrine and Julian's visions in M. L. del Mastro, 'Juliana of Norwich: Parable of the Lord and Servant – Radical Orthodoxy', *Mystics Quarterly* xiv (1988), pp. 84–6.

protects, or enhances, the honour of God, and/or which she wishes to pursue only as long as it is indeed 'worshipfull' to him: the exact interpretation depends on the punctuation of the passage.[32] But with such a genesis, it is not perhaps surprising that the 'mervelous exemple' itself relies so heavily on late-medieval feudal language.

We might further note that Julian particularly associates the adverb 'worshipfully' with heaven: in chapter 55 she sees that Christ 'worshipfully presentith his Fader in hevyn with us; which present ful thankfully his Fader receivith and curtesly gevith it to his Son' (p. 88), while in chapter 58 she argues that in and by Christ 'we arn mytyly taken out of helle and out of the wretchidnes in erth, and worshipfully browte up into hevyn . . . incresid in riches and noblith' (p. 95). Clearly Julian conceives of heaven as a feudal court, a more refined and theologically sophisticated version of the general late-medieval view of heaven, appositely characterised by Christine Carpenter as a place 'organised very much like this world, with God taking the role of ruler, military leader, and justice, and Mary and the "company of heaven" acting as nobles and courtiers'.[33]

To return to chapter 51, however, the 'cyte' of man's soul in which the lord desires to sit, Julian now perceives, can only be restored by 'herd travel'. The servant is engaged in this, for service is often a form of hard work. He is dressed unpretentiously, 'as a labourer which wer disposid to travel' (p. 76): so much so, in fact, that she finds it inappropriate to the lord's honour: 'This is now an onsemely clothyng for the servant that is so heyly lovid to stondyn afor so worship lord' (p. 77). The 'unseemliness' relates both to the status of the servant, who is beloved by his lord, and to the lord himself. Certainly a late-medieval lord would expect to have finely dressed servants: this was just one of the many ways in which he could 'assert his nobility, proclaim his wealth, and advertise his power': a poorly dressed servant would be bad for his reputation.[34] And this servant is indeed badly dressed, in a kirtle that is old, stained, ragged and skimpy.

But more important is the relationship between the two: Julian perceives in the servant 'a ground of love, which love he had to the lord was even like to the love that the lord had to hym' (p. 77). This bond of love (later interpreted as the Holy Spirit) is reciprocal, even identical: the servant serves his lord, not because he is a servant, but because he loves him. When he sees that 'ther was one thing to don which shuld be to the worshipp of the lord', 'for love' he runs 'to don that thing

32 The problem is located in the concessive clause that concludes the first sentence. Does it qualify the whole sentence, or only part of it? G. R. Crampton, ed., *The Shewings of Julian of Norwich* (Kalamazoo, MI, 1994), who places a comma after 'knoyn it', has no punctuation after 'be savid' and therefore seems to relate it only to the clause beginning 'wherby'. Glasscoe and Colledge and Walsh both have a comma, but, if this were replaced with a semi-colon, the concessive clause would be more powerful, qualifying the whole sentence. See *A Book of Showings to the Anchoress Juliana of Norwich*, ed. Edmund Colledge and James Walsh, Pontifical Institute of Mediaeval Studies Studies and Texts XXV, 2 vols (Toronto, 1978).

33 Carpenter, *Locality and Polity*, p. 225.

34 Mertes, *The English Noble Household*, p. 103.

which was to his will and his worship' (ibid.), even though it demands 'the gretest labor and herdest travel that is – he shuld ben a gardiner; delvyn and dykyn, swinkin and swetyn, and turne the earth upsodowne' (ibid.) in order to produce the food that the lord desires and which the servant will eventually carry 'ful worshipfully' before the lord. The lord lacks this 'tresor', which is not available to enhance his 'worship' until the servant has produced it, just as he lacks the 'cyte' where he wishes to take his seat. And both can only be restored to him by his servant's 'travel'.

The shock of the servant's clothing seems to stimulate Julian to notice two more surprising features of the vision that had escaped her so far. Both are trangressions of late-medieval ideas of proper lordship (she calls them 'mervels'). First, the lord has nothing to eat: 'I saw the lord sitten as a man, and I saw neither mete ner drynke wherwith to servyn hym' (p. 77). Secondly, he has only one servant – an extraordinary state of affairs in a society where even an obscure squire might have eighteen servants.[35]

When Julian, however, moves into the exegesis of the lord as God the Father and the servant as both God the Son and Adam/all mankind, it is noticeable that much of this late-feudal language recedes. But Christ's act of redemption is still 'that worshipfull dede be which mankynde was browte ageyn into hevyn' (p. 78), and as the servant he declares his willingness 'to don thy worship whan it is thy will to send me' (p. 79), echoing associations (of worship and heaven and of will and worship) that are familiar from our earlier discussion. The servant's clothing is described as 'not honest', or honourable, to stand directly before his lord, nor was this stance his 'office' while he was a labourer, before he had won his peace 'with his herd travel' (p. 80). And finally, as the exegesis rapidly unravels, gathering up so many reminiscences from the earlier shewings, Julian returns to the transformed and glorified present and describes Christ's clothing as so wonderful it defies description, 'for it is al of very worshipps' (ibid.). In that glorious state, the Son stands before his Father 'rechely clad in blissfull largess, with a corone upon his hede of pretious richess: for it was shewid that we be his corone, which corone is the Fadirs ioye, tho Sons worshippe' (p. 81). In the final sentences the servant has, as it were, been raised up to the lord's level. The Son's clothing is more glorious than the lord's,[36] and it is he who sits 'in his cety', won by his 'travel' but which 'his Fadir had adyte to him of endles purpose' (ibid.).

We may conclude that Julian clearly feels at ease with images and language drawn from late-medieval feudal society. They come naturally to her and she does not linger to explicate them. This strongly suggests that she herself came from a gentry or aristocratic background, and that insofar as she was writing for a specific audience at all, she had in mind one with a similar background. We, on the other hand, live in a very different world. 'Service' is not a concept that comes easily to us. True, it is still in use in theological discourse – there is a

35 Ibid., p. 15.
36 Cf. Glasscoe, *English Medieval Mystics*, p. 248.

whole literature on 'the suffering servant' that I have chosen to ignore that is no doubt relevant to Julian. But we associate 'service' with 'domestic' – dated and probably degrading; or with 'public' and 'community', phrases that would have surely baffled Julian and her contemporaries. For them, service, however altruistic, was not impersonal and abstract but intensely personal and concrete.

We have similar problems with 'worship', both noun and verb. Apart from the occasional use of the noun as an honorific, we now use 'worship' exclusively in its religious senses. 'Lord', too, outside historical writing and the specialised environment of the British House of Lords, is confined to religious discourse. What I am suggesting is not so much that Julian needs to be demythologised or even demystified, but that we should perhaps begin to 'demysticise' her. In the later Middle Ages, a great deal of her language could have been read simultaneously as both secular and religious – to a much greater extent than is obvious to modern readers, especially those reading her in translation. Julian may have written *A Revelation of Love* in an anchorhold, but that anchorhold was attached to a little church only five or ten minutes' walk from what was then, as it is today, a busy urban centre. She was physically separated, but not emotionally removed, from the secular and political concerns of her own time.[37] As the proverb might put it, you can take the mystic out of society, but you can't take the society out of the mystic. We already celebrate her as a visionary and as a citizen of heaven: let us now start to recuperate and reconstruct a 'social' Julian.

[37] In a paper given at Kalamazoo in 2002, Liz Herbert McAvoy also sets out 'to locate Julian's writing firmly within the specific economic and social milieu of mercantile East Anglia', but her emphases are somewhat different from mine: see 'Julian of Norwich and a Trinity of the Feminine', *Mystics Quarterly* xxviii (2002), pp. 68–77 at p. 69.

'HID DIUINITE': THE SPIRITUALITY OF THE ENGLISH SYON BRETHREN

VINCENT GILLESPIE

IN THE YEARS LEADING up to the suppression of Syon Abbey in 1539, Thomas Bedyll, a Commissioner of the King, monitored the activities and attitudes of the house. He regularly reported back on the progress of the campaign against it to his master Thomas Cromwell, chief architect of the dissolution of the monasteries. At this time Syon was one of the wealthiest and most influential monasteries in England and therefore a notable target in the developing war against monasticism.[1] In 1534, early on in the campaign of harassment, Bedyll closely observed sermons given in the abbey church by the Brethren of Syon. Their subject was Henry VIII's claim to supremacy over the Church. Bedyll noted that 'the Confessor there hath preched twice, sythens my Lord of London and I wer at Sion, and dyd his dutie, concernyng the said title accordingly'.[2] The Confessor-General of Syon in 1534 would have been John Fewterer. A scholarly soul who possessed a copy of the first printed Hebrew concordance, Fewterer was also the author of *The Mirror or Glass of Christ's Passion*, printed the very same year that Bedyll's letter was written, which draws in an antiquarian way on the affective contemplative piety of the *Stimulus Amoris*, Ludolph of Saxony and Simon of Cassia.[3] With his interest in the scriptural scholarship of the New Learning and his affinity with the devotional

1 The standard account of the foundation of Syon is still G. J. Aungier, *The History and Antiquities of Syon Monastery, the Parish of Isleworth and the Chapelry of Hounslow* (London, 1840). More recently M. B. Tait, 'The Brigittine Monastery of Syon (Middlesex) with special reference to its monastic uses' (unpublished doctoral thesis, University of Oxford, 1975) studied much unprinted manuscript material and explored the spiritual and cultural life of the house. See also N. Beckett, 'St. Bridget, Henry V and Syon Abbey', in *Studies in St. Birgitta and the Brigittine Order*, ed. J. Hogg, Analecta Cartusiana XXXV:19 (1993), II, pp. 125–50 for a recent perspective on the politics of the foundation. On the fabric, see R. W. Dunning, 'The Building of Syon Abbey', *Transactions of the Ancient Monuments Society*, new series xxv (1981), pp. 16–26.

2 Bedyll's letter, dated 28 August 1534, is transcribed by Aungier, pp. 435–8. 'My Lord of London' would have been the Bishop of London, who had visitation rights at Syon and was involved in persuading the house to accept the supremacy. Letters relating to the suppression of Syon are collected in London, British Library, MS Cotton Cleopatra E. iv and E. vi and others survive in state papers. Some are printed in G. H. Cook, *Letters to Cromwell and Others in the Suppression of the Monasteries* (London, 1965), pp. 33–7. See the excellent account in A. Hutchison, 'Syon Abbey: Dissolution, No Decline', *Birgittiana* ii (1996), pp. 245–59.

3 London: Richard Pynson, 1534; STC 10838.

traditions of the fourteenth and fifteenth centuries, Fewterer exemplifies the cautious and conservative scholarship typical of the Brethren of Syon.[4]

Unsurprisingly, he seems to have been much troubled by the matter of the King's supremacy and more at home with historical precedents than the exigencies and pragmatics of contemporary politics. But a surviving letter written by two Syon Brethren and subscribed by him (in what may have been a politically convenient sickness) urges the monks of London Charterhouse to accept the supremacy, and Bedyll describes him as 'a sad man, bothe tractable and comformable to do every thing according to his duetie'.[5] Bedyll reports that Fewterer is in fear of his life at the obstinacy of those of his brethren who opposed the supremacy, having failed to persuade them to the rightness of the cause as he had promised the authorities to do. 'The vauntperlers and heddes of thair faction' were identified as Richard Whitford and Richard Lache.

Fewterer seems to have known that he was fighting for the life not just of his Brethren but of the very house itself. For threats had already been made and would soon be repeated against the key functions of the house in general and of the Brethren in particular. His letter to the Carthusians recalls that the members of Syon 'haue been in troble, dyspleasure and daunger therfore, as ye nowe bee'.[6] But not all the Syon Brethren shared Fewterer's sense of the necessity of the politics of survival. The opponents of his line seem to have been prepared to lead a vociferous and strenuous campaign against accepting and preaching in favour of the supremacy. Whitford, Bedyll repeatedly complains 'hathe a brasyn forehed, which shameth at no thing' and simply would not toe the line:[7]

4 Ordained in 1507, John Fewterer was a University Preacher in 1510–11 and was still active in Cambridge as late as 1515, yet was elected Confessor-General in 1523. He died in September 1536. His Hebrew Concordance (Venice, 1524) survives as Oxford, Merton College 76 b. 11. For capsule biographies of most of the Brothers mentioned in this article, see the notes on Donors in *Syon Abbey*, ed. V. Gillespie, with *The Libraries of the Carthusians*, ed. A. I. Doyle, Corpus of British Medieval Library Catalogues IX (London, 2001).

5 The letter to London Charterhouse (Aungier, pp. 430–3) has a notably uneasy tone. It exhorts the Carthusians to 'dye not for the cause, salve your selfes and your house, lyve long and lyve welle to the honor of God, welthe by your prayer and edyfying by your lyf to the people'. Fewterer's subscription says that 'yf I ware in good helthe I wolde wryte my full mynde vnto youe', but encourages the Carthusians to be content with 'the charytable wrytyng of my lerned and deuoute brether'. This may be a thin joke, or even a political code, as the first paragraph of the letter is riddled with references to charity, and to behaving 'charytably' over the supremacy, as if encouraging the Carthusians to submit with their fingers crossed, as it were. Later on in August 1537, the pliable Copinger was encouraged by the Visitors of the English Carthusian Province to remove the scruples of two Carthusians of Beauvale (Aungier, pp. 438–9).

6 Aungier, p. 430.

7 Bedyll complains bitterly about Whitford in a letter probably written in December 1535, recounting how he bullied him, threatened him with scandal over his alleged use of indecent language to the nuns in confession, and warned him that 'he myghte be the occasion that frost shalbe layed downe throughe England' (Aungier, p. 87).

> Item, on Sondy last, one Whitford, one of the most wilful of that house, preched and wold speke no worde of the Kinges grace said title; and this man hath but small lernyng, but is a greate rayler. (Aungier, p. 436)

(In Whitford's defence it ought to be said that he was in fact one of the most learned of the early humanist Brethren of Syon, a friend of Erasmus, and the most prolific author in the history of Syon.)

In the same letter from Bedyll to Thomas Cromwell, another Syon brother, David Curson, described with Fewterer as 'the saddest men there, and best learned', is also reported to have preached twice on the subject of the supremacy.[8] On one of these occasions he is said to have included the phrase 'mea culpa' during his sermon 'out of frame, as diverse did report. Percaas he thought no harme thereby, but was a terme that he commonly used and so came into his speche unadvisedly.' Bedyll, no friend of the Birgittines, had apparently taken little trouble to get to know his enemies. For it is most unlikely that Curson used his words 'unadvisedly' or 'out of frame'. The phrase *mea culpa* was used by Syon Brethren when confessing errors to each other in chapter and while receiving due punishment, as the Syon *Additions for the Brethren* record:

> And whan the president hath seyd *Loquamur de ordine nostro* al tho that fele hemself gylty in any open defaute litel or moche, schal fal down prostrat afore the president. To whom the presidente schal say: *Quid dicitis. What say ȝe?* And than al they so prostrate schal answer as it wer but the voyce of oon *Mea culpa*. To whom þan the president schal say aȝen *Surgite. Ryse vp.*[9]

In using the phrase in his public sermon, preached before the entire community and the assembled laity, Curson was perhaps signalling to his Brethren in the most public possible way his sorrow at the words he was being compelled to

8 Bedyll's letter, printed by Aungier, pp. 428–9, reports this favourable assessment of Fewterer and Curson, and says that they both 'shewed thaimselfes like honest men' and that Fewterer would now begin to preach the supremacy. This letter must come early in the sequence of persuasions and threats, before Bedyll starts playing bad cop with the Brethren.

9 For facsimiles and transcriptions of English copies of the *Regula Salvatoris* and the *Syon Additions*, see *The Rewyll of Seynt Sauioure and Other Middle English Brigittine Legislative Texts*, ed. James Hogg, vols II–IV [all published], Salzburger Studien zur Anglistik und Amerikanistik (Salzburg, 1978–80). All citations in this article are from this edition. This quotation is from *Additions for the Brethren*, cap. 1; Hogg, III, pp. 12–13. See now also *The Rewyll of Seynt Sauioure and A Ladder of Foure Ronges By the Which Men Mowe Clyme to Heven*, ed. James Hogg, Analecta Cartusiana CLXXXIII (2003), which reproduces and transcribes Middle English versions of the *Regula Salvatoris* from Cambridge, University Library MS Ff. 6. 33 and London, Guildhall MS 25524 and Latin versions from London, British Library MS Harley 612 and Syon Abbey South Brent MS 7. The standard edition of the versions of the Latin is *Regula Salvatoris*, ed. S. Eklund, Den Heliga Birgitta Opera Minora I, Samlingar utgivna av Svenska Fornskriftsällskapet, Andra Serien, Latinska Skrifter, VIII:1 (Lund, 1975). Fragments of the Rule and Additions were more recently identified among the manuscripts still in possession of the sisters: N. R. Ker and A. J. Piper, *Medieval Manuscripts in British Libraries*, IV (Oxford, 1992), pp. 348–9.

utter. The tension between public and private duty, between monastic obedience and personal integrity is forcefully dramatised in his words and actions. He was fulfilling his office of public preaching (one of the most important offices of a Birgittine brother), and he was also fulfilling the government's injunction that he should speak in favour of the royal supremacy (Bedyll, not always a sound judge of character, considered him pliable to the cause). But he knew himself potentially to be in error in so doing, and wished to signal that error to his listening Brethren and to any of the congregation who were familiar with the procedures of the Syon Brethren. He is both obediently exercising his *magisterium* and putting it immediately under very public correction, as recommended in some versions of the *Regula Salvatoris*:

> Fle all man*ere* pryde and take the to very mekenes, kepe thy mowth and all thy membrys to my worschip. Obeye as I haue bode the. Discusse thy *con*science eu*ery* houre . . . Ryse vp anone if thoue fall.[10]

The Syon Brethren were probably a demanding and high-minded audience. Bedyll further noted that during another sermon on the subject given on St Bartholomew's day by 'one Ricot' (Robert Rygote, a scholar formerly supported by Lady Margaret Beaufort[11]), 'nyne of his brethern, Friers of Sion, departed from the Sermon, contrarie to the rule of thair religion, to the gret sclaunder of al the audience'. The dramatic nature of this scene is worth pausing over: not just the breach of fraternity and solidarity involved in a public walkout by the majority of the priests in the house (nine out of thirteen, or seventeen if the deacons are included), but also the shock and dismay registered by the congregation. This must have felt like the world turned upside down for all those who witnessed it. A similarly shocking incident occurred in 1537 when a lay-brother, Thomas Brownal, publicly rebuked one of the Brethren in the church for preaching in favour of the King's claims. Brownal was thrown into Newgate prison where he died.[12]

Wittingly or unwittingly Bedyll, in focussing on the public preaching of the Brethren, was pinpointing the most politically significant and potentially influential part of their ministry. The public exposition of doctrine in the abbey church was absolutely fundamental to the identity and function of the Birgittine men. His letter suggests, though, that he was indeed aware that he was playing in a high-stakes arena in taking on the Brethren of Syon. A lot was at stake, for the

10 Cambridge, University Library Ff. 6. 33, fols 41v–42r; Hogg, II, pp. 7–8.

11 Rygote claimed in a letter to Henry VIII to be 'sometime scholar to your grandmother'. See M. K. Jones and M. G. Underwood, *The King's Mother: Lady Margaret Beaufort, Countess of Richmond and Derby* (Cambridge, 1992), p. 282, citing *Letters and Papers, Foreign and Domestic, of the Reign of Henry VIII*, ed. J. S. Brewer and J. Gairdner, 21 vols (London, 1862–1910), VII, no. 1092.

12 J. R. Fletcher, *The Story of the English Bridgettines of Syon Abbey* (South Brent, 1933), p. 34. This is probably the same person as 'one of the focares . . . that folisshe felowe with the curlede hede' who is described as interrupting a sermon and being imprisoned for it in a letter to Cromwell by another of his agents, Richard Layton (Aungier, p. 85).

Brethren of Syon had huge reputations for the integrity of their lives and the austerity and authenticity of their preaching. Bedyll's solution was to suggest to Cromwell that:

> [I]t shalbe better, for a season, tyl you retorne to London, to commaunde thaim to surcesse of al preching, or els to provide some remedy in the meane tyme against thaim whiche shal preche and wol not do thair duety; and against them whiche wol fle from the sermon of thair brethern declaring the Kinges grace said title.[13]

His formulation captures precisely the political dilemma in which the Brethren found themselves in 1534: those who 'wol not do thair duety' in their preaching of the King's supremacy refused to do so precisely because they believed their duty lay elsewhere, especially when it came to preaching. The ferment in Syon reported by Bedyll bespeaks a vigorous and rigorous sense of public duty, and a lively sense of personal and pastoral responsibility, all supported by an austere but robustly practical spirituality. But as the debate over the royal supremacy is one of the very few occasions when the Brethren of Syon emerge blinking shyly into the public and political gaze, how can that spirituality and sense of duty best be identified and explored?[14]

The formal legislative texts of the Order do not offer much in the way of help or detail. The order was required formally to observe the Augustinian Rule in its later medieval recension (the so-called *regula recepta*).[15] Bridget's own rule was canonically relegated to secondary and customary status, and its customary provisions were to be further elaborated in *Additions* produced to answer the local

[13] Aungier, p. 436.

[14] In exploring these questions, this paper seeks to address the issues raised in my 'Dial M for Mystic: Mystical Texts in the Library of Syon Abbey and the Spirituality of the Syon Brethren', in *MMT* VI, pp. 241–68, which, while asking some pertinent questions about their life, I now feel to have been overly harsh in its consideration of the Syon Brethren. For other recent attempts to make reparation, see also V. Gillespie, 'Syon and the New Learning', in *The Religious Orders in Pre-Reformation England*, ed. J. G. Clark, Studies in the History of Medieval Religion XVIII (Woodbridge, 2002), pp. 75–95; V. Gillespie, 'Walter Hilton at Syon Abbey', in *'Stand up to Godwards': Essays in Mystical and Monastic Theology in Honour of the Reverend John Clark on his Sixty-Fifth Birthday*, ed J. Hogg, Analecta Cartusiana CCIV (Salzburg, 2002), pp. 9–61; V. Gillespie, 'The Mole in the Vineyard: Wyclif at Syon in the Fifteenth Century', in *Text and Controversy from Wyclif to Bale: Essays in Honour of Anne Hudson*, ed. H. Barr and A. M. Hutchison, Medieval Church Studies IV (forthcoming: Turnhout, 2004).

[15] See the masterly discussions by Roger Ellis, *Viderunt eam filie syon: The Spirituality of the English House of a Medieval Contemplative Order from its beginnings to the present day*, Analecta Cartusiana LXVIII (1984); 'Further Thoughts on the Spirituality of Syon Abbey', in *Mysticism and Spirituality in Medieval England*, ed. W. F. Pollard and R. Boenig (Cambridge, 1997), pp. 219–43; 'The Visionary and the Canon Lawyers: Papal and other Revisions to the *Regula Salvatoris* of St Bridget of Sweden', in *Prophets Abroad: The Reception of Continental Holy Women in Late-Medieval England*, ed. R. Voaden (Cambridge, 1996), pp. 71–90.

needs of particular houses.[16] So the Birgittines thought of themselves as following the Augustinian rule but with a contemplative emphasis and observing a strict eremitical enclosure. The distinctive functions of the Syon Brethren are clearly, if exiguously, described in the *Regula Salvatoris* (which gives far more space and attention to the life of the sisters):

> Thes thrittene preestis owe to entende oonly to dyuyne office and studie & prayer. And implie them w*ith* none oþ*er*e nedes or offices. Whiche also are bounde to expoune iche sonday the gospel of the same day in the same messe to all herers in ther modir tounge.[17]

In pursuance of these duties, they are to be allowed access to books, 'as many as be necessary to doo dyvyne office and moo in no wyse', and also to liturgical and academic books, 'Thoo bookes they shalt haue as many as they wyll in whiche ys to serue*n* or to studye.'[18] But, although the official policy is clear, it is much harder to deduce the tenor and texture of the daily life of the Brethren from the surviving evidence. Some local emphases distinctive to English Syon are described in the *Additions* to the *Regula Salvatoris* composed for both houses (but with a considerable overlap of material between them) by a panel of external (and largely monastic) advisers some time in the first half of the fifteenth century.[19] The *Additions* for the Brethren note, for example, that it is a 'greuous defaute' 'if any despise the comen doctrynes, sette of olde fadyrs and ȝouen to them of ther souereynes to be kepte, or be to negligent to kepe hem'. A 'more greuous faute' for the Brethren is 'if any afferme the reuelacions of saynt birgitte as dremes, or els detracte hem'. It is similarly grievous 'if any publysch or reuele the secretes of the religion to any outewarde persone'. This last provision was presumably to avoid the kinds of criticism and speculation about monastic life that had so marred it during

16 Four versions survive of the *Additions* to the Rule for the English Syon: London, British Library MS Arundel 146 (in Middle English, for the sisters); London, Guildhall Library MS 25524 (in Middle English, for the Brethren); Cambridge, St John's College MS 11 (a fragmentary Latin text for the Brethren), and a post-medieval Latin version produced in Lisbon in 1607. The first three are edited or reproduced by Hogg. For discussion, see Ellis, *Viderunt eam filie syon*, cap. 3 (The Syon Additions).

17 Cambridge, University Library MS Ff. 6. 33, fol. 57r; Hogg, II, p. 38; Eklund, cap. 15, section 174, p. 121. For the passage in the Latin E text, see cap. 13, section 171 (Eklund, pp. 161–2).

18 Cambridge, University Library MS Ff. 6. 33. fols 62v–63r; Hogg, II, pp. 49–50. For the Latin text (P version), see cap. 21, sections 227–8: 'Libri quoque, quotquot necessarii fuerint ad divinum officium peragendum, habendi sunt, plures autem nullo modo. Illos autem libros habeant, quotquot voluerint, in quibus addiscendum est vel studendum' (Eklund, p. 127). The E version, cap. 18, sections 227–8, is substantially the same (Eklund, pp. 204–5).

19 See Aungier and Tait, *passim*. The similar *Liber usum* for the Vadstena Brethren was composed after the General Chapter of the order in 1429, but Syon was not represented at this meeting, probably because of *Mare anglicanum* and English legislation over alien priories. An edition of the Vadstena *Liber usum* is now available: *Liber usuum fratrum monasterii Vadstenensis: The Customary of the Vadstena Brethren*, ed. Sara Risberg, Acta Universitatis Stockholmiensis, L (2003).

the contentions of the late fourteenth century.[20] But such prohibitions, and the traditionally tight discipline of the small cadre of Birgittine men, must surely explain why information on the life of the Syon Brethren is in such short supply.

The *Additions for the Sisters* report the stern admonition that the Abbess must give to those seeking admission to the year of external proof. Although the *Additions for the Brethren* do not record a similar warning being made to male postulants, the Abbess's words may stand as a fair description of 'the dures of the religion' that the Brethren were letting themselves in for:

> Contempte of the worlde, forȝetyng of fader and moder, and of al worldly frendschyp, but as the rewle suffreth and the chirche determyneth, moche fastynge, many water dayes, grete watche, erly rysynge, longe seruyse, dayly labour, streyte sylence, loweste place, harde commaundementes of the souereyne, redy obedience, forsakynge of proper wyll, pacience in aduersite, sufferaunce of alle, sharpe correcciones and many suche other. Whiche may lyghtly be suffred for a whyle, but for to contynewe for terme of lyfe it is harde werke to some.[21]

After formal profession, members of Syon took a vow of obedience 'as it is expressyd in the comen register of the chapter howse', and subscribed (that is signed) their acceptance of it. This vow of obedience is still preserved in the Brethren's *Martiloge* (London, British Library, MS Additional 22285), and was followed by an exhortation delivered by the Confessor-General, or another priest commissioned by him. Reminding the new brother that, as the *Regula Salvatoris* states, 'the begynning of thys religion and of helth of sowle, it is very mekenes, pure chastite and wylful pouerte', the Confessor-General continues with a gloss on these three keystones of the order's life, reminding him that chastity 'stondeth not only in clennes of body, but also of sowle' and that 'wylful pouerte' consists not only of forsaking of worldly goods for God but also forsaking of any will to have property against the rule. But meekness receives the fullest gloss. Meekness is not only ungrudging obedience and a willingness to declare faults in confession or in chapter, but it is also to be content with 'vilenes and abieccion'. He emphasises that meekness is acquired not only from observance of the rule, but also, stressing the collaborative and communal endeavour of the Brethren, from 'the goode ensample of elders . . . lernyng of one mekenes, of another pacience, of another discrete abstinence, of another to kepe ȝour tunge and so forth of other vertues.' Finally he encourages the new recruit to acquire meekness through his daily conduct and *habitus*:

> It is also veray mekenes, yf ȝe kepe silence into tyme ȝe be askyd, yf ȝe be not lyght of laughynge, yf ȝe speke fewe wordys and resonable with sadnes. Also yf ȝe bothe in habite and outewarde wordys schewe mekenes thynkyng alway and in euery place howe ȝe schal be presentyd to the fereful dome of god sayng with the publycan: I am not wordy to lefte vp myne eyen to heuen.[22]

20 These passages are found in Hogg, III, pp. 23, 27, 28 (Brethren's defaults, all repeated for the Sisters).

21 *Additions for the Sisters*, cap. 15; Hogg, IV, p. 80.

22 *Additions for the Brethren*, cap. 17; Hogg, III, pp. 51–2.

This powerful exhortation shows the extent to which the Syon Brethren were meant to follow a 'hid diuinite' fuelled by radical humility and self-abnegation. The prescriptions in *Regula Salvatoris* for the decoration of the church make clear that the life of the house in general, and of the Brethren in particular (because they are more on show to the outside world than the sisters), should be characterised not by opulence or display but by integrity and sadness of life: 'for they shall kepe to them for tresoure neyther golde ne syluyr or p*re*ciouse stones, but the grace of god wyth contynuell studyes, deuoute prayeres and godly praysynges'.[23]

It is hardly surprising, therefore, that we know so little of the individual Brethren after their entry into Syon, and that it is so hard to identify the authorship of the various Latin and vernacular devotional texts believed to have been written by them before the advent of printing. When the translator and redactor of *The Orcherd of Syon*, surely a Syon Brother, writes of himself in ways that play with the governing pomological metaphor of his rearrangement of Catherine of Siena's *Dialogo* ('Grete laborer was I neuer, bodili ne gostli. I had neuer grete strengþe myȝtli to laboure wiþ spade ne wiþ schouel'), this give us a glimpse of his personality, but no hint of his identity, which remains shrouded behind conventional gestures of incapacity ('helpeþ me wiþ preiers, for me lackiþ kunnynge, aȝens my grete febelenes').[24] One unintended consequence of this anonymity is that we may be radically underestimating Syon's role in the production and (more especially) the circulation of vernacular religious texts in the fifteenth century, and are in danger of overstating the role of the nearby Carthusians of Sheen in the active dissemination of texts that can be showed to derive from the Sheen/Syon textual community.[25] Except when exercising their office as preachers, invisibility was the condition of a Syon brother's life.

There are, however, some accounts of that life that have not yet been fully explored. For, in addition to the limited evidence from the legislative texts, valuable insights into the ambitious level of spiritual aspiration which the order set for itself can also be gleaned from the series of daily lections found in the surviving *Martiloge* of the Brethren. This book preserves a record of community decisions, special liturgical observances, lists of benefactors and special friends of the house, obit lists, and places of burial of deceased members.[26] At its heart is a commercially

23 *Regula Salvatoris*, cap. 18; Cambridge University Library MS Ff. 6. 33, fol. 62v; Hogg, II, p. 49.

24 *The Orcherd of Syon*, ed. P. Hodgson and G. M. Liegey, EETS OS CCLVIII (1966), p. 16.

25 The *Speculum devotorum*, an example of a Syon commission from a Sheen Carthusian, is discussed in my 'The Haunted Text: Reflections in the *Mirrour to Deuote Peple*', in *Medieval Manuscripts at Notre Dame*, ed. J. Mann and M. Nolan (forthcoming: Notre Dame, 2004).

26 A new edition of those parts of the *Martiloge* manuscript relating to the history of the house is underway by Dr Claes Gejrot and Dr Virginia Bainbridge. I am indebted to Dr Gejrot for making available to me their preliminary transcriptions. The liturgical *Martiloge* proper has never been edited, though in 1526 Wynkyn de Worde published Richard Whitford's version of it as *The Martiloge in Englysshe after the Use of the*

produced martyrology for the entire liturgical year which was read daily in chapter or refectory. To this standard liturgical book, somebody at Syon added, around the middle of the fifteenth century, a series of short lections, designed to be read daily alongside the *Martiloge* entries. The lections are added by a later and less skilled hand than the scribe of the *Martiloge* itself. Although they are keyed by letter to a particular day's martyrology, they are often clumsily squeezed into the top and bottom margins, and frequently written over the pen flourishing and decoration of the para-liturgical text. The lections are grouped together thematically and are unrelated to the day's martyrological information.

Sound doctrine and good living are inextricably linked together in these texts, and the lections set exceptionally high standards for clerical behaviour. They discuss topics such as the duties of a bishop; the duties of a rector; the role and duties of a preacher; sound teaching and heresy; clerical poverty, common ownership and handling money; dealing with (or, more accurately, avoiding) women; sin, guilt and confession; prayer and contemplation; virtues, temptations and tribulations; good judges; almsgiving; and preparation for death. Drawing (without attribution) on patristic sources such as the *De cura pastorali* and the *Moralia on Job* of Gregory the Great (c. 540–604), the letters of Jerome (c. 342–420), and particularly on the *Sententiae* of Isidore of Seville (d. 636), these lections are rarely more than two or three sentences long. They may have been drawn from the *originalia* (all of which are attested in the great library collection of the Syon Brethren)[27] or perhaps filtered through another intermediate collection of *sententiae* such as those of Taio Caesaraugustanus (bishop of Zaragoza 651–83) or the *Forma institutionis canonicorum* pseudonymously attributed to Amalarius of Metz (c. 780–853). Both of these collections have a high degree of overlap with the *Martiloge* lections. There is, however, no trace of these works in the *registrum* of the Brethren's library and they are rarely (if at all) attested in British medieval library catalogues.[28] Some passages also occur in contemporary compilations like the *Speculum spiritualium* (s. xv[1]: composed in neighbouring Sheen Charterhouse, and found in the Syon

chirche of Salisbury and as it is redde in Syon with addicyons, ed. F. Procter and E. S. Dewick, Henry Bradshaw Society III (London, 1893). Whitford, described in the preface as 'preest and professed broder of Syon', does not translate or include any of the lections discussed here. They are mentioned in passing by Procter and Dewick (p. xxxi) but have otherwise garnered little attention. I hope to publish an edition and commentary in due course.

27 For the sources of the lections, see the following Syon books (references are to the numbering of my new edition). Gregory, *Moralia*: SS1. 339; SS1. 340a; SS1. 341; SS1. 342; SS1. 346b (excerpts); SS1. 346c (excerpts); SS1. 360; SS2. 87; SS2. 126c. Gregory, *De cura pastorali*: SS1. 624m; SS1. 1346; SS1. 1393; SS1. 1397; SS1. 1399; SS2. 260. Jerome, *Epistulae*: SS1. 546; SS1. 747; SS1. 870; SS1. 892b; SS1. 902. Isidore, *Epistulae*: SS2. 153e. Isidore, *Sententiae*: SS1. 910b; SS2. 126a; SS2. 153f. For a summary of recent research on the library, see my introduction to the new edition of the Syon *registrum*: *Syon Abbey*, pp. xxix–lxv.

28 The cumulative *List of Identifications* developed by Richard Sharpe for the Corpus of British Medieval Library Catalogues reports no copy of Taio in the volumes so far catalogued, and only a single copy of Ps. Amalarius.

library) and in older monastic *florilegia* like the *Deflorationes patrum* of Werner von Ellenbach (d. 1126), but the overlap does not appear sufficient for them to be the primary source and probably reflects the commonplace status achieved by many of the *sententiae*.[29] The chances are that the compiler of the *Martiloge* lections either used the *originalia* or some other (as yet unidentified) intermediary *florilegium*, and there are several candidates described in the *registrum* of the Brethren's library. A good example of the kind of florilegial collection on the priestly office that might have supplied the lections is in I. 27 (SS1. 583b: 'De dictis Augustini, Ieronimi & aliorum de dignitate sacerdotum & et de aliis ad sacerdotes pertinentibus'), which is preceded (SS1. 583a) by chapter 139 of John of Mirfield's *Florarium Bartholomei* on 'De sacerdotibus'. But there are others.[30]

The lections stress that the priestly calling is a high vocation only to be approached with humility and following careful self-analysis (perhaps reflecting the importance attached to the year of proof required of all Birgittines):

> Qui regimen sacerdotii contendit appetere ante in se discutiat si vita sit honori congrua. Quod si non discrepat humiliter ad id quod vocatus est accedat. Reatum quippe culpe geminat qui cum culpa ad sacerdotale culmen aspirat. (Fol. 88v, from Isidore, *Sententiae*; also in Amalarius, *Forma insititutionis canonicorum*)

> [Whoever desires to aspire to the priestly rule, first let him examine whether his life is fit for the honour. If it be not discordant, let him humbly approach towards his vocation. Certainly the guilt of the offence is doubled if he aspires to the priestly summit in a blameworthy state.]

A recurrent emphasis throughout the year's worth of readings is the need to match words with deeds ('tam doctrina quam uita' (fol. 93r: 'As the teaching, so the life')) and of living what is taught: 'Sacerdotis predicacio operibus confirmanda est ita ut quod docet verbo instruat exemplo' (fol. 93v: 'The preaching of the priest is to be confirmed by [his] works so that what he teaches by word he may demonstrate by example'). 'Arcus perversus est lingua docentium bene et viventium male. Et ideo quasi ex perverso arcu sagittam emittunt, dum suam pravam vitam proprie lingue ictu confodiunt' (fol. 106v, from Isidore, *Sententiae*; also in Amalarius, *Forma insititutionis canonicorum*: 'Teaching well with the tongue and living badly is a warped bow, and as with those who shoot an arrow from a warped bow, so those of

[29] The *Speculum spiritualium* is reported in the *registrum* of the Brethren's library at SS1. 769 (printed); SS1. 793–4; SS1. 795; SS1. 796. The *Deflorationes patrum* is reported at SS1. 531b; SS1. 536b (both probably printed copies).

[30] Other anonymous or pseudonymous entries in the *registrum* that may point to this kind of priestly *florilegium* include the 'liber notabilis florum ex opusculis doctorum diuersorum & in 2os libros diuisorum cum Capitulis premissis', found at the end of N.29. (SS1. 883l), a book given by Thomas Grant (d. 1471), precentor of St Paul's and a notable upholder of clerical orthodoxy. The 'Tractatus sacerdotibus utilis uocatus Gemma sacerdotum' (SS1. 1384g) might be the *Gemma Crucifixi siue Instructio sacerdoti* attributed to Brother Bernard (s. xii^{ex}). The *registrum* is witness to a consistent interest among the Brethren in their sacerdotal and sacramental practice, with accessions spanning the early manuscript phase of the library right up to the latest printed acquisitions in the 1520s.

depraved life inflict wounds on themselves with their own tongue'). 'Qui bene docet et male vivit tanquam es et cymbalum sonum . . . Qui bene docet et male vivit; quod docet bene viventibus proficit, quod vero male vivit, seipsum occidit' (fol. 107r, from Isidore, *Sententiae*: 'He who teaches well and lives badly is like the sound of brass or a cymbal . . . For him who teaches well and lives badly, his good teaching will be of profit to the living and by his bad living he will kill himself'). Money should never be taken for the exercise of priestly duties, because the riches of the house are the chastity, justice, piety, humility, mildness, innocence, purity, prudence, temperance and charity of its members (fol. 118r). (This last point echoes the argument in the *Regula Salvatoris* that study, prayer and the praise of God represent the abbey's gold and silver.) The cultivation of humility and the avoidance of spiritual and intellectual pride are frequently emphasised. Integrity is all: 'Sacerdotis christi os cum mente concordet' (fol. 109v: 'Let the mouth of Christ's priest agree with his mind').

Passages that might not initially seem relevant to the needs or interests of the Syon Brethren (such as those defining a good and holy bishop) often conclude with the exhortation 'Tu autem', implying that their teachings should be made to apply to the circumstances of the house and of the Brethren's duties. So, for example, the lection that a bishop must be just and holy so that he may dispense justice to the people he leads, giving to each what he deserves (fol. 97v), might be made to refer either to the role of the Confessor-General or to the penitential functions of the Brethren themselves, and the Vadstena Brethren at least had the status of minor penitentiaries, allowing them to absolve some classes of reserved sins denied to ordinary parish clergy and reserved to bishops.[31]

A substantial number of entries in the *Martiloge* lections relate to preaching. In addition to dominical and festal preaching, major opportunities for preaching to the laity at Syon arose on those special days associated with the various indulgences granted to those who attended the house, and in particular with the popular and generous *Ad vincula* indulgence.[32] The pilgrim crowds offered a large potential audience. Apart from occasional (and specially sanctioned) spiritual guidance to high-born women (such as Margaret, Duchess of Clarence) and probably to postulants to the sisterhood, preaching and confession were the main activities that would have brought the Syon Brethren into public view.[33] Though little

31 This passage comes from Jerome's Commentary on the Epistle to Titus and is also included in Ps. Amalarius, *Forma insititutionis canonicorum*. On the Vadstena's Brethren's penitential powers, see *Liber Privilegiorum Monasterii Vadstenensis*, ed. E. Nygren (Hafniae, 1950), p. 236.

32 The preaching office of the Syon Brethren has been carefully and thoughtfully studied by S. Powell, 'Preaching at Syon Abbey', *Leeds Studies in English*, new ser. xxxi (2000), pp. 229–67; see also her 'Syon, Caxton and the *Festial*', *Birgittiana* ii (1996), pp. 187–207, which discusses Syon's possible involvement with printed sermons. Tait, p. 214, notes that Bonde, Fewterer and Reynolds all served as University Preachers at Cambridge before joining the order.

33 On Symon Wynter's relations with Margaret, Duchess of Clarence, see G. R. Keiser, 'Patronage and Piety in Fifteenth-Century England: Margaret, Duchess of Clarence, Symon Wynter and Beinecke MS 317', *Yale University Library Gazette* lx (1985), pp.

evidence of preaching by Syon Brethren now survives, these public sermons were probably popular and influential events. The Brethren's library collection contained hundreds of sermon collections, including several attributed to Syon Brethren themselves, though only one of these has been identified as surviving. The provision in the vernacular *Additions* for the Brethren allowing a preacher three days remission from choir duties 'to recorde hys sermon' suggests that this duty was both accorded a high priority and taken seriously by the Brethren.[34] As the Rule's injunction to 'expoune . . . the gospel' implies, this preaching was intended to be expository rather than elaborative. In the *Reuelaciones Extrauagantes* Christ had given Birgitta precise instructions about the kinds of preaching that her order should undertake. The preachers should use simple and few words, founded on the reading of Scripture; they must avoid verbal pyrotechnics and complexities, and should pay careful attention to the needs and capacities of their audience. Sunday sermons should expound the Gospel, using Christ's own words and those of his mother and of the saints, as well as the *Vitae patrum*, and *miracula sanctorum*. They should address the Creed and provide remedies against temptations and vices. Above all they should avoid dullness and going over the heads of the audience, remembering that Mary was 'simplicissima', Peter was an 'ydiota' and St Francis 'rusticus', but together they have done more for the good of souls than many 'magistri eloquentes'.[35]

The *Martiloge* lections express a similar high-minded evangelicalism:

> Sermo sacerdotis debet esse purus, simplex et apertus, tractans de misterio legis, de doctrina fidei, de uirtute continentie, de disciplina iustitie, plenus grauitate et honestate, plenus suauitate et gracia. (Fol. 78v, from Isidore, *De ecclesiasticis officiis*; also in Ps. Amalarius, *Forma insititutionis canonicorum*)
>
> [The sermon of the priest must be pure, simple and open, dealing with the mystery of the Law, the teaching of the Faith, the virtue of restraint, the rule of justice, full of gravity and honesty, full of sweetness and grace.]

Teaching must be carefully targeted at the needs and abilities of the audience:

> Prima prudentie uirtus est eam quam docere oporteat existimare personam. Rudibus populis seu carnalibus plana atque communia non summa atque ardua predicanda sunt

32–46. The hearing of public confessions by the Syon Brethren greatly worried Bedyll in the last years of the house: 'we think it best that the place where thes frires haue been wont to hire uttward confessiouns of al commers at certen tymes of the yere, be walled up, and that use to be foredoon for euer' (Aungier, p. 87). He complains that 'muche evyl' and 'much treson' about the supremacy and the King's divorce have been spread abroad through these confessionals, and says that he has also 'sequesterd' Whitford and Litelle 'from hering of the ladys confessions'.

34 The Syon *Additions for the Brethren* (Guildhall manuscript) record in a short chapter headed 'Of the offices of the prechours' that 'Eche of the prechours schal besyde the sermon day haue thre hole days at lest oute of the quyer to recorde hys sermon'; Hogg, III, p. 122.

35 *Den Heliga Birgittas Reuelaciones Extrauagantes*, ed. L. Hollman, Svenska Fornskriftällskapets Samlingar, Andra Serien, Latinska Skrifter V (Uppsala, 1956), cap. 23, p. 133, discussed by Powell, 'Preaching'.

> ne immensitate doctrina opprimantur potius quam erudiantur. (Fol. 99r, from Isidore *Sententiae*, also in Ps. Amalarius, *Forma insititutionis canonicorum*)
>
> [The first feature of Prudence is to assess the character of those who are to be instructed. For simple and worldly people, those things to be preached must be plain and commonplace, not elevated or hard, nor should they be weighted down with greater instruction than they can assimilate.]
>
> Cum rector se ad loquendum preparat sub quanto cautela studio loquatur attendat. Ne si inordinate ad loquendum rapitur, erroris vulnere audientium corda feriantur. (Fol. 100r, from Gregory, *De cura pastorali*, also in Taio Caesaraugustanus, *Sententiae* and Ps. Amalarius, *Forma insititutionis canonicorum*, and in Gratian)
>
> [When the rector prepares himself to speak, with what care he must attend to the study of what he is to say. Let him not hastily rush into speaking, lest the hearts of those listening be struck with the wound of error.]

Some of the entries on priestly preaching are hard hitting, reforming in their zeal and perhaps surprising to find in the context of an enclosed religious order:

> Sacerdos semper vocem predicacionis habeat ne superne expectacionis iudicium: silentio offendat. Sacerdos enim in tabernaculum ingrediens moritur si de eo sonitus non auditur. Quia iram contra se occulti iudicis erigit si sine predicacionis sonitu incedit. (Fol. 100v, from Gregory, *De cura pastorali*, also in Taio Caesaraugustanus, *Sententiae* and Ps. Amalarius, *Forma insititutionis canonicorum*, and in Gratian)
>
> [Let the priest always have a preaching voice, lest his silence offend the waiting judgement from above. For a priest entering into the sanctuary dies if no sound is heard from him. Because the wrath of the hidden judge will be raised against him if he proceeds without the sound of preaching.]

At Syon, these patristic guidelines on priesthood and preaching would have provided a congenial parallel with new emphases on preaching and the pastoral care in the post-Wyclif and post-Conciliar world into which the house and most of its members were born.[36]

As preparation for preaching and teaching, particular stress is placed in the *Martiloge* lections on the importance of reading and study, because, it is asserted, no-one who is unfamiliar with the reading of Scripture will be able to access the

[36] In addition to the helpful overview in Anne Hudson's *The Premature Reformation: Wycliffite Texts and Lollard History* (Oxford, 1988), I have found invaluable two superb essays by J. I. Catto, 'Wyclif and Wycliffism at Oxford 1356–1430' and 'Theology after Wycliffism', both in *The History of the University of Oxford: II, Late Medieval Oxford*, ed. J. I. Catto, T. A. R. Evans (Oxford, 1992), pp. 175–261 and pp. 263–80. See also Thomas Gascoigne, a fan of Birgitta and her English house, who is an invaluable witness to the tenor of conservative reform in the first half of the fifteenth century: *Loci e Libro Veritatum: Passages from Gascoigne's Theological Dictionary*, ed. J. E. Thorold Rogers (Oxford, 1881), pp. 34–5. His comments on the causes of heresy, contemporary preaching and priestly life are fascinatingly blunt: cf. pp. 28, 31, 183, 188–91. His text (perhaps a sermon) on *Super flumina babilonis* (pp. 53ff) is a jeremiad on the state of the contemporary church. See my 'Mole in the Vineyard' for further consideration of Syon's role as a bastion of orthodoxy in the post-Conciliar reform movement in fifteenth-century England.

sense of it (fol. 149v). 'Pastorum imperitia voce veritatis increpatur' (fol. 85v: 'The ignorance of the pastors is rebuked by the voice of truth').[37] Just as evil men and sinners are prohibited from priestly functions, so also the uneducated and unskilled are also held back from this office. The former will corrupt good lives by their bad example; the latter will not know how to correct evil men because of their ignorance (fol. 89v). Priests should read the holy scriptures often, pray frequently, exercise their mind towards God, fast and keep vigils (fol. 112r):

> Tu quidem diuinas scripturas sepius lege, immo nunquam de manibus tuis sacra lectio deponatur. Disce quod doceas. Obtine eum qui secundum doctrinam est fidelem sermonem ut possis exhortari in doctrina sana et contradicentes revincere. (Fol. 109v, from Jerome's *Letters*; also in Ps. Amalarius, *Forma insititutionis canonicorum*)

> [Indeed you must read the sacred scriptures again and again, or rather never let the holy reading be put aside from your hands. Understand what you teach. Seize those words which are faithful to Doctrine so that you may exhort in sound teaching and subdue those who argue against it.]

Those who have the skill of understanding but fail to study their reading will stand condemned (fol. 150r). Learning without grace will fill the ears but never the heart, and those who acquire knowledge of the Scriptures only for the sake of the praise it will bring them, rather than for the glory of God, will never touch the hidden truths, which will remain behind a cloud of pride (fol. 151v). Because holy books are written in simple words, human eloquence and dialectical sharpness should be avoided: 'in leccione non verba sed veritas est amanda' (fol. 155v, from Isidore, *Sententiae*: 'it is Truth that is to be loved in reading not words'). For similar reasons, the studies of priests need to be supervised and counterfeit teachings must be examined and corrected to avoid a collocation of sins that would harm the just (fol. 168v). The proud will read and search, but will never find: only the humble will be admitted. Divine eloquence will never be revealed to the arrogant but will remain closed and hidden 'in misterio' (fol. 152v).

As the Syon Brethren were contemplatives with some aspects of active ministry, the lections emphasise the need for reflection and contemplation as much as study and reading:

> Cecus pastor est qui superne lumen contemplacionis ignorat . . . Claudus rector est qui quidem quo pergere aspicit sed per infirmitatem mentis vite viam perfecte non tenere quam videt. (Fol. 105r, from Taio Caesaraugustanus, *Sententiae* or Ps. Amalarius, *Forma insititutionis canonicorum*, often attributed to Gregory)

> [It is a blind pastor who ignores the light of contemplation from above. It is a crippled rector who indeed catches sight of where to proceed but because of an infirm mind does not keep to the way of perfect life which he sees.]

Naturally, prayer is the desired outcome of reading and study, and both are of central importance in the monastic form of living implied in these lections:

[37] This sentence comes from Gregory, *De cura pastorali*, and is also found in Taio Caesaraugustanus, *Sententiae*, and in Ps. Amalarius, *Forma insititutionis canonicorum*.

> Orationibus mundamur; leccionibus instruimur. Utrumque bonum est si liceat; si non liceat melius orare quam legere. Qui vult cum deo semper esse frequenter debet orare frequenter et legere. Nam cum oramus ipsi cum deo loquimur cum vero legimus deus nobiscum loquitur. (Fol. 149r, from Isidore, *Sententiae*, also in *Speculum spiritualium*)
>
> [Let us be cleansed by prayer, instructed by reading. Either is good if permitted; if not permitted, it is better to pray than to read. He who wishes to be always with God must frequently pray and also frequently read. For when we pray we speak to God, but when we read God speaks to us.]

Prayer should be from the heart and not from the lips. It is better to pray silently with the heart and without the sound of the voice (it is not clear how this would have squared with the onerous obligations to liturgical prayer that both houses at Syon sustained). We pray truly when we think of no other things, but there are very few who possess such prayer. Our mind is celestial and we can contemplate God only when our prayer is hindered by no earthly cares or errors. The mind must be purged of all temporal things so that the clean and sharp point of the heart may be directed towards God (fol. 145r).

Despite this contemplative orientation, the lections suggest that the life at Syon is also to be an active and energetic monasticism with no time for leisure, vain words or other distractions. Perhaps because of the active ministry of the Brethren as preachers, the lections emphasise the essential contrast between the active and contemplative lives, and the passages selected suggest that the Syon Brethren should regard themselves above all as contemplatives rather than as exercising some kind of 'mixed life'. Active life consists in good works and pertains to the common multitude of people. Contemplative life consists in gazing at the things above and pertains to very few. Active life consists in using the things of the world well, contemplative life in renouncing them to live solely in the worship and delight of God (fol. 155v). A lection that reflects the instructions in the *Regula Salvatoris* insists that the brothers must always be engaged in prayer or reading or other matters pertaining to the needs of the church, and should become erudite in 'doctrinis sanis . . . et diversarum artium disciplinis' so that no-one in the house may be considered to be idle or useless (fol. 125v). Life in the monastery is to be lived in search of perfection and in a state of purity and integrity, so that the priest may approach the altar like a virgin to her bridal chamber, and the life of the community should be conducted with an eye to the opinion and witness of those outside the house:

> Ita ergo age et vive in monasterio vt clericus esse merearis, ut adolescentiam tuam nulla sorde commacules, ut ad altare Christi quasi de thalamo virgo procedas et habes defloris bonum testimonium. (Fol. 113v, from *Letters* of Isidore and Jerome, also in Ps. Amalarius, *Forma insititutionis canonicorum*)
>
> [Therefore behave and live in the monastery so that you may be worthy to be a cleric, so that you do not stain your youth with anything sordid, so that you may proceed to the altar of Christ like a virgin to her bridal bed, and may have the good opinion of those outside the house.]

Woven into this tapestry of clerical idealism are many assumptions about the responsibility of the priestly office that seem redolent of the reform programme of the English bishops in the early fifteenth century. But there are also many warnings (largely drawn from the *Sententiae* of Isidore) about false teachings and heretical ideas. These warnings are deployed in a way that makes it clear that, in their Syon context, they are addressing a troubled and unstably orthodox environment, where priests have an important role in policing orthodoxy:

> Sacerdotes curam debent habere de his qui pereunt ut eorum redargutione corrigantur a peccatis aut si in corrigibiles existunt ab ecclesia separentur. (Fol. 168v, from Isidore, *Sententiae*)
>
> [Priests ought to have the care of those who come to them so that by confutation of them they may be corrected from their sins or else, if they remain incorrigible, they may be separated from the church.]

Thus it is argued that God's law will never be understood by those who pursue it using the literal sense alone ('carnaliter', fol. 152v), but only by those who see and understand its interior meaning. 'In solis fidelibus religata est lex' (fol. 152v: 'the law was left only to the faithful'). Jews and heretics are not Christ's disciples and do not follow the unity and the peace that Christ gave to his followers, nor do they exhibit the charity that Christ said would be the hallmark of his followers. Those who fail to understand the Scriptures spiritually 'in heresim devoluti sunt in erroribus multis' ('are fallen through heresy into many errors'). The writings of heretics do not give any flavour of the true meaning, but rather lead the understanding into error (fol. 153r). Teachers of error lead their hearers astray by false persuasions and fraudulent arguments. Such is the craftiness of heretics that they mingle truth and lies together, things that are beneficial for salvation mixed with things that are full of error, hiding perverse teachings under the appearance of true persuasions. Even worse, they pass off their writings as the works of authentic teachers:

> Plerumque sub nomine catholicorum doctorum heretici sua dicta conscribunt ut indubitanter lecta credantur. (Fol. 153v, from Isidore, *Sententiae*)
>
> [And commonly under the name of catholic doctors, heretics enroll their own sayings so that undoubtedly what has been read there has been believed.]

(In the context of Syon, of course, this resonates with the characteristic Wycliffite technique of interpolating heterodox opinions into orthodox texts.)

This sample from the extensive range of *Martiloge* lections illustrates how the readings offer a conspectus of the pastoral and theological issues that their compiler thought needed to be reinforced in his audience's understanding of their own distinctive life and calling as Birgittines. Deeply traditional, conventional even, in their reliance on the aphorisms and *sententiae* of patristic wisdom, these readings may illuminate some of the priorities of the spiritual life of the Syon Brethren and also point to some of the concerns facing them. Indeed the ethos of the lections reflects and expands on the core emphases in *The Rule of St Augustine* (some of the lections are in fact also found in Hugh of Saint-Victor's popular Commentary on the Rule, known to be available and used at Syon).[38] The Rule focuses on prayer ('Be assiduous in prayer at the hours and times appointed' 2.1), meditation ('When you

38 SS1. 750a; SS1. 805c.

pray to God in psalms and hymns, think over in your hearts the words that come from your lips' 2.2), common living ('Call nothing your own, but let everything be yours in common' 1.3), and singleness of purpose ('Let all of you then live together in oneness of mind and heart, mutually honouring God in yourselves, whose temples you have become' 1.7).[39] Only briefly outlined in *The Rule of St Augustine*, these vocational imperatives are further fleshed out and meditated over in the *Martiloge* lections.

Although in many ways the individual lections are historical and theological commonplaces, what makes them significant is their resonance as voices from the monasticism of the early Church. The lections articulate Syon's sense of itself as a new monastic beginning after the turmoil of Schism and heresy. Their presentation in the *Martiloge* offered daily injections of clerical idealism to the Brethren as they were gathered together in chapter or at meals. The readings provide a significant insight into the mindset of the fifteenth-century English Birgittine Brethren. They suggest that, certainly by the middle of the century and probably before, Syon was seeking to exercise a high-minded and idealistic model of priesthood that stressed the importance of the lived example of priests reinforcing their teaching; that valued and encouraged scholarship alongside prayer and contemplation; that was fully aware of the dangers of heresy but had learned some of the lessons of the *Wyclifisti* and their critiques of priesthood and monastic life. Some of this idealism was no doubt a reflection of the spirit of the age of the Councils of Constance and Basel. This *zeitgeist* would have penetrated the house through new professions, through the books they brought with them, and through the other books the house continued to acquire by donation and bequest, as well as through the house's wider personal contacts with the clergy, the hierarchy, and the aristocracy.[40] But in Syon it came into contact with an ethos of service, an idealism of priestly life and a discipline of intellectual integrity and moral asceticism that was daily reinforced by the provisions in the *Rules* and the *Additions*, the lections in the *Martiloge* and, perhaps most important of all, the living example of their Brethren.

Thomas Bedyll's anxieties about Syon proved well-founded. Not all would compromise their integrity by accepting the King's supremacy, though only one Brother and one lay-brother paid for it with their lives. The spirit of the Syon Brethren held firm. After Fewterer's death in September 1536, Thomas Cromwell, no doubt hoping for an easy surrender of this flagship house, personally supervised

[39] The textual history of the *Rule of St Augustine* is complex and confusing. The best recent account is L. Verheijen. *La règle de saint Augustin*, Études Augustiniennes (Paris, 1967), which establishes a critical text of the *regula recepta* and distinguishes the different and related versions, all of which share a core of common material. Parenthetic references are to chapters and paragraphs of the eight chapter text, rather than the twelve chapter version published by Migne and used by Ellis in his discussions. The translation, by Robert Russell O. S. A., is based on this edition and that of the *Constitutiones Ordinis Fratrum S. Augustini* (Rome, 1968), and is available online at: <http://www.geocities.com/Athens/1534/ruleaug.html>

[40] This *zeitgeist* is explored a little further in relation to Syon in my 'Mole in the Vineyard' and I hope to consider it in more detail in a future study.

the election of the pliant John Copinger as Confessor-General, but Copinger seems to have died before 1539. It was probably left to the scrupulous David Curson to preside over the final days of the house, which finally had to be suppressed by *praemunire* because its members refused to surrender it.[41] The idealisms of the Birgittine life and its objectives were borne witness to even in the most terrible of circumstances. The Carthusian Maurice Chauncy's vivid account of the martyrdom of the Birgittine Saint Richard Reynolds and the London Carthusians at Tyburn on 4 May 1535 describes Reynolds as 'insignis ille raraeque sanctitatis et doctrinae', a living embodiment of the aspirations of the Rule, the Additions, and the lections. Chauncy records that Reynolds, who was the last to suffer, exhorted and encouraged his Carthusian companions as they underwent their own deaths and, true to the vocation of the Syon Brethren, preached a 'godly and noble sermon' to the crowd while awaiting his turn on the scaffold:

> Pater reginaldus super currum stans mox suspendendus, interim Deum prae oculis suis reliquos socios suos tam horribiliter trucidari viderit, pium valde et isigniter egregium animo constanti, intrepido, et plusquam virili sermonem habuit ad populum, nihil interim haesitans, nihil aut voce, aut verbo titubans, sed nec ullum mortis metusve signum prae se ferens.[42]
>
> [Father Reynolds, that man of rare sanctity and learning, was standing on the cart waiting to be hanged. Keeping God before his eyes as he saw the gruesome murder of his companions, with a constancy and courage more than heroic he preached a godly and noble sermon to the people. He never paused for a word. His voice never faltered. Nothing in his manner suggested fear or the imminence of death.]

Reynolds' behaviour on the scaffold gave eloquent and public testimony to the strength and depth of his inner life. But his actions are entirely consistent with the ideals of the Brethren's life so far as we can discover them. Normally that life was hidden and self-effacing. But, for once, at Tyburn in 1535, there was nothing 'hid' about their 'diuinite'.

41 The pension list at suppression places Curson first among the men with the largest pension of £15, making it probable that he was Confessor-General (though Agnes Jordan, the Abbess, received £200); Aungier, pp. 89–90.

42 M. Chauncy, *The Passion and Martyrdom of the Holy English Carthusian Fathers: The Short Narration*, ed. G. W. S. Curtis (London, 1935), pp. 96–7. This version of Chauncy's account was written in 1570 in exile at Sheen Anglorum. In 1537, Chauncy had been one of the Carthusians sent to Syon to be persuaded by Confessor-General Copinger over the supremacy; see Aungier, p. 438. On the life and death of St Richard Reynolds, see A. Hamilton, *The Angel of Syon* (Edinburgh and London, 1905), which, though dated in style, combines various contemporary accounts of the martyrdom.

INDEX

Page numbers in italic refer to illustrations.